VAT and Financial Services

Fourth edition

Mark Chesham

First published December 2012

This fourth edition published August 2022 by

Spiramus Press Ltd
102 Blandford Street
London W1U 8AG
United Kingdom
www.spiramus.com

ISBN
Paperback 9781913507275
Digital 9781913507282

This publication is based upon the law as at 1 April 2022.

British Library Cataloguing-in-Publication Data.

A catalogue record for this book is available from the British Library.

About the author

Mark Chesham has specialised in advising businesses in the financial services and insurance sectors for over 30 years. He started with HM Customs and Excise, working in a specialist insurance team, before spending 15 years in two of the 'Big 4' accounting firms. He set up his own consultancy practice in 2005 and was Director of Indirect Tax Services at Moore. He now operates as a consultant based in Portugal. He is a member of the the VAT Practitioners Group.

The author can be contacted at mark@cheshamconsultancy.com

Acknowledgements

I would like to thank Anne Humphrey and Linda Adelson for reviewing and commenting on the first edition text. I would also like to thank various clients and contacts for providing a sounding board for questions and a source of information, in particular, Martin Hall at Standard Life, John Brooks at Liverpool Victoria and Garry Davidson latterly of Old Mutual. Also, thanks to the partners at Moore Stephens in Bath who put up with me disappearing to write the original text. If there are any errors or ommissions these are, however, entirely mine.

Contents

Tables of authorities

Cases

Statutes

Regulations

Directives and Treatises

1. Introduction

1.1. Introduction to the first edition, September 2012

"VAT will be a simple tax on the supply of goods and services."
Anthony Barber MP, Chancellor of the Exchequer 1972

"Beyond the everyday world ... lies the world of VAT, a kind of fiscal theme park in which factual and legal realities are suspended or inverted"
Lord Justice Sedley

Anyone who has ever attended a course on VAT or read any publications on the subject will no doubt be aware of both of these quotations. Whilst most people will snigger at the Barber quote – and no doubt he later regretted saying it – for many businesses, VAT is a relatively straightforward tax; a business incurs VAT on expenditure and recovers it from HMRC and it charges VAT on its supplies which it accounts for to HMRC. This then happens all down the chain of supply until that chain reaches the final customer who has to pay VAT but is unable to recover it.

Unfortunately, businesses in the financial services and insurance sectors are not in the category of business for which VAT is a 'simple tax'. Supplies made by financial services and insurance businesses are generally exempt from VAT. This means that there is a restriction on the amount of VAT on expenditure that can be recovered. Calculating how much VAT can be recovered is in itself an art (or maybe a science) which often requires considerable effort to resolve. In addition, the types of supplies made are often difficult to define in the context of VAT, so VAT liabilities and the place of supply of transactions are not always clear.

As a result, many will identify with the views of Lord Justice Sedley – indeed this quotation adorns the walls (and/or the website) of many a VAT adviser! However, perhaps it's better to say that VAT has its own 'factual and legal realities' which I hope this publication helps to translate and explain. Of course, it also needs to be borne in mind that Lord Justice Sedley's comments were made in the context of circumstances in a specific case (*Royal & Sun Alliance Insurance Group plc v C&E Commrs [2001] EWCA Civ 1476 STC 1476*) so VAT is not always so otherworldly. However, it is worth reading his full judgment (paras 54 to 58) to get a real sense of his exasperation in this case!

Many of the problems with VAT originate with the fact that much of the UK legislation was originally written in the 1970s. This is particularly evident for financial services and insurance. Since the 1970s, the environment within which financial services and insurance are sold has changed dramatically, both in terms of the products themselves and the way they are sold (an obvious example being the explosion in services sold over the internet). In addition, many providers of these services now outsource parts of their business (commonly back-office or specialist functions) to third-party providers, many of which are located outside the EU.

In recognition of this, back in 2005, the European Commission commenced a review of the VAT treatment of insurance and financial services. The outcome of this review was intended to be an amendment to the *Principal VAT Directive (2006/112/EC)* to make the legislation 'fit for purpose'.

Three main changes were proposed:

- a rewrite of the VAT exemptions concerning financial services and insurance, to modernise and clarify the legislation;
- an introduction of a mandatory option to tax; and
- a new regime for exempting supplies of cost sharing vehicles.

For various reasons, the last two proposals have effectively been dropped (although the UK finally brought in UK legislation to implement the pre-existing EU requirement for a cost sharing exemption with effect from *Royal Assent to the Finance Bill 2012*).

On the first point, much of the effort has been spent on attempting to produce definitions of exempt financial and insurance services. One area of particular contention has been the treatment of outsourced supplies. The UK has been pushing for a wider and more flexible approach to exempting outsourced services (proposing that exemption should apply for services 'specific to and essential for' the exempt service). However, other member states, in particular Germany, want a stricter approach. For example, the Belgian Presidency proposed that there should be a requirement for the outsourced service to entail 'a change in the legal and financial relationship between the parties' (i.e. between the provider and customer of the financial service) before exemption could apply. Whilst the Belgian proposal would be fine in many cases, it would create issues for services such as claims handling and general back-office support, where a change in the legal and financial relationship between the parties may not occur.

The European Council have indicated that it is unlikely that they will push forward with major reforms of the VAT exemptions at the current time. So, whilst there has been little real progress in the review (and member states probably have much higher priorities at the moment) significant changes in future cannot be ruled out. Also, in the absence of any agreement, it is quite likely that HMRC will amend UK legislation to implement the Andersen's decision,[1] which will result in a further restriction to the scope of VAT exemption for certain intermediary supplies. The Andersen's decision is discussed in more detail in the chapters below, in particular see **Chapter 4**.

Domestically, the Retail Distribution Review is due to come into effect on 1 January 2013. Although this does not in itself have VAT implications, it has led to a focus on the activities and supplies made by IFAs and other Financial Advisers and in an attempt to achieve clarity, the rewrite of some of HMRC's manuals. Unfortunately, at the time of writing some uncertainty still remains (particularly with regard to annual reviews) and the ECJ decision in *Deutsche Bank AG v Finanzamt Frankfurt am Main V-Höchst (Case C-44/11)* may also need to be considered in this context. Further guidance from HMRC was expected in autumn 2012. These issues are looked at in more detail in **Chapter 2**.

This publication is aimed at finance directors and finance controllers in businesses in the financial and insurance sectors and those who advise these sectors. It assumes a reasonable working knowledge of VAT. It is up to date as at 17 July 2012 but VAT is a tax which is subject to regular change, generally as a result of the decisions in European and UK cases. Therefore, readers should always check that there has been no change to case law, legislation or HMRC policy or guidance.

This publication looks at matters specific to the financial services and insurance sectors. One area that it does not cover in any great detail is the VAT treatment of transactions in land and property. It also does not look at matters such as VAT registration and related issues, penalties for errors, nor at the appeals process (other than a brief overview at **7.5**). Information on these matters can be accessed from HMRC or other publications and as always in matters of doubt, advice should be sought from an adviser.

The information in this publication is extracted from various sources, principally EU and UK legislation, HMRC Public Notices, Business Briefs, Press Releases, Guidance Notes and HMRC internal manuals. These are referenced throughout the text. HMRC publications can be accessed via the HMRC website: www.hmrc.gov.uk.

---

[1] *Staatssecretaris van Financiën v Arthur Andersen & Co, ECJ Case C-472/03; [2005] STC 508*

1.2. Introduction to the second edition, June 2015

The disadvantage of a publication of this type is that as soon as you write it, it is immediately out of date. VAT is a tax which never stands still, so revisiting this in early 2015, a number of significant developments have taken place since I wrote the first edition. Furthermore, with tax litigation often taking a number of years to come to any conclusion, many issues remain unresolved so in these cases I have attempted to sign post those issues or cases to keep an eye on.

Since the first edition there have been significant developments in the area of pensions management (and on a related point whether or not an employer can recover VAT charged on investment management fees incurred in respect of pension schemes). This is covered in **2.4.2.1** below. Also, issues around the scope of VAT exemption for payment services (cash handling/cash collection/ debt collection) have moved on with the cases of DPAS, NEC and Bookit (albeit these issues are still unresolved as each case moves forward to further litigation).

I have included a short section on crypto currencies (Bitcoin being the best known of these) at paragraph **2.2.13**. Again, this is a new and developing area and Sweden has now referred questions to the ECJ to establish whether the exchange of cryptocurrencies for traditional currencies is a supply and if so, whether that supply is exempt from VAT. The case (*David Hedqvist, ECJ Case C-264/14*) was heard in June 2015 and the decision is summarised at **2.2.13**.

Other developments over the last year or so have affected VAT grouping, particularly with regards to the treatment of transactions with overseas branches and which entity is entitled to recover historic VAT when the composition of a VAT group changes. Whilst VAT grouping itself is not specifically covered in this publication, these are issues that will be of interest to businesses in the financial sector.

The first issue, regarding the treatment of transactions between parent companies and branches where one or other is in a VAT group, was considered in *Skandia America Corporation, ECJ Case C-7/13*. In brief, the court decided that a recharge of IT services from a US entity to its Swedish branch, which was a member of a Swedish VAT group, was a supply for VAT as the VAT group constituted a separate taxable person. HMRC have reacted by effectively stating that whilst the decision has no impact on UK legislation (UK VAT grouping rules differ from those in Sweden) they will, with effect from 1 January 2016, apply the ruling where the branch/parent is located in a member state that takes the Swedish position on VAT grouping. HMRC have promised to provide a list of the relevant member states. It seems to me that this is a slightly odd, if not contradictory, approach to take – if UK law is correct then why the need to consider the other country's position? I am aware that discussions are ongoing with the European Commission so this may not be the end of the story. Certainly, if the Skandia ruling was applied across the board, it would affect the UK much more than other EU member states owing to the size of the financial services sector in the UK.

The second issue, on which party is entitled to make historic VAT claims when a VAT group has changed or dissolved is ongoing. At the moment, the position would appear to be that it is the representative member that can claim and that it is not possible to assign the right to make the claim (it should be possible to assign the benefit of a claim). However, further litigation is due on these issues (*Taylor Clark Leisure Group [2014] UKUT 0396*) has been appealed by the appellant) so further developments are likely. The message is that when establishing or joining a VAT group, parties should consider putting agreements in place that deal with VAT claims or liabilities that emerge after they have left the group.

Finally, looking a bit further into the future, there will be some key cases being heard in the ECJ on input tax deduction (*Laurentia + Minerva mbH & co, ECJ Case C-109/14* and *Sveda UAB, ECJ Case C-126/14*) and on outsourcing (*Aspiro* formerly known as *BRE Ubezpieczenia Sp. z o.o. ECJ Case C-40/15*), but they will have to wait for the third edition!

1.3. Introduction to the third edition, March 2017

On 23 June 2016, by a narrow margin, the UK referendum decided that the UK should leave the EU (and simultaneously introduced the term 'Brexit' into the lexicon). Parliament subsequently triggered the leaving mechanism (Article 50 of the Treaty of Lisbon) on 29 March 2017, thus setting the clock ticking on a two-year leaving process.

At the moment, that really is as much as we know, so everything else – including the impact on VAT – can only be conjecture or guess work (however educated that guesswork may be). Which all brings to mind the (in)famous comments of Donald Rumsfeld that 'there are known knowns; there are things we know we know. We also know there are known unknowns; that is to say we know there are some things we do not know. But there are also unknown unknowns – the ones we don't know we don't know'

So what we know at the moment is that the referendum decided that the UK should leave the EU, that parliament has triggered the mechanism to start the process and that we remain as members at least until the end of March 2019. What we know we don't know is precisely what impact this will have on the economy, movement of people, the tax system, whether there will be a parliamentary vote on the leave deal (indeed if there will be a deal) or even if there may be a further referendum. And as to the list of unknown unknowns...?

VAT is a European tax and at the moment EU legislation and case law is superior to domestic legislation. The EU has control over VAT rates, VAT exemptions and liabilities and administrative and anti fraud measures. Clearly, leaving the EU will have a significant impact on the UK VAT system. The UK would be free to set its own rates and liabilities and would no longer be required to follow ECJ decisions; in fact, it could if it wished scrap VAT all together (although I wouldn't be holding my breath on that one!).

But at the moment we really cannot be certain. At the time of writing, it is expected that EU legislation will be incorporated into UK statutes by way of a 'Great Repeal Bill' with the assumption that the 'unwanted' bits will be removed over time. So at the moment, it remains 'business as usual' but I expect that changes to the next edition of this book may take a while to complete!

In the meantime, the VAT world continues to turn and since the last edition, there have been significant developments affecting payment processing and card handling services, VAT on holding companies (the Laurentia + Minerva case) and on the right to deduct input tax (the Sveda case) which are now included in the text.

Crowdfunding is a fairly new method of raising funds for activities. HMRC have now issued some guidance on the VAT liabilities affecting transactions in this area, so I've added a brief section on this for the first time.

The decision in Fiscale Eenheid X has further extended the definition of what can constitute a 'Special Investment Fund' (the management of which is VAT exempt) to property-based funds, with a promise from HMRC that changes to UK legislation will follow.

Further litigation is promised in the area of pension fund management with the forthcoming High Court hearing involving the Trustees of the United Biscuits pension scheme, who are challenging the apparent inconsistency that allows insurance companies to exempt the management of defined benefit schemes whereas other managers have to charge VAT. The Supreme Court decision in the ITC case suggests that there will be no claim available direct from HMRC, so if the Trustees are successful in their case, similar issues on recoverability of overcharged VAT will arise. This is outlined in **2.4.2** and **2.4.2.1**.

On partial exemption, the Volkswagen Financial Services case (which looks at the recovery of overhead VAT) has now made its way to the Supreme Court. The Supreme Court has decided that a referral to the ECJ is required although the precise questions to be referred were not agreed at the time of writing.

In the insurance/outsourcing world, the *Aspiro* decision was both unhelpful and possibly a bit surprising. If it was implemented in full, it would have a significant impact on the UK insurance market in particular. However, I suspect much like the Andersens decision in the past (and with Brexit negotiations to come) this one will be kicked into the long grass for now.

1.4. Introduction to the fourth edition, June 2022

On 1 January 2021, the UK completed its exit from the EU. This created a new relationship between the UK and the remaining members and with it created a raft of new legislation. Much of this is outside the scope of this publication but anyone involved in movements of goods whether on a business or personal level will have noticed some significant changes (and no doubt some major irritations too!).

Also, from a practical point of view businesses in the financial services sector who previously operated in the EU (or who wish to do so) under the regulatory 'passporting' arrangements will have needed to consider their position and either look to establish or acquire an EEA based entity or seek separate authorisations in their preferred countries of operation or, as I know a number of smaller business have, maybe withdraw and wait and see what develops.

However, these are issues outside the scope of this publication so I will limit my comments to VAT issues as they currently affect the financial services sector.

The key VAT change is that EU legislation is no longer primary legislation (although many EU VAT principles, obligations and rights have been 'retained') and ECJ court decisions are, in general, no longer binding although 'a court or tribunal may have regard to anything done on or after exit day by the European Court, another EU entity or the EU so far as it is relevant to any matter before the court or tribunal' (*European Union (Withdrawal) Act, 2018* s6(2)). Also, the Court of Appeal decision in *HMRC v Perfect [2022] EWCA Civ 330*, which is an excise duty case but more widely applicable, confirmed that decisions from any referrals to the ECJ made before 31 December 2020 remain binding on the UK even if the decision is issued after that date.

It remains to be seen to what extent the UK courts and tribunals will 'have regard' to EU decisions but I suspect both EU Directives and ECJ decisions will have an influence on UK courts and indeed HMRC interpretations so will remain of interest and relevance to UK businesses. For this reason, I have retained references to EU law and noted those post 31 December 2020 ECJ decisions which I believe affect the sector.

In addition to this general change, there have been some more specific changes, for example the changes to the *VAT (Specified Supplies) Order 1999*, which now treats supplies to persons in the EU in the same way as supplies to persons outside the EU and some changes to the status of EU pension funds. Both have the practical impact of potentially increasing VAT input tax recoveries.

A further EC development that may be of relevance in the future was the EU Commission's review of the VAT rules applying to financial and insurance services which was announced early in 2021. The review was designed to help modernize and simplify the VAT rules applying to these services. The results were published towards in October 2021 and the report can be found at the Europa website. As a very basic summary, most respondents supported the existing exemptions but suggested improvements could be made in areas such as VAT grouping/cost sharing arrangements and perhaps a wider application of an option to tax or zero rate. We now await the Commissions response.

On the subject of consulations, in the Autumn 2021 budget, a consultation on options to simplify the VAT treatment of fund management was announced. The application of the exemption around fund management has caused considerable confusion, no doubt often because of the complexity of fund types in the market (SIFs and non-SIFs) and definitions of 'management'. At the time of writing, we do not know what the results of the consultation will be but any simplification or clarification will I think be widely welcomed.

A further change has been to the status of Cost Sharing Groups, an arrangement that allows persons who carry on certain activities to form a group to share costs without creating sticking VAT. As a result of the ECJ judgements in *DNB Banka AS, C-326/15, Aviva, C-605/15, Commission v Luxembourg, C-274/15* and *Commission v Germany, C-616/15*) HMRC announced a restriction to the types of exempt activities that members of Cost Sharing Groups could undertake. As expected, these excluded financial services and insurance activities. These changes took effect from June 2018. As Cost Sharing groups are no longer available to the financial services and insurance sectors, I have removed the chapter and appendix covering these from this edition. The EU Commission's review above has indicated a degree of support for this arrangement, it is possible that they will be reintroduced for finance and insurance entities in the EU at some point in the future, which in turn may lead to some similar changes in the UK. Until then, I will leave this section out, but anyone interested in the current application can find details in HMRC's Cost Share Exemption Manual on the www.gov.uk website.

2. Financial Services

2.1. Introduction

Readers will be aware that all supplies are treated as taxable for VAT purposes, unless a specific exemption applies. VAT exemption is available for many, but by no means all, financial services. Broadly, exemption is available in respect of dealings in money, securities and the operation and management of accounts or savings schemes. Exemption is also available for related intermediary services.

The EU legislation is found in *Directive 2006/112/EC, Article 135 (1)(b)-(g)*

and equivalent UK legislation is found at *VATA 94, Sch 9, Grp 5*. The EU legislation provides exemption for the following items:

Article 135

1. Member States shall exempt the following transactions:
   - (a) ...;
   - (b) the granting and the negotiation of credit and the management of credit by the person granting it;
   - (c) the negotiation of or any dealings in credit guarantees or any other security for money and the management of credit guarantees by the person who is granting the credit;
   - (d) transactions, including negotiation, concerning deposit and current accounts, payments, transfers, debts, cheques and other negotiable instruments, but excluding debt collection;
   - (e) transactions, including negotiation, concerning currency, bank notes and coins used as legal tender, with the exception of collectors' items, that is to say, gold, silver or other metal coins or bank notes which are not normally used as legal tender or coins of numismatic interest;
   - (f) transactions, including negotiation but not management or safekeeping, in shares, interests in companies or associations, debentures and other securities, but excluding documents establishing title to goods, and the rights or securities referred to in Article 15(2);
   - (g) the management of special investment funds as defined by Member States;
   - (h) ...

This reads across into UK legislation to provide VAT exemption for the following transactions:

1. The issue, transfer or receipt of, or any dealing with, money, any security for money or any note or order for the payment of money.
2. The making of any advance or the granting of any credit.

2A. The management of credit by the person granting it.

3. The provision of the facility of instalment credit finance in a hire- purchase, conditional sale or credit sale agreement for which facility a separate charge is made and disclosed to the recipient of the supply of goods.
4. The provision of administrative arrangements and documentation and the transfer of title to the goods in connection with the supply described in item 3 if the total consideration therefor is specified in the agreement and does not exceed £10.
5. The provision of intermediary services in relation to any transaction comprised in item 1, 2, 3, 4 or 6 (whether or not any such transaction is finally concluded) by a person acting in intermediary capacity.

5A. The underwriting of an issue within item 1 or any transaction within item 6.

6. The issue, transfer or receipt of, or any dealing with, any security or secondary security being –
   (a) shares, stocks, bonds, notes (other than promissory notes), debentures, debenture stock or shares in an oil royalty; or
   (b) any documents relating to money, in any currency, which has been deposited with the issuer or some other person, being a document which recognises an obligation to pay a stated amount to bearer or to order, with or without interest, and being a document by the delivery of which, with or without endorsement, the right to receive that stated amount, with or without interest, is transferable; or
   (c) any bill, note or other obligation of the Treasury or of a Government in any part of the world, being a document by the delivery of which, with or without endorsement, title is transferable, and not being obligation which is or has been legal tender in any part of the world; or
   (d) any letter of allotment or rights, any warrant conferring an option to acquire a security included in this item, any renounceable or scrip certificates, rights coupons, coupons representing dividends or interest on such a security, bond mandates or other documents conferring or containing evidence of title to or rights in respect of such a security; or
   (e) units or other documents conferring rights under any trust established for the purpose, or having the effect of providing, for persons having funds available for investment, facilities for the participation by them as beneficiaries under the trust, in any profits or income arising from the acquisition, holding, management or disposal of any property whatsoever.

7. [.....].

8. The operation of any current, deposit or savings account.
9. The management of –
   (a) an authorised open-ended investment company; or
   (b) an authorised unit trust scheme; or
   (c) a Gibraltar collective investment scheme that is not an umbrella scheme; or
   (d) a sub fund of any other Gibraltar collective investment scheme; or

- (e) an individually recognised overseas scheme that is not an umbrella scheme; or
- (f) a sub fund of any other individually recognised overseas scheme; or
- (g) a recognised collective investment scheme authorised in a designated country or territory that is not an umbrella scheme; or
- (h) a sub fund of any other recognised collective investment scheme authorised in a designated country or territory; or
- (i) a recognised collective investment scheme constituted in another EEA state that is not an umbrella scheme; or
- (j) a sub fund of any other recognised collective investment scheme constituted in another EEA state.
- (k) or (k) a qualifying pension fund

10. The management of a closed ended collective investment undertaken will stop

Note. (k) was introduced via *The Value Added Tax (Finance) Order 2020* and initially in note 6e this included funds established both in the UK and the EU. However, subject to *the VAT (Miscellaneous Amendments to Acts of Parliament)(EU Exit) Regulations 2020*, exemption for for management of funds established in the EU was withdrawn. Consequently, with effect from 1 January 2021, exemption only applies to funds established in the UK.

2.1.1. Place of supply

With effect from 1 January 2010, the place of supply of financial services follows the general rule for the place of supply of services. The place of supply rules are explained further in **Chapter 7**, but in summary this means that the place of supply is where the recipient belongs where the recipient is in business (i.e. for a B2B transaction) and where the supplier belongs for B2C transactions within the EU. B2C transactions in financial services where the recipient belongs outside the EU are also deemed to be supplied where the recipient belongs.

Where a business belonging in the UK sells securities and it is unable to identify the place of belonging of the customer, it has the choice of:

- treating the supply is being made in the UK (and therefore exempt);
- using the place of belonging of a nominee account for the purchaser to determine the place of supply; or
- applying the special 'easement' rules.

Under the easement rules, the following tests are applied in sequential order:

- (a) use the place of transaction (the relevant security exchange) or, if that is not known;
- (b) use the place where the security is listed; or, if that is not known

(c) use the place where the last known broker in the transaction belongs. Further details can be found in *VAT Notice 701/49/*, para 6.16.

2.2. Money and money-related services

The VAT exemption for dealings with money covers the issue, transfer or receipt of money, any security for money or any note or order for the payment of money. Services relating to dealings with securities and secondary securities are covered in 2.3 below.

It should be noted that the supply of coins or banknotes, whether or not legal tender, as collectors' pieces or investment articles is not covered by the exemption and is normally liable to VAT on the full selling price, regardless of whether they sold for more than their face value. However, sales of some gold coins are exempt (with an option to tax) as investment gold, and there is a second-hand margin scheme for supplies of collectors' pieces. Further details on investment gold can be found at **2.11** below and in *VAT Notice 701/21/* and on the second-hand margin scheme can be found in *VAT Notice 718*.

2.2.1. The issue of money

Money can only be issued by a bank or financial institution with a statutory entitlement (most commonly the Bank of England) and a coin or banknote is only issued once. Any exemption for the issue of money is generally overridden by the zero rating available for the issue by bank of note payable to bearer on demand (*VATA 94, Sch 9, Grp 11, Item 1*).

However, in the case of *Royal Bank of Scotland Group plc v C&E Commrs CS [2002] STC 575* exemption applied in relation to fees received by RBS (which was entitled to issue its own bank notes) from other banks whose customers withdrew RBS banknotes from their machines. In this case, the Court of Session ruled that the fees were not consideration for a zero-rated supply of banknotes but for an exempt supply of the provision of facilities to obtain money.

2.2.2. The transfer of money, payment handling and debt collection

The case of *Sparekassernes Datacenter v Skatteministeriet, C-2/95 [1997] STC 932* provided a definition of the meaning of 'transfer', as being:

> a transaction consisting of the execution of an order for the transfer of a sum of money from one bank account to another. It is characterised in particular by the fact that it involves a change in the legal and financial situation existing between the person giving the order and the recipient and between those parties and their respective banks. (para 53).

The SDC case was also applied in *Bookit Ltd v R&C Commrs [2006] STC 1367* which concerned a company arranging cinema bookings and payments (see **2.6.7**).

However, in the case of *HMRC v Axa UK plc, C-175/09 [2010] STC 2825*, the scope of the exemption for the transfer of money was further developed. Axa's services primarily consisted of collecting fees from dental patients by monthly direct debit instalments and passing these (less a charge) on to the dentists. Although this involved a 'transfer' of money, the ECJ saw this as debt collection (which is specifically excluded from exemption). Following this case, HMRC issued Business Brief 54/10 which confirmed that debt collection not only involves the chasing of overdue payments but can be extended to all services involved with collecting payments, regardless of whether those payments are late and outlined HMRC's view of how the decision will apply in practice.

Following from Axa, we then have the case of *DPAS Ltd [2013] UKFTT 676*. DPAS administers dental payments on behalf of dental practices and patients. In 2012, in the light of the Axa decision, it changed its business model so that it had a contract with the patient for plan payment facilities. HMRC were kept informed of these changes. A dispute with HMRC arose on the supply to the patient (both parties accepted that the supply to the dental practices was standard rated) and also whether the change in contract amounted to an abusive practice. The FTT found:

(a) that it was clear to the patient that he was paying the appellant for administration and management of the plan;
(b) the services provided by the appellant were exempt (they were analogous to the services provided to cinema goers by Bookit – see **2.6.7**) and
(c) there was no abuse.

HMRC appealed the case (*DPAS Ltd [2016]; UKUT 373*) and a hearing was originally listed for May 2015 but the decision was reserved pending the outcome of the ECJ case in *Bookit II (Case C- 607/14)* and *NEC (Case C – 130/15)*. See **2.6.7** below for details.

In the end, the Upper Tribunal decided that the decisions in Bookit II and NEC were not sufficient to determine the outcome in this case, so it was referred to the ECJ (Case C – 5/17) for a preliminary ruling as follows:

In the light of Article 135(1)(d) of *Council Directive 2006/112/EC* (the Principal VAT Directive) and the interpretations of that provision given by the Court of Justice in AXA, Bookit II and NEC, the Upper Tribunal (Tax and Chancery Chamber) respectfully refers the following questions to the Court of Justice of the European Union for a preliminary ruling:

1. Is a service, such as that performed by the taxpayer in the present case, consisting of directing, pursuant to a direct debit mandate, that money is taken by direct debit from a patient's bank account and passed by the taxpayer, after deduction of the taxpayer's remuneration, to the patient's dentist and insurance provider, an exempt supply of transfer or payment services within Article 135(1)(d) of the Principal VAT Directive?
2. In particular, do the decisions in Bookit II and NEC lead to the conclusion that the exemption from VAT in Article 135(1)(d) is not applicable to a service, such as that performed by the taxpayer in the present case, which does not involve the taxpayer itself debiting or crediting any accounts over which it has control but which, where a transfer of funds results, is essential to that transfer? Or does the decision in AXA lead to the contrary conclusion?
3. What are the relevant principles to be applied for determining whether or not a service such as that performed by the taxpayer in the present case falls within the scope of 'debt collection' within Article 135(1)(d)? In particular, if (as the Court decided in AXA in relation to the same or a very similar service) such a service would constitute debt collection if provided to the person to whom the payment is due (i.e. the dentists in the present case and in AXA), does that service also constitute debt collection if such a service is provided to the person from whom the payment is due (i.e. the patients in the present case)?

The ECJ subsequently ruled that in answer to the first question, the services supplied did not qualify for exemption as they did not effect the required legal and financial changes; the services wer administrative in nature. In the light of this answer, the court saw no need to address the second question which in itself is a pity as it may have given a bit more guidance on what constitutes – and what does not – 'debt collection'.

In another more recent case, *Target Group Ltd [2021] EWCA Civ 1043* the Court of Appeal confirmed an earlier First Tier and Upper Tier Tribunal decisions that loan administration services constituted taxable debt collection. The Upper Tier Tribunal followed the ECJ decision in DPAS, which was not available at the time of the first hearing, as did the Court of Appeal. The Court of Appeal's decision provides a very good analysis of the development of jurisdiction in this area and is worth reading for anyone involved or interested in these types of supply.

The recent First Tier Tribunal case *Virgin Media Ltd & Anor [2020] UKFTT 30* has also followed the trend and ruled that payment handling services were liable to VAT. The structure involved a tripartite arrangement, with the payment services provided by another VAT group member. However, the tribunal ruled that this was essentially irrelevant as existing legislation views any supply made by a member of a VAT group as being made by the representative member and in these circumstances any 'supply' made by the group member was made to the representative member and formed part of their single taxable supply of media services. But even if these services were supplied separately, they would applying DPAS, still be taxable.

2.2.3. A security for money

In the case of *Dyrham Park Country Club Ltd [1978] VATTR 244 (VTD 700)* the Tribunal defined a 'security for money' as 'a document under seal or under hand at a consideration containing a covenant, promise or undertaking to pay a sum of money'. The Tribunal also held that to be a 'security for money' the document does not have to be 'marketable', 'transferable' or 'negotiable'.

Examples of securities for money include bills of exchange, financial guarantees and promissory notes.

Stocks, shares and bonds are not included within this category (Item 1) but should fall within the exemption allowed for securities (Item 6).

2.2.4. Dealing with money

A supply of services involving dealing with money will be exempt provided that a financial transaction is performed. This will include the common financial transactions carried out by banks, building societies and bureaux de change and similar.

Financial transactions that involve dealing with money will include:

- the acceptance of money on account;
- money transfer services; and
- the exchange of legal tender. See *VAT Notice 701/49/*, para 2.1.

2.2.5. Foreign exchange

Foreign-exchange transactions are normally exempt supplies. Often, the supplier of such services will make profits from a spread between buying and selling prices for the currency or by fluctuations in value over time. Where a person acts as a principal, the consideration received by him for providing a forex service is the net result of the transactions over a given period of time (i.e. the overall profit net of any losses) plus any fees or commission charged (*C & E Commrs v First National Bank of Chicago, Case C-172/96, [1998] STC 850*).

However, in the case of *Willis Pension Trustees Ltd LON/04/1303 (VTD 19183)* where a company which acted as a trustee of the pension fund entered into a number of foreign currency transactions with various banks in order to hedge exposure to adverse exchange rate fluctuations, the Tribunal decided that any profit retained by Willis from foreign exchange transactions did not give rise to a supply for VAT purposes, as it was not consideration for any supply of foreign exchange. HMRC have accepted the decision but say that it will only apply in circumstances identical to those in the Willis case. Therefore, in most cases foreign-exchange transactions are seen as supplies for VAT purposes regardless of whether this is being done as a business on its own account, as supportive of other areas of the business or simply to reduce exposure to foreign-exchange fluctuations.

2.2.6. Automated teller machines (ATMs)

The supply of an ATM itself or the software required to run it is taxable, regardless of whether or not the consideration is based on the ATM's use.

Services provided in connection with the routine operation of an ATM (including filling with cash, maintenance and repair) are also generally taxable supplies. See, for example, the decision in *Concept Direct Ltd (VTD 19721)* which involved a company that located sites for ATMs on behalf of banks and received commission plus a 'swipe fee' each time the machine was used. CDL's supply was found to be taxable as a service of finding and securing sites rather than any exempt supply relating to the issue of money.

In the case of *Cardpoint (C-42/18)* it was ruled that an activity which included installation of ATMs, installation of hardware and software (which verified data and sent an electronic request to a third party to authorize a transaction), replenishing cash supplied by the bank along with general maintenance of the machines did not qualify for exemption. This followed the principles established in Bookit that the exemption for 'transactions concerning payments' had to be more than just physical or technical assistance.

ATM providers will sometimes make charges described as convenience fees, interchange fees or reciprocity fees. Where this charge is for:

- the facility to obtain money;
- the provision of money;
- transaction processing; or
- the operation accounts, the supply is exempt.

The granting of a right to attach an ATM permanently to the ground, or to incorporate it into the fabric of the building, will be an exempt supply (relating to land) unless the grantor has elected to waive exemption. (The 'option to tax' anti-avoidance rules are unlikely to apply in this situation).

VAT Notice 701/49/ para 2.9

2.2.7. Current, deposit and savings accounts

Whilst most of the charges made by banks, building societies or similar organisations relating to the operation of current, deposit and savings accounts are exempt, there are some exceptions. These include:

- the issue of certain types of financial certificate (for example, audit and balance certificates supplied to third parties); and
- the extra cost of special printing or overprinting of cheque books and paying in books.

VAT Notice 701/49/ para 2.10

2.2.8. Dishonoured cheques or direct debit payments

Where a bank makes a charge to its customer because of failure to honour a cheque or direct debit payment, this charge is seen to be part of the overall service of running the customer's account and is therefore exempt.

Where a supplier of goods or services makes a charge (for example where he has borne bank charges) this charge is outside the scope of VAT as it is treated as a form of compensation rather than constituting any supply.

VAT Notice 701/49/ para 2.11

2.2.9. Electronic banking

Electronic banking services are supplied by banks to customers as an addition or alternative to conventional banking services.

In order to determine the liability of an electronic banking service, it is necessary first to determine whether it is a supply in its own right or part of a package of services. Generally, as long as the service would have qualified for exemption if provided by conventional means, it should retain that exemption when provided electronically. However, if any financial service provided electronically is not covered by the exemption, it should be treated as liable to VAT. Examples of taxable services would include the provision of information on share prices and exchange rates etc, the hire of equipment and related charges, such as training and sales of equipment.

VAT Notice 701/49/ para 2.12

2.2.10. Travellers' cheques

The issue and/or encashment of travellers' cheques is exempt.

Unissued or unsigned travellers cheques are neither securities for money nor notes for the payment of money and their supply to or importation by the issuing bank is taxable on their value as stationery.

VAT Notice 701/49/ para 3.4

2.2.11. Deductions from pay

Charges made by an employer for deductions from pay of employees for items such as:

- insurance premiums;
- mortgage repayments; or
- union subscriptions, are exempt from VAT.

Any charges made for deductions from pay in compliance with an attachment of earnings order are seen as reimbursement for expenses incurred in carrying out a statutory duty and are therefore outside the scope of VAT.

VAT Notice 701/49/ para 2.13

2.2.12. Clearing and settlement services

A service supplied by a clearing-house for settling indebtedness between members is an exempt supply.

VAT Notice 701/49/ para 2.8

2.2.13. Crypto currencies – Bitcoin

Crypto currencies can be broadly described as decentralised digital currencies that operate via a peer-to-peer network, independent of any central bank. The network will collectively deal with the issue, processing and verification of transactions. Bitcoin is probably the best known of these crypto currencies.

This is still a new and developing area so VAT treatments may change as the UK and the EU as a whole gets to grips with these new digital currencies. However, HMRC have outlined their provisional views in *Revenue & Customs Brief 09/14*. In summary:

- income received from Bitcoin mining activities (effectively the creation of new Bitcoin) will generally be outside the scope of VAT on the basis that the activity does not constitute an economic activity for VAT purposes because there is an insufficient link between any services provided and any consideration received;

- income received by miners for other activities, such as for the provision of services in connection with the verification of specific transactions for which specific charges are made, will be exempt from VAT under Article 135(1)(d) of the EU VAT Directive as falling within the definition of 'transactions, including negotiation, concerning deposit and current accounts, payments, transfers, debts, cheques and other negotiable instruments';
- when Bitcoin is exchanged for Sterling or for foreign currencies, such as Euros or Dollars, no VAT will be due on the value of the Bitcoins themselves;
- charges (in whatever form) made over and above the value of the Bitcoin for arranging or carrying out any transactions in Bitcoin will be exempt from VAT under Article 135(1)(d) as outlined above; and
- where services are sold in exchange for Bitcoin, VAT will be due in the normal way, with the value being the Sterling equivalent of the Bitcoin at the time of the transaction.

However, it should be stressed that this is only HMRC's provisional view and the VAT (and other tax) position may evolve alongside these new currencies.

In the case of *Skatteverket v David Hedqvist, Case C – 264/14,* the ECJ ruled that the exchange of Bitcoin for another currency is an exempt supply for VAT, in the same way as any other exchange of legal tender and that the consideration is the margin between the sale and purchase price.

2.2.14. Exchanging coins for vouchers

It is quite common for supermarkets to have machines which will accept small coins and issue face value vouchers to the same value to be redeemed in store. In the case of *Coinstar Ltd [2017] UKUT 0256* the Upper Tier tribunal upheld a decision of the First Tier tribunal that commissions earned by the providers of these machines qualified for exemption as consideration for a single supply of the transfer of money or security for money (*VATA 94, item 1, Group 5, Sch 9*).

2.3. Securities

The issue, transfer or receipt of, or any dealing with, any security or secondary security in the UK is exempt from VAT. What constitutes a security or secondary security is set out in *VATA 94, Sch 9, Grp 5, Item 6* (see 2.1 above).

However, despite the wording of the legislation, as a result of the decision of the ECJ in *Kretztechnik AG v Finanzamt Linz, Case C-465/03, [2005] STC*

1118, the first issue of securities, such shares, bonds, loan notes, debentures etc. by a company is not a supply for VAT purposes, as the purpose of that issue is to raise capital. This also includes the issue of units or shares in investment fund.

Transactions in shares which are already in existence are exempt.

2.3.1. Stock lending

In a stock lending transaction one person (the lender) transfers to a second person (the borrower) the legal title, along with all dividends and rights, to securities. The borrower agrees to return to the lender, at a future time, an equivalent number of the same securities as those received.

Stock lending is an exempt supply and consideration for the supply is the fee charged to the borrower.

Where stocks are loaned, the borrower will receive any dividends, but these are not consideration for any supply.

The borrower should not account for VAT on the value of securities returned to the lender, because this is not a supply.

VAT Notice 701/49/ para 6.3

2.3.2. Custody services

Custody services are generally divided into two types: **safe custody services** and **global custody services**.

Safe custody services are liable to VAT at the standard rate. These services mainly concern the provision of the physical services of safekeeping, sometimes referred to as safe-deposit facilities.

A supply of services made in the UK in respect of the safe custody of securities is taxable irrespective of whether the securities are held in the UK, an overseas branch or elsewhere.

If a specific site is leased to a client as opposed to there being a provision of secure storage within a business's own premises, the supply is in the UK if the site is in the UK, but outside the scope of UK VAT if the site is overseas. A business may be required to account for VAT in another member state if the place of supply is elsewhere in the EU.

Global custody services consist of a package of mainly financial services that may include the collection of dividends or interest on securities held, dealing with scrip and rights issues and payment and delivery of stock, as well as physical safe custody as an incidental aspect. In such cases, the supply of the whole service, including the safe custody element, is exempt.

VAT Notice 701/49/ para 6.6

2.3.3. Nominee services

Where a person acts as a nominee (i.e. holds securities in their own name on behalf of the beneficial owner) the services are exempt. This will also include any charges for transferring stock from one nominee to another, which is deemed exempt as a transaction in securities.

VAT Notice 701/49/ para 6.5

2.3.4. Share registrar services

Services of a share registrar may include some or all of the following (this list is not exhaustive):

- all aspects of operating company share registers;
- administration of scrip schemes, share option schemes, profit sharing schemes and dividend reinvestment plans;
- arrangements for advertising the closure of a share offer;
- attending shareholders' meetings and organising polls at such meetings;
- arranging 'break out' for bulk nominee accounts;
- capital gains enquiries, and other correspondence and enquiries;
- conversion of loan stock;
- preparation, designation and despatch of certificates, correction of errors on certificates, and issuing of duplicated documents;
- administrative services in relation to mergers, placings, rights issues, reorganisations and acquisitions;
- processing forms of proxy;
- registration of grants of probate;
- regular reports on share movements; and
- administrative services in relation to savings plan schemes.

These services are liable to VAT at the standard rate and are treated as supplied where the business customer belongs. However, if a share registration service is provided as one element of a single composite supply with other services with different VAT liabilities, the liability of the share registrar service may change.

Where the share registration service is provided to either an authorised unit trust or an open-ended investment company, please see 6.4 below.

VAT Notice 701/49/ para 6.7

2.3.5. Underwriting

The underwriting of an issue falling either within *VATA 94, Sch 9, Grp 5, Item 1* or Item 6 is exempt (*VATA 94, Sch 9, Grp 5,Item 5A*).

A share underwriter guarantees to buy a proportion of any unsold shares when a new issue is offered to the general public, and usually receives either a commission or a fee. The underwriter may also underwrite an issue by agreeing to guarantee that buyers will be found. In both these cases, the underwriter's supply is exempt.

There is no supply for VAT purposes by the issuer who sells the securities to the underwriter (see **2.3** above) but there is a subsequent exempt supply by the underwriter when the securities are sold.

Where the underwriter adjusts their commission or fee to reflect their entitlement to purchase the securities at a special price, the value of the adjustment (discount) must be regarded as part of the consideration for the exempt supply of underwriting services. However, if the underwriter is obliged to purchase further securities which remain unsold and the agreement provides for a price lower than the offer price, that reduction is not regarded as consideration for the underwriting service and should be treated as outside the scope of VAT.

The exemption also applies to supplies made by a sub-underwriter, who agrees to underwrite a proportion of the issue or sale, regardless of whether the sub-underwriter's services are supplied to the underwriter or to the issuer.

VAT Notice 701/49/ para 6.4

2.3.6. Dealer systems and data services

2.3.6.1 Dealer systems

Many securities transactions are carried out by electronic means. Where a dealing system allows the user to insert bid and offer quotes for the securities; allows another user to insert an acceptance and allows the system to match and sell deals, the supply of the dealing system is exempt where it is made by the business that runs that system.

VAT Notice 701/49/ para 6.12

2.3.6.2 Data services

The sale or lease of the data system or of the software or the provision of an electronic data service that simply provides subscribers with a message facility or an information service (e.g. on share prices) is liable to VAT at the standard rate.

VAT Notice 701/49/ para 6.13

2.3.7. Specialist services

In the majority of cases, the exemption for intermediary services (see **2.6** below) does not cover:

- professional services provided by accountants and lawyers; and
- general advisory services (e.g. the provision advice to investors deciding whether to accept or reject a takeover bid).

Other services supplied in connection with share issues, acquisitions and disposals that do not bring together buyer and seller are also taxable, unless they are provided as part of a complete service and are ancillary to an exempt financial service. These services will typically include:

- valuation of assets;
- assessing the direct tax liabilities of a holding;
- investment analysis;
- market sector research;
- share consultancy;
- general financial or investment advice;
- accountancy services;
- tax or legal advice; and
- the supply of a draft prospectus.

Where these services are supplied to either an authorised unit trust or open-ended investment company, see **2.4** below.

VAT Notice 701/49/, para 6.14

2.4. Investment funds and wrappers

Following the decision of the ECJ in *Kretztechnik AG v Finanzamt Linz, Case C-465/03, [2005] STC 1118,* the issue of units in an authorised unit trust are not supplies for VAT purposes (see also HMRC Business Brief 21/05).

A unit trust itself will hold and carry out transactions in securities and the sale of the underlying securities will be an exempt supply by the trust. Whilst investment management services are normally liable to VAT, under *EC Directive 2006/112/EC, Art 135(1)(g),* the management of special investment funds 'as defined by Member States' is exempt. The UK has applied this exemption to the management of those funds falling within *VATA 94, Sch 9, Grp 5 Item 9*:

9. The management of -
   (a) an authorised open ended investment company; or
   (b) an authorised unit trust scheme; or
   (c) a Gibraltar collective investment scheme that is not an umbrella scheme; or

(d) a sub-fund of any other Gibraltar collective investment scheme; or
(e) an individually recognised overseas scheme that is not an umbrella scheme; or
(f) a sub-fund of any other individually recognised overseas scheme; or
(g) a recognised collective investment scheme authorised in a designated country or territory that is not an umbrella scheme; or
(h) a sub-fund of any other recognised collective investment scheme authorised in a designated country or territory; or
(i) a recognised collective investment scheme constituted in another EEA state that is not an umbrella scheme; or
(j) a sub-fund of any other recognised collective investment scheme constituted in another EEA state; or.
(k) a qualifying pension fund

For these purposes, the following definitions apply:

Authorised open ended investment company and authorised unit trust scheme have the meaning given in the *Financial Services and Markets Act 2000, s237(3)*.

Collective investment scheme has the meaning given in *FSMA 2000 s235*.

Gibraltar collective investment scheme means a collective investment scheme to which *FSMA 2000, s264* applies pursuant to an order made under *FSMA 2000, s409(1)(d)*; or a collective investment scheme to which FSMA 2000 applies pursuant to an order made under *FSMA 2000, s409 (1)(f)*.

Individually recognised overseas scheme means a collective investment scheme declared by the financial services authority to be a recognised scheme under *FSMA 2000, s272*.

Recognised collective investment scheme authorised in a designated country or territory means a collective investment scheme recognised under *FSMA 2000, s270*.

Recognised collective investment scheme constituted in another EEA state means a collective investment scheme which is recognised under *FSMA 2000, s264*.

Sub-fund means a separate part of the property of an umbrella scheme that is pooled separately.

Umbrella scheme means a collective investment scheme under which the contributions of the participants in the scheme and the profits or income out of which payments are to be made to them are pooled separately in relation to separate parts of the scheme property.

These provisions do not cover a collective investment scheme, or sub-fund, that is not for the time being marketed in the UK if it has never been marketed in the UK or less than 5% of shares units are held by, or on behalf of, investors who are in the UK.

Qualifying pension fund means a pension fund in relation to which all of the following conditions are satisfied: (a) it is solely funded, whether directly or indirectly, by pension members; (b) the pension members bear the investment risk; (c) the fund contains the pooled contributions of more than one pension member; (d) the risk borne by the pension members is spread over a range of investments; and (e) the fund is established in the United Kingdom.

A pension fund is funded indirectly where contributions are made by a third party on behalf of a pension member. Prior to 1 January 2021, exemption was also allowed for the management of pension funds established in the EU.

VATA 94, Sch 9, Grp 5, Item 9 and notes 6 and 6A

2.4.1. Management of special investment funds

Until 30 September 2008, the UK restricted exemption to the management of authorised unit trust schemes, open-ended investment companies and trust-based schemes. This was changed with effect from 1 October 2008, following an ECJ ruling in the case of *JP Morgan Fleming Claverhouse Investment Trust plc v HMRC (and related appeal), Case C-363/05, [2008] STC 1180 C-363/05* (see **2.4.2** below). The scope of VAT exemption was extended to the management of all similar collective investment undertakings (CIUs) which compete in the UK retail market under comparable conditions.

CIUs are in the business of collective investments (i.e. they pool and invest capital raised from the public and do so for a fee or management charge). It is this management charge this is the subject of the exemption. CIUs may be constituted in various legal forms, but common to all is that investors hold shares or units in the CIU.

In the case of *Fiscale Eenheid X NV cs, Case C – 595/13*, the ECJ held that property-based funds can qualify as 'special investment funds', meaning that the management can be VAT-exempt. However, they must be regulated in the Member State and share certain characteristics with securities-based funds. Management, for the purposes of exemption, will not include services such as day to day management and property maintenance. HMRC announced the following in their updated guidance issued in October 2016:

UK legislation currently confines the scope of the fund management exemption to funds that invest "wholly or mainly in securities". The judgment in Fiscale Eenheid X however means that no restriction should be placed on the nature of the assets in which a fund invests for exemption to apply and UK legislation will be amended in due course to reflect this.

Certain direct contribution or 'DC' pension funds will also qualify as Special Investment Funds as qualifying pension funds (see **2.4** above and **2.4.2.1** below on the ATP case).

Trust-based schemes are no longer included in the exemption.

2.4.1.1 Outsourced SIF management services

In a decision issued in June 2021 in the joined cases of *K v Finanzamt Linz* and *DBK v Finanzampt Linz (Cases C-58/20 and 59/20)* the ECJ looked at whether services such as tax accounting (K) and a supply of a licence to use specialist software (DBK) could constitute management of special investment funds when outsourced to third parties. The decision was that they could, provided they have an intrinsic link to the funds and are provided exclusively for the management of the funds. This

2.4.1.2 Apportionment of platform management funds

In the case of *Blackrock Investment Management (UK) Ltd, Case C-231/19*, the ECJ looked at the treatment of a multi funfunction platform service.

The services are supplied via a software platform called Aladdin. Aladdin is used by Blackrock to provide essential information to portfolio managers to enable them to make investment decisions and is used in the management of both SIFs and non-SIFs.

The Aladdin platform is owned by a US based Blackrock entity which supplies its services to Blackrock in the UK in return for fees that are largely calculated by reference to the value of assets under management. Blackrock accounts for VAT under the reverse charge mechanism.

Blackrock accepted hat the supply of services to them was a single supply but argued that it should nonetheless be entitled to apportion the platform fees and to account for VAT on the part of the fees relating to the management of non-SIFs. It proposed to apportion the fees in accordance with the value of assets under management in the SIF and non-SIF funds. The majority of the funds in this case were non SIFs.

The decision of the ECJ was to rule against apportionment and consequently rule that there was a single supply of services that was taxable on the full amount.

This is an important and complex case and could have implications for many funds and their managers. This case was decided on its own facts and largely decided on how the services were delivered so it may be open to others to consider how they receive services and how those services may be directly related to SIFs or non SIFs. But one key issue – supported by the decision in K and DBK (see **2.4.1.2** above) – is that services such as software can form exempt management as long as it relates to and is essential for the SIF. As mentioned in the introduction to this edition, the EU are currently reviewing how VAT applies to financial services and the UK's is looking more specifically at fund management so the extent and scope of 'management' is almost certainly going to be one of the issues under consideration.

2.4.2. Closed-ended collective investment undertakings

The management of a closed ended collective investment undertaking is exempt (*VATA 94, Sch 9, Grp 5, Item 10*).

The UK VAT legislation was amended from 1 October 2008 following the decision in the ECJ case of *JP Morgan Fleming Claverhouse Investment Trust plc v HMRC, Case C-363/05, [2008] STC 1180* where it was held that the phrase 'special investment funds' could also include closed-ended investment funds, such as investment trust companies (ITCs). Whilst EU provisions give member states discretion as to which special investment funds can benefit from exemption for the provision of management services, in exercising that discretion, member states must have regard to the principle of fiscal neutrality.

A closed-ended collective investment undertaking must satisfy the following criteria:

- its sole object is the investment of capital, raised from the public, wholly or mainly in securities;
- it manages its assets on the principle of spreading investment risk;
- all of its ordinary shares (of each class if there is more than one) or equivalent units are included in the official list maintained by the Financial Services Authority under *FSMA 2000, s74(1)*; and
- all of its ordinary shares (of each class there is more than one) or equivalent units are admitted to trading on a regulated market situated or operating in the UK.

Although the change in law came into effect on 1 October 2008, it was only confirming what should have been the correct position from 1 January 1990, when the exemption was first introduced. Therefore, businesses that had accounted for VAT on fund management services that qualified for exemption had the entitlement to a refund of that VAT subject to the normal capping and unjust enrichment provisions.

VATA 94, Sch 9, Grp 5, Item 10 and note 6. HMRC Brief 35/08

For the trusts or funds incurring the management fees there have been some issues in seeking refunds from the managers, either because refunds were made on a 'net' basis (i.e. the managers would offset irrecoverable input tax when making the refund) or because the managers are no longer in business. This issue was addressed in the Supreme Court decision in *The Commissioners For Her Majesty's Revenue and Customs v The Investment Trust Co [2017] UKSC 29*. This case looked at whether or not it would be possible for funds to recover the overpaid VAT directly from HMRC. However, the Supreme Court has now ruled that the funds can only claim against the manager (the supplier) and that a claim from HMRC would only ever be possible if it were virtually impossible or excessively difficult to claim from the supplier. Furthermore, they ruled that any such claim was ruled out in any event by statute (*VATA 94 s80*) and that this treatment was fully compatible with EU law.

2.4.2.1 *Pension fund management*

One of the main changes since the publication of the first edition has been in the area of pension fund management. Until recently, pension fund management was always seen as a taxable supply (unless provided by an insurance company as the management of pension funds is a class of insurance[2]). However, this was challenged before the CJEU in *Wheels Common Investment Fund Trustees and Others, Case C-424/11*, following a referral from the UK FTT. Briefly, Wheels and the NAPF argued that the exemption afforded by the JP Morgan case noted in **2.4.2** above, should also extend to the management of occupational pension funds. HMRC argued that a pension fund is not a special investment fund (SIF) because it is not a collective investment undertaking available to a private investor which is directly in competition with authorised investment funds, closed-ended collective undertakings (i.e. investment trust companies and venture capital trusts) or overseas equivalents that market to the general public in the UK. The ECJ ruled that they were not 'special investment funds' within

---

[2] Class of insurance Part II VII (see **Appendix A**)

Article 135(1)(g) of *Council Directive 2006/112/EC*. However, the ruling was restricted to answering questions referred to it by the UK VAT tribunal which in this case was solely about defined benefit (DB) schemes. A question remained regarding the management of defined contribution (DC) schemes. Furthermore, the decision of the FTT has been stayed pending the outcome of the United Biscuits case (see below) as Wheels were allowed to amend its appeal and stand behind United Biscuits.

Before turning to DC schemes, the issue of managing DB schemes was also examined in the case of *Fiscale Eenheid PPG Holdings BV c.s. v Inspecteur van de Belastingdienst/Noord/kantoor Groningen, Case C-26/12*. The question regarding whether or not exemption applied to the management of the DB fund was not specifically answered, as this had been addressed in the Wheels case. However, what PPG did consider was the recoverability of VAT incurred by an employer that related to the pension fund. In PPG the ECJ ruled that an employer would be entitled to recover VAT incurred on administration and pension management costs, provided there was a direct and immediate link between these services and the employer's own supplies. Historically, HMRC had distinguished between the costs of administering the fund and costs relating to the investment activity of the fund, with only VAT on the former being input tax of the employer. In light of the PPG case, HMRC have now changed their approach and will allow the employer to recover VAT on investment-related activities provided the employer bears the cost and the service also includes some pension administration (investment management services alone are seen as having a direct and immediate link to the supplies of the investments themselves). HMRC's initial response can be found in Revenue & Customs Brief 6/1. They subsequently updated their view in Revenue & Customs Brief 17/15 where they looked at particular issues around tripartite arrangements, Corporation Tax deductions, trustees providing services to employers and VAT grouping. In addition, they confirmed that the transitional period (under which a taxpayer can opt to use the old rules) is extended to 31 December 2017.

The management of DC schemes was considered in the case of *ATP Pension Service A/S, Case C-464/12*. In this case, unlike in the Wheels and PPG cases, the ECJ ruled that the management of these funds fell within the exemption

> ...if they are funded by the persons to whom the retirement benefit is to be paid, if the funds are invested using a risk-spreading principle, and if the pension customers bear the investment risk. In that regard, it is of little consequence that the contributions are paid by the employer; that the amount paid in is based on collective agreements between labour market

> organisations; that there are different ways of paying out the funds invested; that contributions are deductible under income tax law; or that it is possible to add an insurance element which is ancillary to the other services provided;...

Following the ATP decision, HMRC issued *Revenue & Customs Brief 44/14* announcing that there would be changes to UK legislation to reflect the ECJ ruling and that they were considering whether the case had any wider implications. In their updated guidance notes, issued in October 2016, HMRC confirmed:

> 'In light of the ATP judgment, it is now accepted that pension funds that have all of the following characteristics are SIFs [Special Investment Funds] for the purposes of the fund management exemption so that the services of managing and administering those funds are exempt from VAT:
>
> - they are solely funded (whether directly or indirectly, e.g. by an employer) by persons to whom the retirement benefit is to be paid (i.e. the pension customers)
> - the pension customers bear the investment risk
> - the fund contains the pooled contributions of several pension customers
> - the risk borne by the pension customers is spread over a range of investments
>
> In addition to funds that contain the pooled assets of defined contribution occupational pension schemes, such as that at issue in ATP, funds that contain the pooled assets of personal pension schemes and that have all of the above characteristics will also fall within the VAT exemption for fund management services.'

VATFIN5120

As a result, *The VAT (Finance) Order 2020* added qualifying pension funds to *VATA 94, Sch 9, Grp 5 Item 9*. A qualifying pension fund is defined (in note 6 to that item) as:

> a pension fund in relation to which all of the following conditions are satisfied—
>
> (a) it is solely funded, whether directly or indirectly, by pension members;
>
> (b) the pension members bear the investment risk;
>
> (c) the fund contains the pooled contributions of more than one pension member;
>
> (d) the risk borne by the pension members is spread over a range of investments; and
>
> (e) the fund is established in the United Kingdom or in a member State.

Subsequently, the *VAT (Miscellaneous Amendments to Acts of Parliament)(EU Exit) Regulations 2020*, removed 'or in a member state' from e with effect from 1 January 2021.

as Another relevant case involves the Trustees of the United Biscuits pension scheme which appealed to the High Court challenging the point that insurers can exempt management of DB schemes whereas other managers must charge VAT on the basis that this offends the concept of fiscal neutrality. *United Biscuits (Pension Trustees) Limited v HMRC (HC14A01221)*. In essence the appellant argued that the differentiation in treatment offended fiscal neutrality and that as a consequence, HMRC had been unjustly enriched at the appellants expense and that furthermore they were entitled to a remedy directly from HMRC as it would be impossible to claim back the unlawfully levied VAT elsewhere. The High Court dismissed the case but the appellants were given leave to appeal to the Court of Appeal who in turn referred the following question to the ECJ:

> 'Are supplies of pension fund management services as are provided to the applicants by (a) insurers and/or (b) non insurers 'insurance transactions' within the meaning of Article 135(1)(a) of Directive 2006/112/EC'?

The Advocate General's opinion was that they do not and in the decision in the case (*United Biscuits (Pension Trustees) Limited & Anor (Case C-235/19)*) the ECJ agreed giving the answer to the question that Article 135(1)(a) must be interpreted as meaning that 'investment fund management services provided to pension funds which do not provide any indemnity from risk, cannot be classified as 'insurance transactions'…'. Although the court never looked at the fiscal neutrality point, this decision seems to resolve the long running saga of the differing treatments of pension fund management.

2.4.3. Wrapper products

'Wrapper' products hold investments in a tax efficient wrapper making them free of income and capital gains tax and are aimed at stimulating the general public to save and invest money. Examples of these products include (or have included) Individual Savings Accounts (ISAs), Child Trust Funds (CTFs), Personal Equity Plans (PEPs) and Self Invested Personal Pensions (SIPPs).

2.4.3.1 *Individual Savings Accounts (ISAs)*

An ISA is a tax-free annual investment product, launched on 6 April 1999 to replace the Personal Equity Plan and the Tax Exempt Special Savings Account (TESSA). When launched, it was made up of three components: cash, insurance, or stocks and shares and could be a mix of these components. An ISA comprising one component only was called a 'mini'

ISA, whilst an ISA allowing for more than one component was called a 'maxi' ISA.

1. Cash mini ISA - there is usually no charge connected with a cash ISA. The ISA manager's service to the investor is exempt as the operation of a bank account. However, where the ISA is based on cash unit trusts it is treated as a stocks and shares mini ISA for VAT purposes and the ISA management charges are taxable at the standard rate.
2. An insurance mini ISA is an investment linked to a life insurance policy ensuring the life of the ISA holder. See **Chapter 3** for more details on the liability of insurance-related services.
3. A stocks and shares mini ISA is generally intended for savers who do not need immediate access to savings. The VAT treatment for the stocks and shares components of both ISAs and PEPs is the same.
4. A maxi ISA could comprise a mixture of cash, insurance and stocks and shares components but most tend to consist solely of stocks and shares. Where a maxi ISA consisted of multiple components, each component, although packaged together for tax purposes, is usually managed and charged for separately. The VAT liability of supplies made in respect of the stocks and shares component of a maxi ISA is the same as that for a stocks and shares mini ISA.

From 6 April 2005, the ISA structure was changed. The separate ISA insurance component was removed and insurance products were given the same ISA treatment as other collective investment schemes within the ISA stocks and shares component. This means that there are now only two ISA components: cash or stocks and shares.

The VAT liability of charges to customers is as follows:

1. Cash ISAs – these operate like bank accounts and therefore consideration received by the provider, such as any fees charged for operation of the account, will be exempt under *VATA 94, Sch 9, Grp 5, Item 8*.
2. Share ISAs – customers may be charged for execution of the purchase of shares or for portfolio management once the shares are purchased and held in their ISA. Arranging the purchase of securities is exempt under *VATA 94, Sch 9, Grp 5, Item 5*. Portfolio management is excluded from that exemption and is therefore taxable at standard rate. *Deutsche Bank AG v Finanzamt Frankfurt am Main V-Höchst (Case C-44/11)*
3. Insurance ISAs – it is understood that very few insurers have ever offered this product. However, contributions to insurance ISAs are

likely to be treated as insurance premiums and exempt under *VATA 94, Sch 9, Grp 2, Item 1.*

HMRC Finance Manual VATFIN5600

2.4.3.2 ***Child Trust Funds (CTFs)***

The CTF was introduced in April 2005 and is an account that may be either a 'stakeholder account' or a 'non-stakeholder account'. The accounts must be held with an account provider as approved by HMRC. The government provides the initial contribution in the form of a voucher and others may also contribute to the account.

There is a maximum 1.5% annual charge if the CTF is a stakeholder account, which is normally charged by the CTF provider and which is deductible from the child's fund. Non-stakeholder accounts have a range of charges. CTFs may be provided as savings accounts and charges for their operation will be exempt under *VATA 94, Sch 9, Grp 5, Item 8*. However, if they are provided as other wrapper products, the VAT liability will depend on the liability of the particular product.

2.4.3.3 ***Personal Equity Plans (PEPs)***

PEPs were introduced in 1987 and replaced by the ISA from 6 April 1999. A PEP was treated the same as a share ISA for VAT purposes. From 6 April 2008, all remaining PEPs became share ISAs.

2.4.4. AUTIF administrative agreement

An agreement was entered into on 1 April 1994 between HMRC and the Association of Unit Trusts and Investment Funds (AUTIF) – now the Investment Management Association – regarding the VAT treatment of PEP manager's charges. This agreement was subsequently used as a guide to determine the VAT treatment of charges in respect of other wrapper products. However, the AUTIF agreement has since been withdrawn and the tax treatments are now outlined in the VAT Finance Manual, VATFIN5000 which is available from the HMRC website.

2.4.5. Wrap accounts

A wrap account is an arrangement that holds a range of investments, whether within tax efficient wrappers or not, providing a single point of contact and management for investors and their agents.

A wrap manager is usually a separate legal entity within a financial services or insurance group that offers to hold, manage and administer the whole or part of an individual's portfolio. The wrap account may typically be an interest-bearing bank account, with a set of sub-accounts, allowing payments to be made and received within broad product silos. The manager will generally nominate a third-party discretionary investment manager along with an execution-only broker. The discretionary investment manager normally offers (or is required by the wrap manager to offer) nominee account services. Often it will also offer safe custody services.

Typically, charging structures for wrapper products are transaction charges, based on the value of investments within the account, including dividends, interest and principal amounts along with annual charges. The VAT liability of a wrap will depend on the nature of the supplies made.

2.4.5.1 *Nominee accounts*

The simplest form of a wrap account is a nominee account. Investors will usually make investments through a bank or building society account or via an Independent Financial Adviser (IFA) or other intermediary. Many of these will operate nominee account arrangements.

As far as the provider (e.g. the fund manager) is concerned, it receives a purchase instruction registered in the name of a nominee account. The fund manager does not need to have, and usually does not have, a relationship with the underlying investor. The intermediary will receive ongoing reporting/disclosures from the provider, which it will forward (appropriately customised/apportioned) to the underlying investors, of which there may be hundreds, or even thousands.

Charges for the services of acting as a nominee (i.e. holding securities on behalf of a beneficial owner) are exempt.

2.4.5.2 *Fund supermarkets*

Fund supermarkets are another facility offered by many wrap accounts. They provide access to a variety of collective funds managed by different fund managers. In effect, the investor is like a shopper in the supermarket, with the products being the funds and the supermarket the shop. They may offer advice or analytical decision or fund selection tools or simply provide 'execution only' services.

Fund supermarkets allow investors to purchase fund shares/units from a variety of fund managers, usually at discounted prices. Such shares/units may be wrapped within a PEP or ISA, or held as standalone investments. The investor has a contractual relationship with the supermarket, and does not deal direct with the fund manager. Likewise, fund managers have no knowledge of individual investors – they simply deal with net, bulk orders from the supermarket's nominee account to sell or buy shares/units.

Typical services undertaken by the supermarket may include:

- fund transaction clearance and settlement;
- receipt and payment of fund distributions;
- maintenance of investors' fund information (share/unit balances, dividend and distribution information and transaction history);
- issue of all confirmations, statements, prospectuses and literature to investors;
- sending of any tax vouchers to investors, including the amount of dividend and interest paid; and
- holding (by the supermarket, or its nominee/custodian), of the shares/units subscribed for by investors, together with any reinvested dividends and distributions.

Investors usually pay no fee to the supermarket itself. Instead, the supermarket usually receives commission from the fund manager, which may be taken in the form of a rebate of the management fee. In this case, the 'commission' represents a bulk discount for a large nominal investor, and, as such, is not a taxable supply. At the time of writing, this is an area under review with regards to the impact of the Retail Distribution Review (RDR), so it is possible that there may be some changes to how supermarkets operate and as a consequence, how they account for VAT. For more details on the impact of RDR generally, see **2.6.5.1.**

HMRC Finance Manual VATFIN 5500

2.4.6. Crowdfunding

Crowdfunding is a method of funding a project or new business venture through a collection of small contributions from a large number of people (the crowd via the internet.

The project owner normally utilises a specialist online platform to advertise their project to the general public in the hope of generating interest and raising funds.

HMRC have now issued some initial guidance on the likely VAT aspects of Crowdfunding:

> HMRC understands, there are two main crowdfunding models; the non-financial model and the financial return model.
>
> **1. The non-financial return model**
>
> The two main non-financial models are the reward model and the donation (no reward) model.

1.1 Reward model

The contributor, in return for providing a monetary contribution to the project or venture will receive goods or services (non-monetary reward).

VAT treatment

Where a contributor receives goods or services that have an intrinsic value (e.g. clothing, tickets, dvd) in exchange for support given, there is a supply for VAT purposes. The VAT treatment will follow the liability of the goods or services provided.

1.2 Donation (no reward) model

The contributor makes a monetary contribution to the project or venture and expects nothing in return.

VAT treatment

Where a contributor freely makes a contribution where they expect and receive nothing in return, the contribution is treated as a donation and is not liable to VAT. The position is the same where all that the funder receives is something of symbolic value. For example, an acknowledgement such as a mention in a programme or something similar.

2. The financial return model

The two main types of financial return model are investment based and loan based.

2.1 Crowdfunding - Investment based

In exchange for their investment, the contributor receives financial remuneration in the form of equity securities (such as shares) or debt securities (such as bonds or debentures) issued by the business who launched the funding campaign.

VAT treatment

Following the decision of the ECJ in Kreztechnik, the issue of securities by the business to the contributor, will not be a supply for VAT purposes provided the purpose of the issue is to raise finance.

Where there is a sale, transfer of or trading in existing shares and this is done in furtherance of a course of business, then this is treated as exempt under item 6 Group 5 schedule 9 VATA 94.

Where the contributor has received financial remuneration in the form of shares issued by the business, any dividends paid to the contributor will be outside the scope of VAT.

Where the contributor has received financial remuneration in the form of a debt security such as a bond or debenture issued by the business, interest received by the contributor as holder of the security will be exempt under item 2 Group 5 schedule 9 VATA 94.

Where a fixed term debt security such as a bond is held to its maturity date the repayment received on redemption will be outside the scope of VAT.

For further information on the VAT treatment of securities see VATFIN4250.

2.2 Crowdfunding - loan based

Otherwise known as peer to peer lending, the contributor will lend money to a business/entrepreneur they select on the crowdfunding platform in return for interest payments and a repayment of capital over time.

VAT treatment

The contributor is granting credit in the form of a loan and in return will receive interest. The value of the supply is the gross interest or other sum received but not the repayment of the loan itself. The interest received on the money loaned is consideration for an exempt supply of credit.

VATFIN 5550

2.5. Derivatives

Derivatives are financial instruments, whose prices are dependent upon, or 'derived' from, an underlying security. Therefore, to establish the correct VAT treatment the key is to understand what the underlying security or product is. Derivatives can be divided into two types; financial derivatives (based on financial assets such as currencies, securities and interest rates) or commodity derivatives (based on an underlying raw material or commodity). Both of these are covered below.

2.5.1. Commodity futures, options and other derivatives

A commodity is a raw material such as grain, coffee, metal or oil that is traded on a commodity market. This can be based in the country of the commodities' origin or on a terminal market (i.e. a commodity market in a trading centre, such as London). Commodity prices often fluctuate widely and therefore commodity exchanges will help both producers and users of the commodity to hedge against the price risk with outside speculators and investors.

2.5.1.1 *Derivatives, Commodities and Terminal Markets*

Where a transaction is traded on the terminal market (listed in the *Value Added Tax (Terminal Markets) Order 1973* and *VAT Notice 701/9/*, para 4, and in **Appendix F** of this book) then zero-rating is available in certain circumstances:

1. Futures transactions in commodities, ordinarily dealt with on a market listed in VAT Notice 701/9/, para 4 between two market members or a market member and non-member, provided the transactions do not lead to a physical delivery of the goods.
2. Actuals transactions between two market members which results in goods being delivered, provided that the market is the:

- London Metal Exchange (LME) and the transaction is between members entitled to deal in the 'ring';
- London Cocoa Terminal Market, London Coffee Terminal Market, London Meat Futures Market, International Petroleum Exchange in London (IPE), London Potatoes Futures Market, London Soya Bean Meal Futures Market, London Sugar Terminal Market, the London Vegetable Oil Terminal Market or the London Wool Terminal Market, and the transactions is a sale registered with the International Commodities Clearing House Ltd or its successor;
- London Rubber Market, the London Bullion Market or the London Platinum and Palladium Market, and the transaction is between members of the respective market;
- London Grain Futures Market, and the transaction is a sale registered in the Clearing House of the Grain and Feed Trade Association Limited; or
- Liverpool Barley Futures Market, and it is a sale registered at the Clearing House of the Liverpool Corn Trade Association Ltd.

'Delivery' is not defined but is regarded by HMRC as taking place when instructions are given for the goods to be physically removed from the warehouse or vault. If a futures transaction leads to the delivery of the goods, VAT at the appropriate rate must be accounted for on the basis of the original contract price.

3. The grant by or to a market member of an option to acquire any goods (other than investment gold) ordinarily dealt with on the market where either the right is exercisable at a date later than that on which it is granted or where the sale resulting from the exercise of the right would be a sale falling within (1) or (2) above, is also zero rated. When an option is exercised, the resulting transaction should be considered under (1) or (2) above.

2.5.1.2 *Commodities traded off-exchange*

Commodity futures and actuals

- A commodity future traded outside one of the terminal markets, follows the liability of the underlying commodity.

Commodity options

- Payment for the right to buy a commodity, rather than a contract to buy a commodity, is a standard rated supply of services. If the option is subsequently exercised there will be a separate supply of the commodity itself.

VAT Notice 701/9/ provides more details on commodities and terminal markets.

2.5.2. Financial futures

Financial futures transactions are exempt. For details of the VAT liabilities affecting agents or intermediaries involved in the sale or purchase of financial futures refer to **2.6**.

Futures contracts can be divided into cash-settled contracts and non-cash-settled contracts:

- Cash-settled contracts are contracts where there are no underlying deliverable securities or contracts, and are only capable of financial settlement. These include short-term interest rate futures, FTSE 100 futures, other stock index futures, weather derivatives and other cash-settled contracts. The supply of cash-settled contracts for consideration is exempt from VAT. Where a futures contract runs to maturity, there is no further supply for VAT purposes. Cash settlements under these contracts are not consideration for a supply and must be excluded from partial exemption calculations and VAT returns.
- Non-cash-settled contracts are contracts where there are underlying deliverable securities. These include gilts, Treasury bonds (T-bonds) and other securities (not being securities for money). The supply of a non-cash-settled contract is exempt. If a contract runs to maturity there is a separate exempt supply of the underlying security. Transactions on exchanges are treated as being made between either the member and the client or the member and the relevant clearing house. The value of the supply of the securities is the price that was agreed when the contract was made.

2.5.3. Financial futures - exchange trading

2.5.3.1 Fees charged by members

Members of certain exchanges (e.g. LIFFE) deal as principals and the commission charged by the member to the client transacting a financial futures contract is the value of the member's supply. A member may charge for each leg of the transaction, or for a round-trip in a closed-out transaction. The full value of each charge will be the value of the supply for VAT purposes. The turn or commission is consideration for an exempt supply of financial futures by the member acting as a principal.

Where a member acts for another member in executing a transaction then he is a principal and the turn or commission charged is exempt.

Transactions between members on their own account are not treated as supplies for VAT purposes.

2.5.3.2 *Client to member transactions*

There is no supply by a client to a member in a closed-out financial futures transaction. The reason for this is that the client purchases an equal and opposite contract and is the recipient of the supply rather than the supplier.

2.5.3.3 *Margin payments*

Margin payments (whether initial or variation) fall outside the scope of VAT. They are treated as payments on account in respect of a potential future liability.

2.5.4. Financial options

Financial options are exempt. The sale of an option over a financial instrument is a supply of services separate from the underlying transaction to which the option relates.

There are three main types of financial options contracts:

- Options based on financial futures contracts. These are options on short-term interest rate futures, index-based futures or cash-settled futures and are exempt. (These are options on cash-settled contracts, see **2.5.2** above.) There is no further supply when option is exercised to obtain or supply the underlying futures contracts.

- Equity options. These are options that have equities, rather than financial futures contracts, as the underlying instrument and they are exempt from VAT. If such an option is exercised there will be a further exempt supply of equities. (These are options on non-cash settled contracts, see **2.5.2** above).

- Index-based options. Unlike equity options, index-based options do not provide for delivery but are cash-settled. This type of option is VAT exempt (as an option on a cash-settled contract, see **2.5.2** above).

Where a financial option is sold for a premium there is the grant of a right. The value of the supply is the premium charged and the supply is exempt.

2.5.5. Other types of trade: trading by locals

Locals are traders registered to members of exchanges who act in an independent capacity to some degree, but as the embodiment of the member to whom the local is registered. Locals can be employees, self-employed or engage in a joint-venture or partnership with the member. The VAT treatment is dependent on the status of the local.

- Employee locals. Employee locals may manage or trade on an account for their member and will be on the member's payroll. Payments from the member to the local are outside the scope of VAT.

- Self-employed locals. Self-employed locals may trade on their own account. When the local makes a trade it is the member who is the principal to the contract. However, when the trade is completed there is another contract between the member and the local, now in the same position for VAT purposes as a third-party client, in which both parties are also principals (i.e. there is a back-to-back arrangement). The supply made by the member to the client is an exempt supply of a financial futures contract. Self-employed locals may also act as the embodiment of the member with which the local is registered. For VAT purposes the local is acting as an agent.
- Joint ventures and partnerships. Where the local and the member are engaged in a joint-venture partnership, every trade executed by the local is a trade of the member to whom the local is registered in the rules regarding transactions by members will apply to this initial transaction. The VAT liability of the remuneration received by the local under the joint-venture partnership arrangement will depend on the nature of the agreement between the parties.

2.5.6. Other types of trade: trading over-the-counter

Financial futures and options can also be traded over-the-counter (OTC). These are non-standard contracts traded off-exchange. Trading both financial futures and options OTC is exempt.

2.5.7. Other types of trade: trading on non-UK exchanges

The value and liability of any supplies made in respect of transactions in financial futures and options contracts traded on non-UK exchanges will depend on whether the business acts as a principal or an agent. The rules of the overseas exchange and local legislation may also have a significant effect on how the transaction should be viewed for UK VAT purposes. Each transaction will need to be determined on its own merits.

2.5.8. Interest rate swaps

For VAT purposes, during the term of an interest rate swap there is a continuous supply of services and, to the extent that any money changes hands, there is an exempt supply under *VATA 94, Sch 9, Grp 5, Item 1.*

2.5.9. Currency swaps

Currency swaps are similar to interest rate swaps but have a different VAT treatment. Currency swaps provide both a currency and an interest hedge. As with interest rate swaps, during the term of the swap, there is a continuous supply of services and, to the extent that any money changes hands, there is an exempt supply under *VATA 94, Sch 9, Grp 5, Item 1.*

However, for VAT purposes no supply takes place in relation to the exchange of the principal amounts of underlying loans in currency swaps.

2.5.10. Financial Spread Betting (FSB)

FSB is very similar to sports spread betting. In effect, it involves speculating by placing a bet on an index (e.g. the FTSE 100 index or the price of a specific commodity or series of commodities). As with sports spread betting, FSB is exempt under *VATA 94, Sch 9, Grp 4,* but liable to Betting Duty (currently at a rate of 3%). Any winnings are outside the scope of VAT.

2.5.11. Contracts for differences (CFDs)

A CFD provides a speculator with the opportunity to buy or sell the risk / reward associated with the performance of a share or equity without the need to own the underlying asset. Where a CFD is provided for consideration (a turn or commission), this is an exempt supply of financial services. The CFD is treated as a cash-settled contract for the purposes of defining the VAT liability of an intermediary's supply (see **2.6** below for more details).

VAT Notice 701/49/, paras 8.1 – 8.11

Further information and guidance on the VAT treatment of financial derivatives can also be found in HMRC's Finance Manual at *VATFIN6000.*

2.6. Intermediary services

Article 135 (1)(b)-(f) of Directive 2006/112/EC provides VAT exemption for the following services:

(b) the granting and the negotiation of credit and the management of credit by the person granting it;
(c) the negotiation of or any dealings and credit guarantees or any other security for money and the management of credit guarantees by the person who is granting credit;
(d) transactions, including negotiation, concerning deposit and current accounts, payments, transfers, debts, cheques and other negotiable instruments, but excluding debt collection;
(e) transactions, including negotiation, concerning currency, banknotes and coins used as legal tender, with the exception of collectors' items, that is to say, gold, silver or other metal coins or banknotes which are not normally used as legal tender or coins of numismatic interest;
(f) transactions, including negotiation but not management or safekeeping, in shares, interests in companies or associations, debentures and other securities, but excluding documents establishing title to goods, and the rights of securities referred to in Article 15 (2)

In the EU legislation, negotiation is effectively equivalent to intermediation, so that, for example, exemption for credit is provided for the person providing the credit and the person who negotiates (i.e. acts between the parties in) the provision of credit.

Under UK legislation, exemption is allowed for the provision of intermediary services in relation to transactions within items 1, 2, 3, 4 and 6 of *VATA 94, Sch 9, Grp 5* providing the person is acting in intermediary capacity.

'Intermediary services' means bringing together, with a view to the provision of financial services, persons who are or may be seeking to receive financial services and persons who provide financial services. Where the transactions fall within items 1, 2, 3 and 4 of *VATA 94, Sch 9, Grp 5,* the intermediary must also be performing work preparatory to the conclusion of contracts for the provision of those financial services.

However, supplies of market research, product design, advertising, promotional or similar services for the collection, collation and provision of information in connection with such activities are specifically excluded from the exemption under the UK legislation. It is worth noting, however, that EU legislation does not specifically exclude these items from exemption. So, arguably, UK legislation is not in line with the EU VAT Directive.

'Work preparatory to the conclusion of contracts' refers to work done of a specialised nature (for example, helping to set the terms of the contract or making representations on behalf of a client) and would not include work done of a general nature such as administrative and clerical formalities.

Note however, that preparatory work is not a requirement for exemption with regard to the arrangement of Item 6 transactions, so that a simple introduction of a person in respect of a transaction in securities may be sufficient.

'Acting in an intermediary capacity' means acting as an intermediary, or one of the intermediaries, between a person who provides financial services and the person who is or may be seeking to receive financial services.

Exemption is available regardless of whether or not a contract for financial services is finally concluded. Provided that the intermediary is acting as such and providing intermediary services, exemption should still apply.

An intermediary needs to be independent of the parties entering into a contract for financial services and should not be simply a subcontractor of one of the parties. For example, in *CSC Financial Services Ltd v C & E Commrs, Case C-235/00, [2002] STC 57*, CSC supplied services to Sun Alliance in respect of PEPs. CSC dealt with telephone enquiries and reviewed application forms. However, as the customers had already been approached by Sun Alliance, CSC were deemed not to be acting in an intermediary capacity because they were not providing a negotiation service (which the ECJ saw as including providing a distinct act of mediation, bringing together the parties together or pointing out opportunities for the conclusion of a contract). CSC was effectively standing in the shoes of Sun Alliance when it took calls and was carrying out administrative and clerical work that would normally have been done by Sun Alliance.

2.6.1. Securities broking

The introductory service of bringing together a person who wishes to buy securities and persons selling securities is exempt. As noted above, there is no requirement to perform preparatory work to achieve exemption for arranging Item 6 transactions. Exemption applies even if the intended transaction does not take place.

The exemption applies to arranging issues or the placement of securities, whether as offers for sale, rights issues, cash offers, vendor placings or bids with underwritten cash alternatives, including the service of coordinating an issue where a number of participants are involved in the share or other placings. However, the provision of advice is taxable.

VAT Notice 701/49/, para 6.10

Where a broker acts as an execution-only broker, buying or selling securities on a client's instruction but without offering any advice, the supply is exempt. If the broker provides advice and this advice is incidental to any transaction in securities then the supply remains exempt.

Where a broker arranges a securities transaction, the contract note can be split to show as separate items the basic charge for the execution service and any compliance and regulatory charges which are made to cover the cost of meeting regulatory requirements. These additional charges are part of the consideration for the exempt supply. This rule does not apply to any statutory levies such as stamp duty that are a liability of the client. These are outside the scope of VAT and should not be accounted for as part of the exempt supply.

VAT Notice 701/49/, para 6.11

2.6.2. Soft commissions

'Soft commissions' are arrangements under which an intermediary can use his income from a provider to fund, either directly or indirectly, some of his client's costs in recognition of the amount of business the client has, or will, put his way.

Soft commissions are treated as being outside the scope of VAT as they do not represent consideration for any supply.

2.6.3. Corporate finance

Advice alone (e.g. on raising capital or on defending takeover bids) is taxable at the standard rate.

Where that advice leads to, or is associated with, a transaction in securities carried out by the client, then the services may qualify for exemption as the provision of intermediary services for a transaction in securities, provided it meets the criteria outlined in **2.6** above. These principles may be applied to abortive contracts.

However, depending on whether there is a single or multiple supply, it may be necessary to apportion the supplies between the taxable advice and the exempt intermediary supply.

VAT Notice 701/49/, para 9.7

2.6.3.1 Types of corporate finance deals

These are examples of services provided by a corporate finance business ("CFB"), which may involve exempt supplies as an intermediary under Item 5.

Clear or specific mandate agreements

The CFB's client may choose to issue, sell or purchase securities or take out a loan. The CFB is engaged to negotiate the transaction. If the CFB's service meets all the criteria for exemption (bearing in mind that for transactions in securities there need be no preparatory work) and there is a single supply, this is an exempt intermediary service. Other companies may be sub-contracted for their advisory services in the sale of the securities. Unless they themselves are acting as an intermediary (e.g. bringing together the parties) their supply will be taxable at the standard rate.

Where the agreement is aborted, and the services provided would have been exempt had the transaction gone through, the services remain exempt.

Open mandates

An open mandate arises when an organisation is engaged for its specialist skills, but it is not known at the time of engagement if there will be any resulting specific exempt transaction. For example, a merchant bank could be asked to evaluate methods of refinancing a business and eventually decides that the best way to do so is by issuing shares in the company (an exempt Item 6 transaction).

The merchant bank offers advisory services under the agreement to evaluate methods of finance and these will be supplies for VAT purposes only when those services are paid for. These supplies will be liable to VAT at the standard rate until any such time as an exempt transaction is actually envisaged. This is a complex area and it is open to some debate, because the point at which the services change from being advisory to intermediary in nature is often unclear.

If the business subsequently decides to effect a transaction that is exempt (e.g. a share issue), then the intermediary's services will be exempt except to the extent that any specific charge for the advisory element may be identified. It is important to look at how the services are supplied: there may be a new agreement with the bank outlining a change in engagement terms (in which case the advisory services supplied under the first agreement will be liable to VAT) or an exempt transaction will be envisaged from the outset, albeit that it is not known exactly what (with the advisory services then seen as part of this single exempt supply).

Where an agreement is aborted, the VAT liability depends on the nature of the service supplied. Exemption is not permitted for advisory services – only for work which has specifically been undertaken in relation to an exempt supply (and provided all the criteria are met). If an exempt transaction was envisaged, and the work already carried out reflects this, the fee will be exempt regardless of whether or not the transaction was concluded.

Services provided to a target company

A company may need to defend itself against a hostile take-over bid and engage another party to help deal with this. Such services are often advisory and will be taxable. However, as with the situation above, the services may involve raising capital (perhaps by issuing shares) or arranging a de-merger or sale of a subsidiary in order to defend the take-over. Where such services are supplied to a company in connection with an agreed bid, these may involve only advice (which is liable to VAT at the standard rate). However, it could be that the adviser eventually becomes involved as an intermediary for the take-over, for example, by setting up the terms and conditions for the final deal. Provided the appropriate criteria are met, such services would fall within the exemption.

HMRC Manual VATFIN7460

2.6.4. Financial investigations

Financial investigations include activities such as checking the validity of documents, normally on behalf of a financial institution.

These services are taxable at the standard rate.

VAT Notice 701/49/, para 9.6

2.6.5. Independent Financial Advisers (IFAs)

IFAs can:

- provide general financial advice only,
- act as an intermediary in the supply of a financial product or, most commonly,
- do both.

Where an IFA provides general financial advice only, the supply is taxable at the standard rate. (However, see below for the meaning of 'advice' in the context of retail investment products under RDR – see **2.6.5.1** below).

Where an IFA acts between his customer and the provider of a financial product, then provided the intermediary criteria outlined at **2.6** above are met, the supply will be exempt.

Where an IFA both provides advice and acts in an intermediary capacity between his customer and the provider of a financial product, the IFA needs to establish which of the two elements predominates. Where the advice directly results in the customer taking out a financial product, or intending to take a financial product, and all of the criteria for intermediary services are met, then the whole of the supply (including the advice element) will be exempt. In these circumstances, the advice element is likely to be seen as ancillary to the exempt intermediary service.

However, if the advice outweighs the work done to arrange the contract, then the intermediary services are ancillary to the advice, with the result that VAT is due on the whole supply.

VAT Notice 701/49/, para 9.9

The liability of IFA charges was considered in the case of *Bloomsbury Wealth Management LLP ([2012] (UK FTT 379).*

Bloomsbury was an IFA providing services to high net worth individuals. The services in question involved Bloomsbury holding an initial meeting to discuss the client's requirements. They would then recommend funds to the client. If the client decided to proceed, Bloomsbury would introduce them to the appropriate fund manager, with a view to the client making an investment. Bloomsbury would also perform a quarterly 'rebalancing' of the investments, based on the client's instructions.

A fee was charged to the client only if it decided to invest. Having originally charged VAT on the fees, Bloomsbury took the view that they were in fact exempt, as the consideration for a supply of financial intermediary services. Accordingly, a VAT refund claim was submitted to HMRC.

HMRC rejected the claim on the basis that the fees related to a supply of standard rated services. Their first line of argument was that Bloomsbury was introducing the client to the fund manager so that the client could receive fund management services. The Tribunal quickly dismissed this, on the grounds that it was 'extremely unlikely' that the client's principal aim was to purchase fund management services.

HMRC's second argument was that Bloomsbury's services were predominantly advisory and therefore taxable. This was also rejected by the Tribunal, which said that, as no fee was charged to the client for the meeting if it decided not to proceed, the meeting (and therefore the advisory element of the service) could not be the element which was most important to the client (i.e. it was not an aim in itself). It was the introduction of the client to the fund manager, with a view to the client making an investment, which was the predominant nature of the service. Consequently, the Tribunal decided that Bloomsbury's fees were consideration for an exempt supply of financial intermediary services.

Although HMRC has decided not to appeal this decision, it is possible that it may be overtaken by the ECJ ruling in the case of *Deutsche Bank* (see **2.10.2**).

2.6.5.1 *Retail Distribution Review*

The FSA's Retail Distribution Review (RDR) came into effect on 31 December 2012. The announcement created some concern within the adviser community as to any VAT impact. HMRC issued guidance in their internal manuals and whilst some uncertainties still remain, particularly with regard to ongoing services, a number of issues have been clarified.

RDR introduction

The key objectives of RDR are to:

- improve the clarity with which firms describe their services to consumers;
- address the potential for adviser remuneration to distort consumer outcomes; and

- increase the professional standards of advisers.

The new rules require advisers to move in most cases from receiving commissions to fees agreed with customers in respect of all Retail Investment Products as defined by the FSA.

These products are:

- a life policy;
- a unit;
- a stakeholder pension scheme;
- a personal pension scheme;
- an interest in an investment trust savings scheme;
- a security in an investment trust;
- any other designated investment which offers exposure to underlying financial assets, in a packaged form which modifies that exposure when compared with a direct holding in the financial asset; or
- a structured capital-at-risk product,

whether or not any are held within an ISA or a Child Trust Fund (CTF).

Retail Investment Products do not include protection-only insurance or charges for trading in securities.

The new rules apply to all product distributors and providers across the retail investment market involved in advised-sales. They also apply to advised-sales via platforms.

Meaning of 'Advice'

It is important when considering the VAT treatment of services in this area to understand the meaning of 'advice' for regulatory purposes. From a VAT perspective general financial advice is not synonymous with the term 'advice' for the purposes of the RDR rules. The RDR is primarily concerned with the distribution (i.e. sale) of financial products to the retail market. The RDR's focus is to ensure that there is no hidden bias in product recommendations by making certain that intermediaries (termed 'advisers') clearly disclose the nature of their service and set the level of their charges by reference to the amount of work done, rather than being motivated by the level of fee associated with a particular product type or product provider.

The term 'advice' under RDR thus covers a broad range of functions including primarily recommendation, referral and intermediary work around product distribution which would continue to be exempt under general principles. General financial advice would continue to be taxable in the same way.

VATFIN7660

Services of an adviser

HMRC have identified a six-stage process that an adviser may go through in respect of a Retail Investment Product:

1. gather information about the customer (fact-find);
2. carry out research to find suitable investment options;
3. provide the customer with reports, financial health-checks, forecasts;
4. recommend specific investment products to the customer, including the prices at which these can be arranged;
5. act between the product provider(s) and the customer with a view to arranging the sale of the Retail Investment Products agreed with the customer; and
6. where applicable, i.e. where the customer agrees to an ongoing review service, monitor the customer's ongoing position to ensure that the products continue to meet the requirements of the customer.

Where the customer is seeking the arrangement of a Retail Investment Product and the adviser performs the arrangements as outlined at stage 5 above (regardless of whether the sale of the product is finally concluded) and is able to provide evidence that they have done so; the services in stage 1-6 (which fall within the agreement concluded with the customer) will be VAT exempt.

Where there is no evidence of such product arrangement services or where one or more of the stages are contracted for under a separate agreement, so that the service provided to the customer is that of general advice or recommendation only, any charges to the customer will carry VAT at the standard rate.

The VAT liability depends on what is done by the adviser and it makes no difference whether a fee is levied up front or over the life of a product (as for example with Regular Contribution products).

VATFIN7665

Ongoing services

This is where there is still some element of uncertainty at the time of writing. The HMRC manual reads as follows:

> If, after the arrangements of the sale of Retail Investment Products, the customer signs up to ongoing review services, some or all of the process may occur again. The adviser should be able to determine and evidence where they are in the process with that customer. The VAT liability of ongoing services will depend upon the services the customer has agreed the adviser should perform, as outlined at VATFIN7665.

VATFIN7670

What was not entirely clear was the position where annual reviews were agreed at the start of the process. In practice, HMRC have accepted that annual reviews agreed as part of the initial contract for the supply of the advised products will be treated as part of the overall (exempt) supply. This should also include review services which clients can opt in to at a later date. Review services agreed at a later date will be liable to VAT unless part of a distinct intermediation process. HMRC seem to draw a distinction between 'ongoing' portfolio management provided by Discretionary Fund Managers (which are usually liable to VAT unless the fund constitutes a SIF) and 'periodical' reviews provided by IFAs.

Evidence

Advisers will need to keep evidence to support the tax treatment that they apply to the services supplied to customers. In the absence of sufficient evidence that an exempt supply has been made, VAT will be due.

Employee benefit consultants (EBCs) and others

HMRC have issued *R&C Brief 9/13* regarding the position affecting consultants such as EBCs following the implementation of RDR. Prior to RDR, EBCs would have been paid for their services via commissions received from pension providers. Under RDR (subject to certain transitional arrangements) these commissions have been banned from 1 January 2013. Instead, EBCs are now likely to receive consultancy charges paid from the pension provider plus, in some cases, fees from the employer. HMRC's view is that both types of payment are fees in respect of advisory or administration services provided to the employer so should attract VAT at the standard rate.

2.6.5.2 *IFA networks*

Many IFA firms operate as networks through agreements with persons known as Appointed Representatives (ARs) for whom the authorised IFA firm takes regulatory responsibility. These arrangements enable the AR to carry out regulated activities without the need to be directly authorised by the Financial Services Authority (FSA).

The network arrangements are permitted under UK legislation and are subject to strict regulatory rules. In particular the following should apply:

- the network appoints the ARs and trains them to operate in accordance with FSA requirements;
- in all dealings with the client the ARs make it clear, both orally and on any paperwork, that they are acting on behalf of the network;
- the network has the contractual relationship with the financial product providers and at all times the AR acts on the network's behalf;

- the network maintains a high level of control over the ARs, carrying out regular checks and audits and imposing sanctions were appropriate;
- the network accepts responsibility for the actions of the ARs and handles all customer complaints;
- the network holds liability insurance to cover any claims resulting from the activities of the ARs and is legally liable for any sanctions imposed under the *Financial Services and Markets Act 2000;*
- all fees or commissions for regulated activities are paid by the clients or product providers to the network and form part of the income of the network for accounting and direct tax purposes; and
- the network pays the ARs for their services and these payments can be adjusted at the discretion of the network should, for example, the AR be found to have failed to conduct the business in accordance with the regulatory requirements.

When networks operate in this way, in effect a 'sub-agency' or 'sub-contract' arrangement exists between the network and the ARs. The network acts as principal, making supplies of financial intermediary services to the financial product providers and supplies of advice and/or financial intermediary services to the clients. The networks effectively subcontract their functions to the ARs who interact directly with the client and the product providers in the provision of individual supplies on behalf of the network.

Therefore:

- all payments received from product providers or clients relating to supplies of financial intermediary services provided via the AR is the network's VAT exempt income. Onward payments made to the AR are consideration for the exempt intermediary service supplied to the network by the AR;
- any fee paid directly to the network or via the AR, that relates to advice-only services is the network's standard rated income. Any onward payments made to the AR are consideration for the provision of taxable services by the AR to the network. VAT will be due if the AR is registered for VAT;
- any optional services supplied by the network to their ARs for additional consideration (e.g. compliance or IT services) are separate supplies and the appropriate VAT liability will apply; and
- any non-regulated services provided by ARs fall outside the network arrangements altogether and are made directly by the AR (or IFA) to the client or product provider.

This VAT treatment will not apply to any supplies made by networks that do not operate in the way outlined above (e.g. those which are not authorised entities and are set up to provide marketing and/or compliance support services to directly authorised IFA firms). In cases of doubt, businesses are advised to contact HMRC.

VAT Notice 701/49/, para 9.10.

2.6.6. Affinity card arrangements

These schemes are quite common particularly with charities or interest groups. Under these arrangements, the charity or interest group will endorse a credit card and recommend its use to their members, supporters or customers. The charity or interest group then receives a commission, normally based on the numbers of cards taken out and/or subsequent usage of the card.

Charities have been granted a concession to recognise that an element of such payments could be charitable and this can be applied subject to certain rules. (*VAT Notice 701/1/, para 5.3*).

For non-charity organisations however, affinity card schemes are subject to the normal VAT rules. As a result, whether commission income is exempt from VAT will depend on the nature of the service supplied to the credit card provider. If the business introduces its members, supporters or customers to a credit card provider, brings the two parties together and carries out independent negotiation services as a distinct act of intermediation, then VAT exemption should apply.

Marketing and promotional services supplied in isolation or clerical functions such as providing a list of names or access to a database are viewed by HMRC as always being standard rated.

See the cases of *BAA plc v C & E Commrs, CA 2002, [2003] STC 35* and *Institute of Directors v C & E Commrs, CA 2002, [2003] STC 35* which were heard together.

VAT Notice 701/49/, para 4.9

2.6.7. Credit and debit card handling services

One of the main areas of developing case law over the last few years has involved the treatment of card handling services. In the case of *Bookit Ltd v R & C Commrs, CA [2006] STC 1367*, a company arranged advance bookings for cinema seats by telephone or internet, checked seat availability and took details of the customer's credit or debit card. They charged an administration fee of 50p per ticket. The court held that the company was making an exempt supply because its service involved a transfer of funds by virtue of transmitting the card information with the necessary security information to Girobank.

As a result of this case, HMRC accepted that where an agent, acting for the supplier of goods or services, makes a charge to the customer over and above the price of the actual goods and services, for a separately identifiable service of handling payment by credit or debit card and that service includes the transfer of funds to its account, the additional charge is exempt from VAT. (*Business Brief 18/06*). However, see below for developments on this case.

In the case of *National Exhibition Centre Limited [2013] UKFTT 289*, the FTT allowed VAT exemption for booking fees charged to customers (in this case, the appellant charged a standard rated facilities fee to promoters for acting as an agent of the promoter but also a separate booking fee to the customer). Again, see below for developments in this case.

In the case of *Way Ahead Group Ltd [2014] UKFTT 178*, the FTT held that card handling fees collected by the Appellant from purchasers of tickets are exempt from VAT where the Appellant was acting as agent in sales of event tickets by event promoters.

However, compare the case of *Everything Everywhere (formerly T-Mobile UK) Case C-276/09*, where an additional charge was made to customers for paying by cheque (rather than by automated methods) these payments were ruled not to be separate supplies but additional consideration for the principal taxable supply of telecoms services. See also the case of *CRC v Axa UK plc, C-175/09 [2010] STC 2825*, where the ECJ ruled that the operation of a payment plan was excluded from exemption and *DPAS Ltd [2013] UKFTT 676* where the appellant changed its business model to fall outside the scope of taxable debt collection (see **2.2.2**).

The *Bookit* case subsequently returned to the *FTT, Bookit Ltd [2014] UKFTT 856*, as some of the facts stated in the Court of Appeal appeared not be correct for supplies made in the period 2009 to 2012. As a result, a reference was made to the ECJ (*Case C-607/14*) asking the following questions:

1. With regard to the exemption from VAT in Article 135(1)(d) of Council Directive 2006/112/EC as interpreted by the Court of Justice in *Case C-2/95 Sparekassernes Datacenter (SDC) v Skatteministeriet*, what are the relevant principles to be applied in determining whether or not a "debit and credit card handling service" (such as the service that is supplied in this case) has "the effect of transferring funds and entail[s] changes in the

legal and financial situation" within the meaning of paragraph 66 of that judgment.

2. As a matter of principle, what factors distinguish (a) a service which consists in the provision of financial information without which a payment would not be made but which do not fall within the exemption (such as in *C-350/10 Nordea Pankki Suomi*), from (b) a data handling service which functionally has the effect of transferring funds and which the Court of Justice has identified as therefore being capable of falling within the exemption (such as in SDC at paragraph 66)?

3. In particular, and in the context of debit and credit card handling services:

Does the exemption apply to such services which result in a transfer of funds but which do not include the task of making a debit to one account and a corresponding credit to another account?

Does entitlement to the exemption depend on whether the service provider itself obtains authorisation codes directly from the cardholder's bank, or alternatively obtains those codes via its merchant acquirer bank?

A reference on similar issues was made in the *National Exhibition Centre Ltd* case *(Case C-130/15)(*see above*)*. In this case the questions asked were:

1. With regard to the exemption from VAT in Article 13B(d)(3) of the Sixth Directive ... as interpreted by the Court of Justice in *Case C-2/95 Sparekassernes Datacenter v Skatteministeriet*, what are the relevant principles to be applied for determining whether or not a service has "the effect of transferring funds and entails changes in the legal and financial situation" within the meaning of paragraph 66 of that judgment? In particular:
   1.1. Is the exemption applicable to a service, such as that performed by the taxpayer in the present case, which does not involve the taxpayer debiting or crediting any accounts over which it has control, but which is, where a transfer of funds results, the cause of a transfer of funds made by an independent financial institution?
   1.2. In a case where payment is made by credit or debit card, does the answer to Question 1.1 depend on whether the service provider itself obtains authorisation codes directly from the cardholder's bank, or alternatively obtains those codes via its merchant acquirer bank?
   1.3. What factors distinguish (a) a service which consists in the provision of financial information without which a payment would not be made but which does not fall within the exemption (such as in *Case C-350/10 Nordea Pankki Suomi*), from (b) a data handling service which functionally has the effect of transferring funds and which

the Court of Justice has identified as therefore being capable of falling within the exemption (such as in SDC at paragraph 66)?

2. What are the relevant principles to be applied for determining whether or not a service such as that performed by the taxpayer in the present case falls within the scope of the "debt collection" exclusion from the exemption in Article 13B(d)(3) of the Sixth Directive? In particular, if a service of processing payment by a particular method (e.g. debit or credit card) would, pursuant to the principles in *Case C-175/09 Commissioners for Her Majesty's Revenue and Customs v AXA UK plc*, constitute "debt collection" in circumstances where the supply of that service was to the person to whom that payment was due (i.e. the person receiving the payment), will that service also constitute "debt collection" in circumstances where the supply of that service is to the person from whom the payment is due (i.e. the person making the payment)? Further, in the circumstances of this case, does a "debt" even exist to be "collected"

Although the *Bookit* and *NEC* cases were not heard together, the judgments were essentially the same – VAT exemption is not available for card handling services or payment processing services supplied by service providers handling ticket sales, even if a separately disclosed charge is made to the customer purchasing the tickets.

The case law in this area has now developed further (see **2.2.2** for comments on the DPAS case and others) in clarifying between exemption (e.g. effecting the transfer of funds so as to change the financial position between parties – assuming this doesn't fall within the definition of 'debt collection') and taxable supplies (e.g. the transmission of information to enable another party to undertake those changes). Certainly anyone involved in this area should take note of these cases and seek specific advice.

2.6.8. Individual voluntary arrangements and company voluntary arrangements

In the case of *Paymex Ltd v HMRC (2011) (TC01210)* a company provided insolvency practitioners (IPs) to run and maintain individual voluntary arrangements for consumers. The Tribunal ruled that Paymex were providing exempt financial services under *Directive 2006/112/EC, Article 135 (1)(d).*

Following the decision, HMRC announced in *Business Brief 35/11* that although the *Paymex case* related to consumer IVAs, they accepted that it applied to all IVAs. At this time they stated that they did not see it as applying to company voluntary arrangements (CVAs).

However, following a review, HMRC announced in *Business Brief 03/12* that in their view the VAT exemption arising from the *Paymex* ruling applies to:

- individual voluntary arrangements;
- company voluntary arrangements;
- partnership voluntary arrangements; and
- protected trust deeds (applicable only in Scotland). Other IPs' services remain liable to VAT at the standard rate.

2.6.9. Derivatives

Where a person acts as a broker or intermediary for a supply of financial derivatives the supply will be exempt in the following circumstances:

- For *cash-settled contracts*, the supply is exempt provided they (a) act between the person selling and the person buying a cash-settled financial derivative; (b) bring the parties together; and (c) carry out some form of preparatory work to the conclusion of the contract.
- For *non-cash-settled contracts*, their supply is exempt provided they act between a person selling and the person buying non-cash-settled financial derivatives and they bring the parties together.

VAT Notice 701/49/, para 8.12

2.7. Supplies relating to the provision of credit

The following supplies are exempt:

(a) The making of any advance or the granting of any credit (VATA 94, Sch 9, Group 5, Item 2).

This covers most normal types of credit transactions, e.g. loans and overdrafts. The value of the supply will be the gross interest or other payment received but not the repayment of capital loaned. This will also include interest received on money deposited.

VAT Notice 701/49/, para 4.1

(b) The management of credit by the person granting it (VATA 94, Sch 9, Group 5, Item 2A).

The management of credit by a person who does not grant it is, however, taxable.

Typically, supplies by a third-party of taxable credit management will include the following:

- credit checking, this includes debt profiling, assessing credit worthiness, electoral roll checks and obtaining references;
- valuation of assets such as property, land, or vehicles;

- authorisation services, including those that go beyond just checking the applicant's signature or agreeing credit or payment within limits set by the person providing the credit;
- taking decisions on credit applications on behalf of the credit provider;
- creating and maintaining records on behalf of the credit provider in order to enable them to fulfil their legal obligations, such as those relating to credit applications, payments and credit transactions; and
- monitoring a payment record or dealing with overdue payments.

VAT Notice 701/49/, para 4.10

(c) The provision of the facility of instalment credit finance in a hire-purchase, conditional sale or credit sale agreement for which facility a separate charge is made and disclosed to the recipient of the supply of goods (*VATA 94, Sch 9, Group 5, Item 3*).

Please see **2.7.5** below for further information on hire-purchase agreements.

(d) The provision of administrative arrangements and documentation and the transfer of title to the goods in connection with the supply described in item 3 if the total consideration therefor is specified in the agreement and does not exceed £10 (*VATA 94, Sch 9, Group 5, Item 4*).

Although the legislation specifies a £10 limit, in the case of *Wagon Finance Ltd (VTD 16288)* the Tribunal held that administration fees in connection with credit transactions were exempt from VAT regardless of the £10 limit, as the company was providing customers with the facility of instalment credit within *VATA 94, Sch 9, Group 5, Item 3*. HMRC decided not to appeal this decision and now accept that the exemption applies to any connected credit ancillary charge unless the contract explicitly states that the charge relates, wholly or partially, to the supply of goods. (See *Business Brief 27/99*).

2.7.1. Credit, debit and charge cards

Credit, debit and charge cards include MasterCard, Visa, American Express, Diners Club, Connect and Switch. Banks and financial services institutions issue these cards under the umbrella of these organisations. Additionally, certain companies provide in-house card schemes for retailers or retail outlets.

The supply by the person carrying on a credit card, chargecard or similar business is exempt when made to a person who accepts the card when presented to him in respect of payment for goods or services (*VATA 94, Sch 9, Group 5, Note 4*).

The consideration for the supply usually takes the form of a discount on the amount reimbursed to the retailer or provider of the goods or services. *C&E Commrs v Diners Club Ltd and Another, CA [1989] STC 407.*

Retailers are required to account for VAT at the time of supply and on the full price charged to the customer. If the retailer charges for accepting payment by any of the cards mentioned above, the charges are further consideration for the supply of goods or services. VAT is chargeable at the same rate as that applying to the goods or services supplied.

Cardholders have the option of either paying off the outstanding balance in full or paying on an instalment basis, with interest being charged on the outstanding amount. The following charges associated with credit, debit and charge cards are consideration for exempt supplies:

- interest charged on the outstanding balance;
- annual membership, joining and subscription charges or charges made by card companies to the cardholder for the issue of the card;
- as above, the charge made to merchants by credit card companies (normally taking the form of discounts from the amounts the card companies reimburse the merchant);
- joining fees charged to merchants by the card companies;
- interchange fees; and
- imprinter/terminal rental charges when provided as an ancillary part of other exempt card services.
- The following charges are consideration for taxable supplies:
- imprinter/terminal rental charges when this is an optional or additional service by card company to the merchant or retailer; and
- the consideration for a sale of goods (e.g. imprinter/terminals in connection with any card scheme).

VAT Notice 701/49/, paras 4.7 and 4.8

2.7.2. The provision of outsourced services to a loan provider

Where a business provides a package of outsourced services to a loan provider that consist of services prior to and after the granting of a loan, the supply is exempt provided all of the following services are a central part of the supply:

- the operation of bank accounts on behalf of the credit provider;
- arranging the transfer of funds to the borrower; and
- the processing of loan repayments (and any additional charges and fees) by direct debit or cheque.

Where one or more of these services are provided along with one or more taxable credit management services listed above, the supply may qualify for exemption depending on the nature of the whole service being provided.

See *C & E Commrs v Electronic Data Systems Ltd, CA [2003] STC 688* and *VAT Notice 701/49/, paragraph 4.11.*

2.7.3. Deferred payments and discounts

In the ECJ case of *Muys' en De Winter's Bouw-en Aannemingsbedrijf BV v Staatssecretaris van Financiën, Case C-281/91* it was held that:

> ... the expression 'the granting and the negotiation of credit' in *art 13B(d)(1) [now Article 135 1(b) of Directive 2006/112/EC]* was, in principle, wide enough to encompass credit provided by a supplier of goods in the form of deferment of payment for the goods. The wording of *art 13B(d)(1)* did not confine its scope to loans and credit granted by banks and financial institutions. Moreover, that interpretation accorded with the objective of the Sixth Directive to guarantee taxpayers equality of treatment which would otherwise have been defeated if a purchaser was taxable on credit provided by his supplier but credit provided by, for example, a bank was exempt. Accordingly, a supplier of goods or services who allowed a client to defer payment, on the payment of interest, in principle granted a credit which was exempt from VAT by *art 13B(d)(1).*

Consequently, where a supplier of goods or services allows its customers to defer payment for an additional charge, if the charge relates to periods before and up to the time of the supply, the charge is seen as further consideration for the supply of goods or services.

However, where the supplier agrees to defer payment beyond the time of supply, any additional charge for doing so is deemed consideration for an exempt supply of credit.

VAT Notice 701/49/ para 4.5

Where a business offers a discount on condition that the customer pays for the supply of goods or services within a specific time, the value for VAT is the discounted amount regardless of whether or not the customer takes up the offer. See *VAT Notice 701/49/ para 4.4* and *VAT Notice 700, para 7.3.*

However, it is worth noting that HMRC did not follow their own guidance when arguing against a repayment claim in the VAT Tribunal case *Saga Holidays Ltd (2004) [2004] V & DR 94.* In this case, Saga had failed to take account of discounts and submitted a repayment claim. HMRC agreed to refund overpaid amounts but only in circumstances where customers have actually received discounts. Where discounts had not been taken advantage of, HMRC rejected the claim. The Tribunal agreed with HMRC, taking the view that the appropriate legislation (*VATA94, Sch 6, para 4(1)*) should be interpreted as meaning that the consideration is only reduced where the discount is actually achieved.

2.7.4. Penalties for late payments

Where a customer is not explicitly allowed to defer payment and a late payment penalty is imposed, the penalty is not consideration for a supply and is outside the scope of VAT.

VAT Notice 701/49/ para 4.4

2.7.5. Hire-purchase, conditional sale and credit sale agreements

Subject to *VATA 94, Sch 4, para 1(2)(b)* if possession of goods is transferred under agreements which expressly contemplate that the property also will pass at sometime in the future (determined by, or ascertainable from, the agreements but in any case not later than when the goods are fully paid for) there is a supply of goods. The three most common ways of supplying goods with credit are:

(a) hire-purchase (HP) agreements;
(b) conditional sale agreements; and
(c) credit sale agreements.

Legally, under an HP agreement, goods are hired for periodic payments and the hirer has an option to purchase. Under conditional sale agreements, goods are sold with the price payable in instalments and the goods remain the property of the seller until the full price is paid (or another condition is met by the customer). Under a credit sale agreement, the goods immediately become the property of the customer, the price for the goods being payable in instalments.

In each case VAT is due on the full value of the goods at the time of supply. The 'tax point' for the exempt supplies of credit are treated as taking place each time a payment is received unless HMRC approve an earlier date. It is common for application to be made to treat the supply of goods and exempt services as taking place at the same time as this is simpler to administer.

VAT Notice 700, para 15.11

It is worth noting the case of *Mercedes-Benz Financial Services UK Ltd [2014] UKUT 0200* which involved Agility Finance, a flexible arrangement under which the customer can choose to keep or return the vehicle at the end of the agreement. The First Tier Tribunal had ruled that this constituted a supply of goods (with VAT due in full at the time the agreement was signed). However, the Upper Tribunal overturned this decision, ruling that this constituted a supply of services with VAT due on each instalment. The case has now moved to the Court of Appeal who in order to attempt to resolve this issue have referred the following questions to the ECJ:

1. What is the meaning of the words "a contract...which provides that in the normal course of events ownership is to pass at the latest upon payment of the final instalment" in *Article 14(2)(b) of the EU VAT Directive (2006/112)*?
2. In particular, in the context of the present case, does the phrase "in the normal course of events" require a tax authority to do no more than to identify the existence of an option to purchase which can be exercised no later than upon payment of the final instalment?
3. Alternatively, does the phrase "in the normal course of events" require the national authority to go further and to determine the economic purpose of the contract?
4. If the answer to (3) is yes:
(a) Should the interpretation of Article 14(2) of the EU VAT Directive (2006/112) be influenced by an analysis of whether the customer is likely to exercise such an option?
(b) Is the amount payable on exercise of the option to purchase relevant for the purposes of determining the economic purpose of the contract?

The ECJ in its decision set two conditions to establish whether the supply is one of goods under Article 14(2)(b): first, a requirement for the contract to have a clause that expressly refers to the transfer of ownership of the goods; and second, on an objective assessment of the contract at the point that it is signed, an intention that ownership of the goods will pass automatically through the normal performance of the contract.

Where only the first test is met and there is no automatic transfer of ownership but it is just one of a set of options (e.g. it sits alongside an option to return the car and/or extend the hire) then the the supply will not fall within Article 14(2)(b). However, the supply will still fall within Article 14(2)(b), where it is the 'economically rational' decision to exercise an option to purchase. That could be the case where the instalments paid under the contract correspond to the market value of the goods including the cost of financing and the customer will not be required to pay a substantial additional fee in order to exercise the option to purchase.

The ECJ has provided some clear and useful guidance, but as usual national courts will need to determing how this is applied on a case-by-case basis.

2.7.5.1 *Transactions not involving finance companies*

When agreement is made to supply goods under (a), (b) or (c) above without the involvement of a finance company (i.e. self-financed credit) any charge for credit disclosed as a separate charge to the customer is exempt. The consideration for the taxable supply of goods is the price stated in the agreement before any deposit is paid.

If goods are supplied on interest-free credit there is no exempt supply for VAT purposes (as there is no charge for credit).

Any other charges are exempt unless the contract explicitly states that the charge relates, in whole or in part, to the supply of goods. Fees relating to the goods (e.g. option fees or fees for transfer of title) are not exempt unless the charge for them is £10 or less (see **2.7(d)** above).

2.7.5.2 *Transactions involving finance companies*

Where a finance company finances the instalment credit then it becomes the owner of the goods. Therefore, the supply of goods is made by the supplier to the finance company and not the customer. This supply is a taxable supply of goods. The finance company then makes a supply of goods and a supply of credit to the customer. The supply of credit is exempt if the credit charge is disclosed to the customer in writing.

If the finance company does not become owner of the goods (e.g. the purchase is financed by a loan) then there is a supply of goods to the customer rather than to the finance company, even where the finance company makes payment direct to the supplier. This supply is taxable and VAT is due on the full selling price charged to the customer even where a lesser amount is paid by the finance company to the supplier. The finance company then makes a separate supply of credit to the customer.

See *C&E Commrs v Primback Ltd, Case C-34/99, [2001] STC 803* and *VAT Notice 700, paragraph 8.4*

2.7.5.3 *Transfers of HP or conditional sale agreements*

(a) *Transfers by the owner*

If the owner of the goods assigns his rights, interests and ownership under hire-purchase or conditional sale agreement to a bank or finance company (e.g. under a block discounting arrangement) the transfer is outside the scope of VAT. (*Value Added Tax (Special Provisions) Order 1995, Art 5 (4)*).

If the owner assigns his rights etc. to the dealer (for example under a recourse agreement) the transfer is a single supply of goods and is taxable.

(b) *Transfers by the customer*

If a customer buys goods under a hire-purchase or conditional sale agreement and subsequently transfers his rights and obligations to another customer, he is making a standard rated supply of services to the new customer. There is no supply by the owner to the new customer. VAT is due on the open market value of the supply (the total amount payable by the new customer to the owner to complete the agreement plus any amount paid to the original customer to secure the transfer).

In the case of *Philip Drakard Trading Limited v C & E Commrs, QB [1992] STC 568,* a company (P) had held two vehicles under a hire-purchase agreement. Due to financial problems, it was unable to make the payments required by the agreement and it therefore transferred the vehicles to a sole trader (M), who promised to settle the hire-purchase agreement. P's MD indemnified the hire-purchase company against any loss. HMRC issued an assessment on the basis that P had supplied the vehicles to M, the consideration being the amount outstanding under the hire-purchase agreement. The Tribunal dismissed P's appeal and the QB upheld this decision. Where a person paid off the settlement figure under a hire-purchase agreement to a finance company, it was reasonable to conclude that he did so on behalf of the hirer, since only the hirer had the contractual right to pay the amount in question to acquire ownership. The essence of the agreement was that P would supply the vehicles to M and that M would discharge P's debt to the hire-purchase company.

2.7.5.4 Repossession of goods

(a) *Goods supplied under hire-purchase or conditional sale agreements*

Title in goods supplied under these agreements does not pass until all payments due under the agreement have been made. However, any VAT due on the goods is payable at the start of the agreement. Where goods are subsequently repossessed or returned and the agreement ends early, if the agreement results in the customer becoming liable to pay nothing further or a lesser amount than the remaining instalments, an adjustment can be made to any VAT accounted for at the start of the agreement. Where the reduction in price contains elements of capital and interest, any reasonable method of apportionment can be used providing it is consistent and reflects the accounting methods used in the business.

If the customer is VAT registered, he should be sent a document regarding the adjustment to ensure that he makes a corresponding adjustment to his input tax recovery.

(b) *Goods supplied under credit sale agreements*

Title to goods supplied under credit sale agreements passes to the customer at the outset of the agreement. The return of goods is therefore treated as a supply from the customer to the finance company and the value of the original supply is unaffected.

2.7.5.5 Sale of repossessed goods

Repossessed goods are goods which have been:

- voluntarily returned under an HP agreement;
- repossessed under the terms of a finance agreement; or
- returned by a customer under the Consumer Credit Act once they have made 50% of the total payments due.

VAT Notice 718, para 13.8

The sale of returned or repossessed goods will be subject to VAT on the full selling price. However, if the goods are works of art, antiques or collectables or second-hand goods repossessed under the terms of a finance agreement or boats and aircraft repossessed by a mortgagee under the terms of a boat or aircraft mortgage, and

- they are sold in the same condition at disposal as they were when repossessed or acquired (the cleaning of goods is allowed as is the addition of any missing instruction manuals);
- if the goods had been supplied in the UK by the person from whom they were obtained, that supply would not have been chargeable with VAT or would have been chargeable on less than full value;
- if the goods have been imported into the UK they must have borne VAT which has neither been reclaimed nor refunded;
- the goods must not have been reimported having previously been exported as a zero rated supply;
- for motor cars, the VAT on any previous supply acquisition or importation must have been wholly excluded from credit,

then, if these conditions are met, the disposal is outside the scope of VAT.

If these conditions are not met then VAT is due on the full amount realised on the sale. However, if the goods were second hand when the finance agreement was entered into, the repossessed goods can be sold under the margin scheme.

VAT (Special Provisions) Order 1995, SI 1995/1268, Art 4 covers general provisions on disposals. *VAT (Cars) Order 1992, SI 1992/3122, Art 4* covers disposals of repossessed cars.

In the case of *British Credit Trust Ltd [2014] UKFTT 0744*, the tribunal held that VAT on legal costs and fees relating to the repossession can be directly attributed to the taxable disposal.

2.7.6. Pawnbrokers

There is no supply if a person redeems a pledge within the agreed redemption period.

With regard to unredeemed pledges, the following rules apply (see

Consumer Credit Act 1974, sections 120 and 121):

(a) *Loans not exceeding £75 with a six-month redemption period*
Ownership of the pledge passes to the pawnbroker if the goods are not redeemed within the six month statutory redemption period. A disposal of the goods to a third party after that time is a taxable supply.

However, if the goods are restored by the pawnbroker to the original owner within three months of the end of the redemption period, the transaction is treated as a redeemed pledge and there is no supply the VAT purposes. (*Value Added Tax (Treatment of Transactions) Order 1986, Art 3*).

The restoration of an unredeemed pledge more than three months after the redemption period is a taxable supply.

(b) *Other loans*
Where the loan is over £75 or where the redemption period is greater than six months, ownership of the pledge does not pass to the pawnbroker at the end of the redemption period. As a result, the onward supply to a third party is not a taxable supply by the pawnbroker. It is, however, a taxable supply by the pledgor if he is a taxable person and the pledge is something acquired in the course of his business.

Other charges made by pawnbrokers, e.g. interest payments, valuation fees and charges for selling unredeemed pledges are all generally treated as exempt supplies as relating to the granting of credit.

HMRC Manual VATFIN3180

2.8. Debts and related services

2.8.1. The sale of debts

Where a business sells a debt to a third party, this is an exempt supply under *VATA 94, Sch 9, Group 5, Item 1*. The value of the supply is the amount paid by the purchaser.

VAT Notice 701/49/, paragraph 5.1

2.8.2. Factoring and invoice discounting

Factoring, including invoice discounting, is essentially a form of debt collection and is treated as a taxable supply. However, factors and invoice-discounters offer a range of services and these usually include the prepayment of part of the value of the debt. Any consideration attributable to this is in respect of an exempt supply of credit.

Under a factoring arrangement, the client assigns his debt to the factor. The assignment is not a supply for VAT purposes but the creation of an equitable interest that enables the factor to fulfil his contracted functions. The factor opens a client account to which he credits the face value of the debts he has been assigned and debits his charges. These charges may be consideration for a number of standard rated administrative, clerical and accounting services. The balance, less an agreed retention is available for the client to draw on. Depending on the extent to which he does so, the factor debits a further charge (often described as 'discount') and this is consideration for the exempt supply of credit.

The factor may operate on a 'recourse' or 'non-recourse' basis.

In a recourse agreement, the factor will put the responsibility for bearing any loss on the client. If the debtor defaults the factor will reassign the debt to the client.

In a non-recourse agreement, the factor will accept the risk of the default. The charge for this service is standard rated although it will usually be reflected within an enhancement to the administration, factoring or service charge.

The VAT treatment of the various services supplied by a factor to his client can be summarised as follows:

(a) *Standard rated*

- administration service charge (this may cover the provision of all sales ledger management service, credit advice, debt collection service and the provision of management information)
- guarantee of payment

(b) *Exempt*

- discount or interest charge
- electronic transfer of funds (if charged for separately)

(c) *Not a supply*

- assignment or reassignment of debt

A factor cannot claim bad debt relief on the debts assigned to him by his client. The client cannot claim bad debt relief for debts assigned to a factor but can do so if the factor reassigns the debt to him. See also *Regency Factors Ltd v HMRC [2019] UKFTT 144* where a claim to bad debt relief failed under a 'with recourse' agreement because of the time and way factoring charges were deducted.

VAT Notice 701/49/, paras 5.2-5.8

2.8.3. Debt negotiation

A business provides exempt debt negotiation where they bring together the credit provider with the debtor and act between them in an attempt to mediate a change to the payment terms. This follows the Tribunal decision in *Debt Management Associates Ltd (VTD 17880).*

In *Business Brief 30/03,* HMRC outlined the type of service that may be included as debt negotiation services:

- taking details of income and expenditure, along with details of the creditor(s) and the amount outstanding, and preparing and presenting a payment plan to the creditor;
- agreeing to act on behalf of such a debtor with the creditor in negotiating the payment plan; or
- agreeing to receive payments from the debtor and passing these payments on to the creditors (with or without first extracting a fee or commission for doing so).

HMRC take 'negotiation' to refer to the activity of an intermediary providing a distinct act of mediation with the purpose of doing all that is necessary in order for or two parties to enter into a contract without the person who is acting as the intermediary having any interest of his own in terms of the contract. Therefore, providing the person is bringing together the two parties, acting between those parties and attempting to mediate a change in the payment terms, they are deemed to be negotiating debts.

2.8.4. Debt collection

Supplies made by a debt collection agency or by a business involved in debt collection are taxable at the standard rate. Debt collection includes a collection of debts of any nature, even if payment of the debt has been received before, or after their due date.

Although debt collection services undertaken on behalf of the creditor company may involve some negotiation of the repayment of the debt by the debtor to the creditor this is not an exempt debt negotiation service. For example, if the business:

- issues letters to the debtor on behalf of the creditor demanding payment; or

- seeks to chase the debt in some other form (e.g. by contacting the debtor by telephone etc); or
- attempts to locate a debtor on behalf of the creditor; or
- provides accounting services to the creditor (i.e. monitors the debtors payment account and notifies the creditor of any default payments),

these services are taxable at the standard rate. Any debt negotiation services are ancillary to the principal service of debt collection.

VAT Notice 701/49/, paragraph 5.10

2.8.5. Insolvency practitioner services

Supplies made by Insolvency Practitioners are normally taxable. Any negotiation and/or payments and transfer services are ancillary to the main supply and follow the liability of that supply.

VAT Notice 701/49/, paragraph 5.11

See **2.6.8** above regarding individual voluntary arrangements and company voluntary arrangements.

2.9. Islamic finance

According to Islamic law (known as *Sharia'a*) the following are prohibited:

- the charging or receipt of interest ('riba');
- uncertainty or deception, for example an ambiguity or lack of clarity in the terms of the contract that can give rise to speculation ('gharar');
- gambling or speculation. For example, any transaction undertaken the purely speculative purposes ('maisir'); or
- unethical investments. For example, dealing activities or commodities include pork, pornography, arms and munitions, conventional financial services, cinema, tobacco, gambling or alcohol.

As a consequence, many Muslims have been unable or unwilling to obtain conventional credit finance in order to purchase goods and/or services because those products break Sharia'a law. In order to be able to provide Sharia'a compliant products financial institutions such as banks, along with boards of Sharia'a scholars, have worked together to create various products, which are summarised below and in HMRC Finance Manual *VATFIN8000*. One of the ways financial institutions have found to circumvent the prohibition against the charging and/or receipt of interest is to use 'profit' obtained from the various investments. This mechanism is outlined below.

2.9.1. Price plus 'profit' products

There are three products that use the 'price plus 'profit'' principle; a basic product (called 'Murabaha') one involves commodity transactions (called 'commodity Murabaha') and reverse of this (called 'reverse Murabaha').

2.9.1.1 Basic Murabaha

This product can be used to fund the purchase of a variety of assets, including cars, white goods, televisions and property (both residential and commercial).

This product works by the customer entering into an agreement with the bank under which the bank will purchase the assets for the sale price, taking title whilst the customer takes possession of the asset as agent for the bank. The bank then sells the asset to the customer for the sale price plus a profit. The customer defers payment by instalment over a set period of time or agrees to pay the total price at a specified future date. Title to the asset will always pass from the bank to the customer at the beginning of the arrangement.

For VAT purposes, the sale is treated in the same way as a credit sale (see **2.7.5** above). There are two supplies being made by the bank; one of the goods or property and the other of the facility to defer payment.

Consideration for the supply of the goods or property will follow the normal liability rules. The 'profit' element will be treated as consideration for the facility to defer payment and will be exempt under *VATA 94, Sch 9, Group 5, Item 3*.

2.9.1.2 Commodity Murabaha

This product is basically a loan facility from a financial institution but rather than lending the money and charging interest, it uses commodities and deferred payments to achieve the same end effect. There are two ways in which this product can operate:

(a) Assuming the customer requires a loan of £20,000, the financial institution (e.g. a bank) will purchase commodities from a supplier for £20,000, will take title and then immediately sell to the customer for, say £22,000 (the base price plus 'profit'). The customer can either defer payment over a set time or until a specified future date. The customer takes title to the commodities and using the banker as agent, immediately sells the commodities for £20,000 to the purchaser (the bank makes no charge to the customer for acting as agent). All of this is done 'on spot' to avoid the risk of either a rise or fall in the commodity price. The £20,000 cash is credited to the customer's account. The £2,000 'profit' on the sale of the commodity by the bank to the customer is the bank's income from the deal.

(b) Assuming the customer requires a loan of £20,000, the financial institution or bank, using an agent, purchases commodities from a supplier for £20,000, takes title and immediately sells to the customer for £22,000 (base price plus 'profit'). The customer can defer payment, either over a set period or until a specified future date. The customer takes title to the commodities. As above this is done 'on spot'. The £2,000 'profit' on the sale of the commodity by the bank to the customer is the bank's income from the deal.

2.9.1.3 *Reverse Murabaha*

This product is the reverse to the commodity Murabaha and is normally used to effect a loan between financial institutions. As with the commodity Murabaha outlined above, this product can operate in one of two ways:

(a) Assuming Bank A requires a loan of £20 million, Bank B will purchase commodities from a supplier for £20 million, Bank A acting as agent for Bank B but making no charge for doing this. Bank A takes title to the commodities and sells them immediately to Bank B for £25 million (a base price plus 'profit'). Bank B can defer payment, either over a set period or until a specified future date. Bank B takes title to the commodities and immediately sells the commodities for £20 million to an end purchaser. All of this is done on spot to minimise the risk of a rise or fall in the commodity price. The £20 million cash is credited into bank A's account.

(b) Assuming Bank A requires a loan of £20 million, Bank B purchases commodities from a supplier for £20 million, takes title, and immediately sells to bank A for £25 million (the base price plus 'profit'). Bank A can defer payment, either over a set period or until a specified future date. Bank A takes title to the commodities. Bank A, with Bank B now acting as an agent, immediately sells the commodities for £20 million to an end purchaser. This is done 'on spot'. The £20 million cash is credited into Bank A's account.

The VAT treatment of commodities is outlined at **2.5** above. The 'profit' element retained by the bank is treated as consideration for the facility to defer payment and is exempt under *VATA 94, Sch 9, Group 5, Item 2*.

2.9.2. Lease and lease plus purchase

2.9.2.1 *Lease only (Ijara)*

This is a basic leasing product that can be used to lease a variety of assets, including cars, white goods, televisions and property (both residential and commercial). With this product, the financial institution (e.g. a bank) acquires title to the asset and leases it to the customer. At no time does title to the asset pass to the customer nor is it expected to pass. If the customer wishes to purchase the asset at a later date a separate agreement is drawn up.

Consideration for the supplies made under this arrangement will be treated in the same way as other forms of leasing agreement. Where the agreement is for a supply of services other than property, the supply would be taxable. For supplies of property these will follow the rules applying to property.

2.9.2.2 *Lease plus purchase (Ijara-wa-Iqtina)*

This product is basically the same as Ijara above, except that title to the asset is expected to pass to the customer at some point, normally at the end of the contract period. It can be used to purchase both goods and property.

Where the product is used in respect of goods other than property, it is treated in the same way as a hire-purchase/conditional sale arrangement (see **2.7.5** above). There are two supplies being made by the bank or financial institution; one of the goods and one of the facility to defer payment. Consideration for the supply of the goods will follow the normal liability rules. The additional charge over and above the price of the goods will be treated as consideration for a deferred payment facility and will be exempt under *VATA 94, Sch 9, Group 5, Item 3.*

In respect to property, where the bank is the absolute legal and beneficial owner of the property, the transaction will be treated in the same way as for goods (i.e. a hire-purchase or conditional sale) except that the normal rules for property will apply to the sale of the asset. The additional charge above the price of the property will be treated as consideration for a deferred payment facility and thus exempt under *VATA 94, Sch 9. Group 5, Item 3*. Where the bank is unlikely to be the absolute legal and beneficial owner of the property, but takes title only by way of security, the assignment of the title by the customer to the bank operates by way of a mortgage. Any payments made by the customer to the bank will be repayments of the loan and where the amount repaid is greater than the capital sum advanced, will be consideration for a grant of credit and exempt under *VATA 94, Sch 9. Group 5, Item 2.*

2.9.3. Shared ownership (diminishing Musharaka)

This product involves the use of two written contracts, a lease agreement ('Ijara') and a diminishing ownership agreement ('Musharaka'), where two or more parties share ownership of an asset.

As an example, where a customer wishes to purchase a residential property for £500,000, they will pay a deposit of, say, £50,000 to the vendor of the property and then enter into a diminishing ownership agreement with the bank, under which the bank pays the outstanding £450,000. The bank takes title to the property by way of a sub sale between the vendor and the bank. The customer now has a 10% beneficial interest in the property, with the remainder being with the bank. The bank allows the customer to defer payment of £450,000 over a period of 25 years. It does not (and indeed cannot) add interest to the £450,000 and so under this contract the customer pays back the exact amount paid out by the bank.

At the same time as the customer enters into the diminishing ownership agreement, he also enters into a lease agreement, whereby the bank agrees to lease its share of the house to the customer for a variable amount of rent. The lease agreement runs concurrent with the diminishing ownership agreement.

It is also likely that the customer will be expected to pay outgoings related to the property in addition to all administrative and legal costs, arrangement fees, Stamp Duty Land Tax, HM registry fees and VAT (if applicable).

Both the amount repaid under the diminishing ownership agreement and the amount paid under the lease agreement are amalgamated and used to calculate how much of the bank's share of the property has been purchased per month by the customer. As the bank's share in the property decreases so does the amount paid under the lease agreement.

At the end of the 25 years, assuming all the conditions within the two contracts have been met, the bank will pass title in the property to the customer under the diminishing ownership agreement, normally for an additional payment.

For VAT purposes, there are two supplies:

(a) the gradual sale of the equitable interest; and
(b) the lease of the property.

The VAT treatment will follow the normal rules for property.

2.9.4. Agency (wakala)

This investment product functions in the same way as Mudaraba (see below) with the exception that with a Mudaraba all the profit is divided between the parties whereas with a Wakala the investor receives only the agreed ratio against investment. Anything made above that ratio is kept by the financial institution and not given to the investor.

So, for example, an investor may agree to invest a sum with a bank for an agreed return (for example 5%). The bank will pool investors' funds with the funds of other investors plus its own capital and invest in Sharia'a compliant assets. At the end of a given period, the bank will return the invested sum to the investor along with the agreed 5%. Any revenue above the 5% is retained by the bank; if the bank does not make the agreed percentage return, then the investor gets what has been made whilst the bank gets nothing.

Where the bank makes the investment decisions any charges made by the bank to the investor will follow the rules outlined above of investments. The additional profit made by the bank will be outside the scope of VAT.

Where the bank follows the instructions of its clients the additional revenue made by the bank on the investment of the capital will be taxable at the standard rate. This is because what the bank is doing is a form of portfolio / investment management.

2.9.5. Sharia'a compliant current and savings accounts

Current accounts operate in the same way as a conventional current account except that there is no overdraft facility and no interest added by the bank to the account for funding credit. The VAT treatment will follow the exemption for the operation of any current, deposit or savings account (*VATA 94, Sch 9, Group 5, Item 8*).

For savings accounts operated under an unrestricted Mudaraba contract, the product operates broadly as outlined in **2.9.4** above.

As with conventional savings accounts, the aim of the product is to give investors an agreed return on their investments. The bank will pool the investors' money with that of other investors and the banks own money and invest it in Sharia'a compliant equities. At the end of each month the gross income is calculated, various deductions made, the banks share of the income calculated and the remainder credited to the customer's account.

The VAT treatment will be the same as that outlined in **2.9.4** above.

2.9.6. Intermediary services

The rules regarding intermediary services will be the same as for conventional financial products (see **2.6** above).

It should be noted that where someone introduces customers to products that do not involve financial services (for example, transactions in land or property) the VAT exemption for financial intermediary services will not apply and any fees charged will be liable to VAT at the standard rate.

VATFIN8000

2.10. Standard rated services

There is a range of services which although connected to financial services do not qualify for VAT exemption. These include (and the list is not exhaustive):

- bookkeeping services;
- debt collection and credit control;
- depository and trustee services;
- equipment leasing;
- executor and trustee services and the administration of estates;
- investment, finance and taxation advice;
- management consultancy;
- merger and takeover advice;
- portfolio management (see **2.10.1** below);
- registrar services (see **2.3.4** above);
- safe custody services (see 2.3.2 above) and safe transportation services; and
- the activities of service companies, e.g. administration, payment of salaries and wages.

VAT Notice 701/49/, paragraph 1.6

2.10.1. Discretionary investment or fund management and 'portfolio management'

Discretionary investment management or discretionary fund management describes an arrangement under which an investment or fund manager provides a service to a client of using the manager's 'discretion' (or expertise) to invest funds to achieve the best result for their client, subject to the level of risk to which the client is happy to expose their capital. After being authorised by the client, the manager makes all the decisions in respect of the pooling and investment of capital.

Unless involved in the management of Special Investment Funds (see **2.4.1**) which qualify for exemption, discretionary investment management services are currently taxable in the UK. This will cover all charges to the client, including those described as initial charges, annual management charges or performance charges.

However, there are certainly some questions over the blanket treatment of discretionary fund management where it involves model portfolios (prebuilt collections of investments). I understand that some advisers have agreed exemption with HMRC on the basis that what is being managed (the model portfolio) qualifies for exemption. Unfortunately, none of these agreements have been made public so it is difficult to be certain on the scope and extent of any ruling and of course will depend on what is being managed and what, if any, level of managers discretion is required. I suspect this is an area which will develop over the next year or so as advisers look more closely at the cost of VAT to themselves and their clients and of course it may be affected by the outcome of HMRC's fund management review.

It has also been common for many advisers to separate out the 'execution' element of any arrangements in order to treat that part as VAT exempt. HMRC have been aware of these arrangements and have accepted that fees for such services are exempt. This treatment is now under threat as a result of the ECJ case of *Deutsche Bank AG v Finanzamt Frankfurt am Main V-Höchst (Case C-44/11) [2012] STC 1951* which looked at the treatment of discretionary investment management or portfolio management services.

2.10.2. Deutsche Bank AG v Finanzamt Frankfurt am Main v Höchst (Case C-44/11) [2012] STC 1951

Deutsche Bank provided discretionary investment management or portfolio management services to individuals. There were two elements to their supplies: (i) asset management, and (ii) the purchase and sale of securities. The fee charged was split between the two elements.

The referral to the ECJ asked the following three questions:

1. Is the management of securities-based assets (portfolio management), where a taxable person determines for remuneration the purchase and sale of securities, and implements that determination by buying and selling the securities, exempt from tax only in so far as it consists in the management of investment funds for a number of investors collectively within the meaning of Article 135(g) of Directive 2006/112/EC or also in so far as it consists in individual portfolio management for individual investors within the meaning of Article 135(1)(t) of Directive 2006/112/EC (transactions in securities or the negotiation of such transactions)?

2. For the purposes of defining principal and ancillary services, what significance is to be attached to the criterion that the ancillary service does not constitute for customers an aim in itself, but a means of better enjoying the principal service supplied, in the context of separate invoicing for the ancillary service and the fact that the ancillary service can be provided by third parties?

3. Does Article 56(1)(e) of Directive 2006/112IEC cover only the services referred to in Article 135(1)(a) to (g) of Directive 2006/112/EC or also the

> management of securities-based assets (portfolio management), even if that transaction is not subject to the latter provision?

And in answer, the ECJ ruled:

> 1. A securities-based assets management service, such as that at issue in the main proceedings, namely where a taxable person for remuneration and on the basis of his own discretion takes decisions on the purchase and sale of securities and implements those decisions by buying and selling the securities, consists of two elements which are so closely linked that they form, objectively, a single economic supply.
> 2. Article 135(1)(f) or (g) of Council Directive 2006/112/EC of 28 November 2006 on the common system of value added tax must be interpreted as meaning that securities-based asset management, such as that at issue in the main proceedings, is not exempt from value added tax under that provision.
> 3. Article 56(1)(e) of Directive 2006/112 must be interpreted as covering not only the services referred to in Article 135(1)(a) to (g) of Directive 2006/112, but also securities-based assets management services.

So, in answering the second question first, the ECJ have ruled that discretionary investment management is a single supply – which suggests that the UK's position in allowing 'execution' services to be separated out and treated as VAT exempt is incorrect. They have ruled that the supply is taxable (upholding the UK's position). Finally, they have ruled that the place of supply rules outlined in Article 56(1) cover these services as they are services of a financial nature.

HMRC responded to the decision in *R&C Brief 11/13*. In the brief they state:

> Whilst all portfolio management services are subject to VAT, the UK currently treats separate charges for effecting the purchase and sale of securities as exempt from VAT on the basis that they are consideration for separate supplies.
>
> As a result of the judgment, it is clear that fees charged by portfolio managers on an annual or other periodic basis for the purchase and sale of securities can no longer be treated as exempt from VAT, regardless of whether or not a separate charge is made.
>
> However, the ECJ in *Deutsche Bank* only considered the VAT position of periodic fees charged on a flat fee basis where there was no direct link to the transactions being executed. Where, therefore, fees are charged strictly on a transaction-by-transaction basis (that is, per purchase or sale of investments) exemption will continue to apply. This is conditional upon the portfolio management services being contracted for on that basis and the transaction charges being separately identified in any VAT invoice. This

VAT treatment will apply irrespective of whether the portfolio is managed on a full discretionary or on an advisory basis.

Probably most notable is that HMRC still accept exemption for execution services, provided they are contracted for separately, separately identified on any invoice and fees charged on a transaction-by-transaction basis.

2.10.3. Discretionary investment management and IFAs

Where an IFA introduces a client to a discretionary investment management or fund management service, that introduction is generally taxable on the basis that the underlying supply is itself taxable.

However, note the decision in *Bloomsbury Wealth Management LLP ([2012] UK FTT 379* discussed at **2.6.5** above.

2.11. Investment gold

Investment gold is exempt, subject to an option to tax.

2.11.1. Definition of investment gold

Investment gold is:

(a) gold of a purity not less than 995 thousandths that is in the form of a bar, or a wafer, of a weight accepted by the bullion markets;

(b) a gold coin minted after 1800 that:
- is of a purity of not less than 900 thousandths;
- is, or has been, legal tender in its country of origin; and
- is of a description of coin that is normally sold at a price that does not exceed 180% of the open market value of the gold contained in the coin; or

(c) an investment gold coin as specified in section 3 *Notice 701/21A Investment gold coins*.

2.11.2. Exemption

The following supplies are exempt:

(a) a supply of investment gold;

(b) a supply which confers the right to take possession of investment gold. This includes supplies of unallocated investment gold, loans, swaps, forward and future contracts concerning investment gold. This does not include options. Also see *Notice 701/9 Derivatives and terminal markets*; and

(c) a supply of services by an agent which consists of attempting to bring about a supply within (a) or (b) above for a named principal, whether or not the agent is successful.

2.11.3. Notification

The first time a trader makes an exempt supply of investment gold which exceeds £5,000, or where the value of supplies of exempt investment gold to any one customer is over £10,000 in any 12-month period, they are required to notify HMRC within 28 days at the following address:

HM Revenue & Customs
Written Enquiries Section
Alexander House
Victoria Avenue
Southend
Essex SS99 1BD

Where notification is required but the trader is not registered for VAT, the following information must be provided:

1. Name of company, partnership or sole proprietor
2. Company incorporation number or details of partners
3. Address(es)
4. Phone number
5. Contact name
6. Accountant's name, address and phone number
7. Associated VAT registration numbers

The business will be sent an acknowledgement by the Gold Team which should arrive within 28 days. If the acknowledgement is not received within 28 days, the trader must check that HMRC have received the notification. There is no requirement to notify HMRC of subsequent supplies.

2.11.4. Option to tax

A business may wish to opt to tax in order to reclaim attributable input tax.

2.11.4.1 When can a trader opt?

A trader can only opt to tax supplies of investment gold made to another taxable person. They can also opt to tax investment gold coins if they produce the coins. Supplies of investment gold to non-taxable persons will always be exempt. Where a business supplies gold for industrial purposes, it may opt to tax those supplies subject to agreement from HMRC, and this agreement must be sought in advance of the transaction.

2.11.4.2 Notification

A trader must notify HMRC of any intention to opt to tax. Written acknowledgement will be issued within 28 days. If no acknowledgement is received, the trader must check that HMRC received the notification.

2.11.4.3 Agents

Where an agent acts for a named principal and the principal has opted to tax, the agent may opt to tax their services in so far as they are related to the principal's "opted" supplies of investment gold. Again, notification as per **2.11.4.2** is required.

2.11.4.4 Invoices

Invoices for opted transactions must be annotated 'we have opted to tax this transaction'.

2.11.5. General record keeping requirements

Traders dealing in exempt investment gold over the thresholds outlined in 2.11.3 are required to issue invoices and maintain certain records. These requirements have legal force and are outlined in *paragraphs 6 and 7 of VAT Notice 701/21/.*

3. Insurance

3.1. Introduction

Insurance transactions can be split into three main areas:

1. services supplied by those providing insurance cover;
2. services supplied by those arranging insurance cover; and
3. other expert services related to the provision of insurance.

Insurance itself can be split between general (non-life) and long-term (or life) insurance. Reinsurance contracts are contracts taken out by an insurer to indemnify themselves against risks they have insured (in effect, insurance taken out by an insurer). Consequently, unless otherwise stated, all references in this chapter to insurance include reinsurance.

The way that insurance is sold has changed dramatically over the last 10 to 15 years. Much insurance is now sold online, meaning that much of the intermediary provision is now automated. Similarly the Lloyd's insurance market has developed with the introduction of corporate members.

3.1.1. Definitions

There is no legal definition of insurance. However, in *Medical Defence Union Ltd v the Department of Trade [1979] 2 All ER 421,* the judge held that there must be three specific elements present in the contract of insurance:

- the contract must provide that the insured would become entitled to money for money's worth of occurrence of supplement;
- the event must be one which involves some element of uncertainty in the subject matter of the contract; and
- the insured must have insurable interest. Therefore, if the insured risk occurs, the policyholder stands to suffer some loss.

The FSA's *Perimeter Guidance Manual (PERG) 6 Guidance on the Identification of Contracts of Insurance* notes:

> **PERG 6.3.3**
> The courts have not fully defined the common law meaning of 'insurance' and 'insurance business', since they have, on the whole, confined their decisions to the facts before them. They have, however, given useful guidance in the form of descriptions of contracts of insurance.
>
> **PERG 6.3.4**
> The best established of these descriptions appears in the case of *Prudential v. Commissioners of Inland Revenue [1904] 2 KB 658*. This case, read with a number of later cases, treats as insurance any enforceable contract under which a 'provider' undertakes:
>
> (1) in consideration of one or more payments;

(2) to pay money or provide a corresponding benefit (including in some cases services to be paid for by the provider) to a 'recipient';
(3) in response to a defined event the occurrence of which is uncertain (either as to when it will occur or as to whether it will occur at all) and adverse to the interests of the recipient.

HMRC will generally accept that a supply is insurance if it is something that requires authorisation under the *Financial Services and Markets Act 2000 (FSMA)*. In addition, they will also accept that some funeral plans and vehicle breakdown cover are insurance, even though they are specifically exempted from authorisation.

Under the provisions of the FSMA, with some specific exceptions, it is illegal for UK businesses to provide insurance without authorisation. However, for the purposes of VAT, exemption applies to all supplies of insurance and reinsurance, regardless of the status of the provider. This was a change introduced from 1 January 2005 as consequence of the decision in *Card Protection Plan Ltd v C&E Commrs, ECJ Case C-349/96, [1999] STC 270*. Here, the ECJ held that it was illegal under EC law for the UK to restrict the scope of VAT exemption to those permitted under national law. However, whilst an unauthorised provider of insurance may be able to benefit from VAT exemption (at least up to 1 January 2021) they are likely to face investigation and potential prosecution under the FSMA.

Some further assistance in establishing what constitutes insurance can be found in the case of *Mapfre Warranty SpA – Case C-548/13*. This case involved car breakdown warranties. The taxpayer, an insurer, was seeking to argue that the warranties were not exempt. However, the Advocate General, referring to a previous ECJ decision in *BGZ Leasing Sp z o.o. Case C-224/11*, has opined that all the characteristics of an insurance transaction were present in the warranties. The ECJ has now decided that warranties with the characteristics of an insurance contract should be treated as VAT exempt (see **3.9.1**)

In the case of *Supercar Drive Days Ltd [2018] UKFTT 31*, the appellant argued that the provision of insurance Collision Damage Waivers (CDW) constituted a VAT exempt supply of insurance. HMRC argued that they were taxable as they simply reduced an insurance liability to zero. The First Tier Tribunal ruled that they were not insurance transactions largely by reference to the terms and conditions of the contract which did not put the appellant in the position of being a broker or agent. It was also interesting to note that the FTT held that the correct interpretation of 'insurance transactions' derives from EU law (*Card Protection Plan*) and not from UK law (HMRC's view) in *Prudential* and *Medical Defence Union Ltd*.

3.1.2. Legislation

The principal EC legislation concerning insurance transactions is found at Article 135 1(a) of *Council Directive 2006/112/EC*. This states that:

Member States shall exempt the following transactions:

(a) insurance and reinsurance transactions, including related services performed by insurance brokers and insurance agents;...

This is translated into UK legislation in *VATA 94, Schedule 9, Group 2*, which provides VAT exemption for:

1. Insurance transactions and reinsurance transactions
4. The provision by an insurance broker or insurance agent of any of the services of an insurance intermediary in a case in which those services -
   (a) are related (whether or not a contract of insurance or reinsurance is finally concluded) to an insurance transaction or a reinsurance transaction; and
   (b) are provided by that broker or agent in the course of his acting in an intermediary capacity....

Note: Items 2 and 3 were removed from Group 2 following the judgment in *Card Protection Plan Ltd v C&E Commrs, ECJ Case C-349/96, [1999] STC 270.* These items used to cover the provision of insurance by insurers or reinsurers belonging outside the UK and the provision of a form of insurance by the Exports Credit Guarantee Department (ECGD), a public body that was not registered as an insurance company. These items are no longer required as Item 1 covers all insurance and reinsurance transactions regardless of where the insurer or re-insurer is based and whether or not the insurer or reinsurer is authorised.

The UK legislation then has a series of notes clarifying where the exemption does and does not apply on services provided by brokers, agents and other parties involved in the supply of insurance and reinsurance:

NOTES

(1) For the purposes of item 4 services are services of an insurance intermediary if they fall within any of the following paragraphs—
  (a) the bringing together, with a view to the insurance or reinsurance of risks, of—
    (i) persons who are or may be seeking insurance or reinsurance, and
    (ii) persons who provide insurance or reinsurance;
  (b) the carrying out of work preparatory to the conclusion of contracts of insurance or reinsurance;
  (c) the provision of assistance in the administration and performance of such contracts, including the handling of claims;

(d) the collection of premiums.

(2) For the purposes of item 4 an insurance broker or insurance agent is acting 'in an intermediary capacity' wherever he is acting as an intermediary, or one of the intermediaries, between—

(a) a person who provides [insurance or reinsurance], and

(b) a person who is or may be seeking insurance or reinsurance or is an insured person.

(3) Where—

(a) a person ('the supplier') makes a supply of goods or services to another ('the customer'),

(b) the supply of the goods or services is a taxable supply and is not a zero-rated supply,

(c) a transaction under which insurance is to be or may be arranged for the customer is entered into in connection with the supply of the goods or services,

(d) a supply of services which are related (whether or not a contract of insurance is finally concluded) to the provision of insurance in pursuance of that transaction is made by—

(i) the person by whom the supply of the goods or services is made, or

(ii) a person who is connected with that person and, in connection with the provision of that insurance, deals directly with the customer,

and

(e) the related services do not consist in the handling of claims under the contract for that insurance,

those related services do not fall within item 4 unless the relevant requirements are fulfilled.

(4) For the purposes of Note (3) the relevant requirements are—

(a) that a document containing the statements specified in Note (5) is prepared;

(b) that the matters that must be stated in the document have been disclosed to the customer at or before the time when the transaction mentioned in Note (3)(c) is entered into; and

(c) that there is compliance with all such requirements (if any) as to—

(i) the preparation and form of the document,

(ii) the manner of disclosing to the customer the matters that must be stated in the document, and

(iii) the delivery of a copy of the document to the customer,

as may be set out in a notice that has been published by the Commissioners and has not been withdrawn.

(5) The statements referred to in Note (4) are—

(a) a statement setting out the amount of the premium under any contract of insurance that is to be or may be entered into in pursuance of the transaction in question; and

(b) a statement setting out every amount that the customer is, is to be or has been required to pay, otherwise than by way of such a premium, in connection with that transaction or anything that is to be, may be or has been done in pursuance of that transaction.

(6) For the purposes of Note (3) any question whether a person is connected with another shall be determined in accordance with *section 1122 of the Corporation Tax Act 2010.*

(7) Item 4 does not include—

(a) the supply of any market research, product design, advertising, promotional or similar services; or

(b) the collection, collation and provision of information for use in connection with market research, product design, advertising, promotional or similar activities.

(8) Item 4 does not include the supply of any valuation or inspection services.

(9) Item 4 does not include the supply of any services by loss adjusters, average adjusters, motor assessors, surveyors or other experts except where—

(a) the services consist in the handling of a claim under a contract of insurance or reinsurance;

(b) the person handling the claim is authorised when doing so to act on behalf of the insurer or reinsurer; and

(c) that person's authority so to act includes written authority to determine whether to accept or reject the claim and, where accepting it in whole or in part, to settle the amount to be paid on the claim.

(10) Item 4 does not include the supply of any services which—

(a) are supplied in pursuance of a contract of insurance or reinsurance or of any arrangements made in connection with such a contract; and

(b) are so supplied either—

(i) instead of the payment of the whole or any part of any indemnity for which the contract provides, or

(ii) for the purpose, in any other manner, of satisfying any claim under that contract, whether in whole or in part.

3.1.3. Place of supply

With effect from 1 January 2010, the place of supply of insurance services follows the general rule for the place of supply of services meaning that the supply is made where the customer belongs.

The 'place of supply' rules are explained further in **Chapter 7**.

Although VAT is not payable on insurance transactions, the place of supply is important as it determines whether or not VAT is recoverable on related costs.

Where the place of supply is the UK, the supply of insurance is exempt from VAT and VAT recovery is not available. Where the place of supply is outside the UK, the supply is outside the scope of VAT.

If the place of supply is outside the UK (i.e. the policyholder belongs outside the UK), then the supplies are outside the scope of VAT but VAT on related costs is recoverable.

There is one main exception to this rule and this affects insurance directly related to the export of goods to a place outside the UK. In these cases, even if the recipient or insured belongs in the UK, whilst the supply is still exempt, the insurer is entitled to recover VAT on related costs.

Some insurance policies may have multiple insured parties and name more than one party as being the insured under the contract. In such cases, the place of supply will be determined by the place of belonging to the principal insured. Where there is no one principal insured and the insured parties are a mix of EU and non-EU, the place of supply should be treated as being where the majority of insured parties belong or the location of the party which is the principal beneficiary under the contract.

With effect from 1 October 2016, the place of supply of certain insurance repair services has changed to where those services are effectively used and enjoyed (see *R&C Brief 15/2016*). The repair services affected are those on moveable goods (e.g. cars and equipment) but not buildings or fixtures and fitting performed as a result of an insurance claim to the insured person.

3.1.4. Consideration and time of supply

Generally, the value of any supply of insurance is based on the value of gross premium payable to the insurer or re-insurer. The gross premium includes:

- any brokerage commission retained by the broker or intermediary involved in arranging the business;
- any claims payments;
- any reinsurance payments to reinsurers; and
- any taxes (although insurers can choose to exclude the value of Insurance Premium Tax (IPT) from their partial exemption calculation. See **3.10.6** for further details).

For reinsurance, the value of the supply is the gross premium after deduction of:

- reinsurance commission (also known as treaty, flat, ceding or overriding commission). This is a commission agreed between the reinsurer and the ceding insurer (the reinsured) to cover the acquisition costs of the insurer in obtaining the business. This is treated as a discount; and

- profit commission (which may be called contingent commission), which is payable by the reinsurer to the ceding insurer (the reinsured) if the business proves to be profitable. This is regarded as a contingent discount and reduces the amount which the insurer pays for the reinsurance.

For insurance brokers and agents, the value of the supply for VAT purposes will be based on the gross brokerage or commission received or the full value of any fee charged. No deduction should be made for any commissions paid to other brokers or intermediaries.

As insurance is exempt from VAT, the tax point or time of supply is not an issue in determining when any VAT becomes due but it can be important in determining when VAT can be recovered.

The tax point for supplies of insurance and reinsurance can be summarised as follows:

- for short-term or one-off risks, a basic tax point occurs when an insurance contract is finalised and signed;
- an actual tax point will arise if any of the premium is received in advance of the basic tax point; and
- renewable policies for long-term risks are generally deemed to be continuous supplies of services, where the tax point is the date of the receipt of each premium.

3.1.5. Recovery of input tax

Probably the key VAT issue that arises for businesses in the insurance sector is whether or not VAT incurred on expenditure can be recovered.

VAT recovery is principally driven by the place of supply rules.

As noted above, VAT recovery is only available where costs are related to:

- any taxable supplies made; or
- any insurance supplies made where the recipient of the insurance services (the policyholder) belongs outside the UK (EU prior to 1 January 2021); or
- a supply of insurance directly linked to the export of goods to a place outside the UK (EU prior to 1 January 2021).

However, the complication for insurers and intermediaries is that the majority of costs incurred do not directly relate to a specific VAT category of supply. The vast majority of costs will relate to insurance transactions involving both UK and non-UK policyholders along with other activities carried out by the business (e.g. investments in securities and land and property). The recoverability of VAT on these overhead (or residual) costs will then be driven by the partial exemption method that the business employs. This is considered in more detail in 6.6 which looks at partial exemption.

3.2. General (non-life) insurance

General insurance covers insurance falling within the classes in Schedule 1, Part I to the *Financial Services and Markets Act 2000 (Regulated Activities) Order 2001*. (See **Appendix A** for details).

A supply of general insurance is exempt from VAT where the recipient belongs in the UK.

Where the recipient belongs outside the UK, the supply is outside the scope of UK VAT but with credit for related input tax.

3.2.1. Insurance linked to the export of goods

An insurance policy related to the export of goods to a place outside the UK is exempt but with recovery of related input tax where the insured belongs in the UK. It is outside the scope with recovery of related input tax where the insured belongs outside the UK.

This treatment effectively replicates zero rating for the supply (as the legal note to *VATA 94, Sch 8, Group 7* regarding the application of zero rating for international services excludes insurance and financial services from zero rating under that provision).

In order for this to apply:

- the goods must be being exported by the recipient of the insurance;
- the insurance must be directly linked to the specific goods being exported; and
- the insurance must cover the risks of the person who owns the goods or is responsible for their export.

VAT Notice 701/36/, para 6.6.2

Prior to 1 January 2021 when the rules changed on the UK's departure from the EU, HMRC took the view that this only included movements from a place within the EU to a place outside the EU (i.e. it does not cover movements of goods from one place outside the EU to another place outside the EU). Presumably now, this logic would mean that it would only apply to movements from or to the UK and not entirely outside the UK. However, this may be arguable. Care also needs to be taken on the directly linked point. For example, covers relating to loss, damage, theft or delay in delivery of goods should be covered but insurance of a warehouse storing goods for export would not (both because the insurance does not relate to specific goods being exported and because the person insured (the warehouse owner) would not be the exporter of the goods). Also, some insurance covers may cover a mix of imports and exports and include both UK and non-UK movements, in which case an apportionment may be necessary to identify the export element.

3.2.2. Marine aviation and transport (MAT) insurance

Insurance falling within certain classes of risk defined in *paragraphs 1, 4 – 7, 11 and 12 of Part I of Schedule 1 to the Financial Services and Markets Act (Regulated Activities) Order 2001*, is categorised as Marine, Aviation and Transport (MAT) insurance.

The following classes of risk are covered:

- accident (relating to MAT risks only);
- aircraft;
- ships;
- railway rolling stock;
- goods in transit;
- aircraft liability; and
- liability of ships.

However, it does not cover risks relating to:

- motor vehicles;
- oil and gas rigs permanently fixed to the seabed;
- policies relating to laid up ships or ships under repair;
- grounded aircraft or aircraft under repair; or
- port and airport owners and operators liability.

The rules relating to the place of supply of MAT insurance are the same as for other general insurance (see above). Often MAT premiums will cover risks located both inside and outside the EU, e.g. transport of goods is often insured on a worldwide basis. As a consequence, an agreement is in place with HMRC to provide guidelines to deal with this type of business.

The guidelines have been in place since July 1993, providing three codes that can be used to identify the VAT status of supplies of MAT insurance:

X is used where the supply of insurance is not directly related to an export of goods to a place outside the UK and the insured belongs within the UK. As a consequence, there is no entitlement to deduct related input tax.

Z is used where either the insurance is directly linked to the export of goods to a place outside the UKor the insured belongs outside the UK. As a consequence, there is an entitlement to deduct related input tax.

M is used where the insurance does not directly relate to the export of goods, took place outside the UK, and the policy has no clear principal insured and at least one, but not all, of the insured parties belongs outside the UK. The M (mixed) code gives an entitlement to treat 50% of the input tax incurred on related goods as recoverable.

Establishing the place of supply for MAT insurance can occasionally be difficult. The following rules are used to determine whether the X or Z code is appropriate, based on the location of the insured or insureds:

- **Single insured** – Where there is only one insured party the address shown on the brokers slip, or equivalent, should be used to determine where the insured belongs. If there is no address shown, the location of the insured should be determined by reference to the broker or other intermediary. If the insured has more than one address, the one on the slip, or equivalent, should be used unless it can be shown that this is simply there for administration purposes.
- **Multiple insureds** – It is not uncommon for there to be multiple insureds, (e.g. in certain marine covers where owners, managers or time charterers may be shown on the slip). In these cases, the principal party should be identified where possible and their place of belonging used to establish the correct VAT code. Where a principal insured cannot be identified, the places where all the insured parties belong should be ascertained and business coded X, Z or M in accordance with the location of the insured parties.
- **Unidentified insureds** – If the place of belonging of the insured cannot otherwise be determined, VAT coding should be decided by reference to the country of origin of the business, the address of the broker, the address of any overseas agents and any additional information on the slip. Where these matters are not clear or there is conflicting evidence, HMRC would expect best judgement to be used.

If it is impossible to determine whether the X or Z code should be used after following the guidance above, then the M coding can be used. However, the M coding should only be used as a last resort.

VAT Notice 701/36/, para 6.7

3.2.3. Protection and Indemnity (P & I) Clubs

A P&I Club is a mutual association of shipowners established to insure its members, specialising mainly in third-party liability cover and insurance of the balance of collision risk is not covered by the company or the London market. P&I Clubs are non-profit-making and operate on a system of contributions (or 'mutual premiums') normally based on the previous year's costs, used to meet claims, reinsurances and administration costs. If claims are higher than expected, there may be pro rata supplementary payments (or 'additional calls'). If there is a surplus, there may be returns to members or the surplus may be transferred to a reserve to cover losses in other years. More than 90% of the world's ocean-going tonnage is insured by the 13 P&I Clubs who are members of the International Group of P&I Clubs. These members are based in UK, Bermuda, Scandinavia, Luxembourg, the United States and Japan.

P&I Clubs will delegate day-to-day management to professional Managers. For a number of the larger Clubs based outside the UK the Managers will delegate in turn, a substantial part of their day-to-day operations to representatives or Club agents in the UK. The Managers and their representatives are responsible for the day-to-day underwriting of risks, the handling of claims, and the administration of the Club's funds in accordance with the Club's policies.

P&I Clubs are deemed to be making supplies of insurance and the liabilities and place of supply will follow the normal rules.

P&I Club Managers are required to be separately registered from any clubs they manage. As noted above, Managers carry out the day-to-day running of the club; employing staff, establishing the level or weighting of contributions and often providing premises and facilities. If they are empowered to accept risks on behalf the club, they are deemed to be providing the services of an insurance intermediary. Unless they make other supplies, the VAT recovery rate of the manager will follow that of the Club that they manage.

A P&I Club agent acts for a P&I Club Manager when the manager has no presence in the UK. P&I Clubs agents, however, are viewed by HMRC to be supplying taxable management services to the Manager. These services are usually deemed to be supplied where the recipient of the supply belongs. Where such services are supplied to P&I Club managers belonging outside the UK, therefore, they are outside the scope of VAT with input tax recovery.

VAT Notice 701/36/, paras 3.4 and 10.2

3.2.4. Engineering inspection services

Inspection services are often carried out under an engineering insurance contract. They can take two forms – inspections which are for the benefit of the:

- insurer and are designed to provide reassurance to the insurer that all conditions attached to the insurance contract are being complied with; and
- insured, perhaps to identify ways to reduce cover or prevent the need for a claim.

If, as a condition of the insurance, an insurer reserves the right to inspect the insured plant wholly for the purpose of the control of the risk, then such inspections would normally constitute an overhead of the insurer, rather than a separate supply of inspection services to the insured.

Where an insurer provides inspection services to a policyholder and those inspection services are provided on their own, they are subject to VAT at the standard rate.

From 1 April 1997, where inspection services were provided with insurance, insurers were required to tax the inspection element separately. However, insurers should consider the impact of the tests laid down in *Card Protection Plan Ltd v C&E Commrs, ECJ Case C–349/96, [1999] STC 270* to determine whether there is a single or multiple supply, and if there is a single supply whether it is one of exempt insurance for taxable inspection services. (See also **7.6.5** on single v mixed supply).

If an insurer subcontracts the engineering inspection to a third party, that person will make a standard rated supply of services to the insurer. Where the insurer makes an onward exempt supply of insurance with ancillary inspection services, the VAT charged by the third party will not be recoverable.

The VAT liability of any commission earned by an intermediary in respect of a contract for engineering insurance with inspection services will follow the liability of the contract itself.

VAT Notice 701/36/, para 4.5 and VATINS7210

3.2.5. Block policies

The decision in *Card Protection Plan Ltd v C&E Commrs, ECJ Case C-349/96, [1999] STC 270* had significant implications for suppliers of block policies. Card Protection Plan Ltd (CPP) held a block insurance policy under which they were given authority by the insurer to arrange for their customers to become insured under the policy. The court ruled that CPP were making supplies of insurance transactions to their customers even though they were not themselves insurers. As a result of the CPP decision, HMRC now regard supplies made by block policyholders as insurance transactions for the purposes of VAT exemption even though they would not be seen as insurance for regulatory purposes. As a consequence, block policyholders act as principals when effecting insurance transactions rather than as intermediaries arranging supplies of insurance.

For these purposes, a block policy has the following characteristics:

- there is a contract between the block policyholder and the insurer which allows the block policyholder to effect insurance cover subject to certain conditions;
- the block policyholder, acting in their own name, procures insurance cover for third parties from the insurer;
- there is a contractual relationship between the block policyholder and third parties under which the insurance is procured; and
- the block policyholder stands in place of the insurer in effecting the supplies of insurance to the third parties.

Examples of block policies may include:

- A removal company taking out a block policy to provide insurance to its customers against the risk of damage to their belongings during a house move; or
- a pony club arranging insurance under a block policy to provide cover to their members against the risk of injury or third-party liabilities whilst taking part in equestrian events.

Block policies may also cover the risks of the block policyholder as well as those of their customers (e.g. the removal company's policy may also cover its own risk of damaging customer's property).

As a block policyholder act as a principal in the supply of an exempt insurance transaction, the whole consideration received by the block policyholder is treated as the income of the business rather than just the amount of any commission or fee. This may have implications for the calculation of recoverable input tax under the partial exemption method. It may also have implications for the VAT treatment of supplies made which consist of insurance transactions with other goods or services (see **3.9.4**).

See also the First Tier Tribunal case, *Wheels Private Hire Ltd [2015] UKFTT 363 (TC)* where a taxi firm arranged cover for its drivers.

VAT Notice 701/36/para 2.5

3.3. Life assurance

Life assurance is used to describe insurance contracts which fall within the *Financial Services and Markets Act 2000 (Regulated Activities) Order 2001, Schedule 1, Part II*. (See **Appendix A** for details).

Life assurance contracts fall into three main categories:

1. protection policies, designed to provide a benefit in the event of death before an agreed date or loss of income due to long-term illness, injury or disability, either by way of a lump sum payment or monthly income;
2. investment policies, where the main objective is to facilitate the growth of capital by regular or single premiums. The premium is invested in a collective investment product or fund. Consequently, as well as a payout in the event of death, the policyholder receives an investment return based on the performance of the product or fund; and
3. pensions products, where pensions administration services are provided both to individuals and to commercial institutions for the benefit of its employees.

For VAT purposes, life assurance is treated in the same way as general insurance. Therefore, the VAT liability is based on the location of the insured party.

When it comes to the recovery of input tax, using the location of the insured as a basis to determine recovery often leads to an unfair result. A life insurance policy will often last for a number of years (25 years or more is not uncommon). As the policy is only sold once, the costs incurred (a) in selling the initial insurance product, and (b) in periodical collection of premiums are relatively small. As the intention of the policy is to provide some long-term financial benefit to the policyholder (and this will be the case with both protection and investment policies) much of the life assurer's time and resource is spent in managing premiums received to maximise benefit to both the policyholder and the business itself. Therefore, having a partial exemption method which determines recovery purely on the basis of the location of the policyholder at the time of the initial sale of the policy does not properly reflect the 'use' of those costs.

As a consequence, many life assurers will want to ensure that the partial exemption methods they use accurately reflects the 'use' of the input tax they incur. Further details on partial exemption can be found in **Chapter 5**.

3.3.1. Sale of part-paid endowment policies

The sale of part-paid endowment policies is not exempt under the insurance exemption because the risk covered by the underlying insurance remains that of the original policyholder. However, there is a financial transaction taking place and the consideration received is exempt as a financial supply.

VAT Notice 701/36/, para 3.9

3.3.2. Broker managed funds offered by life assurance companies

Life assurance backed broker managed funds are provided under a contract between the life company that operates the fund, the policyholder and the broker who arranges the policy. In addition to arranging the policy, the brokers (usually referred to as Broker Fund Advisers) with authorisation from the policyholder, provide investment advice to the life assurance company, recommending the switching of monies invested by the policyholders between the various funds operated by the life assurer or, if permitted, directly into other forms of investment such as shares or gilts.

In addition to any commissions from the insurance company for arranging the policy, the broker fund adviser will receive fees for providing investment advisory services. They may also be entitled to a performance fee based on any increase in the value of the investment.

Any commissions received for arranging the policy will be exempt from VAT. However, fees for investment advice are likely to be taxable.

VAT Notice 701/36/, para 10.7

3.4. Friendly Societies

Friendly Societies are mutual organisations, accountable to their members and registered under the FSMA. Their primary purpose is the provision of insurance against distress in the event of accident, sickness, old age and widowhood. Insurance capital is provided by members' subscriptions.

Friendly Societies vary by size and range of activity. Some societies will have a single product; others offer a range of savings, insurance and banking services. Some will provide services via subsidiaries. Friendly Societies focus on the retail market (i.e. individuals and families) rather than the commercial market.

Where members' subscriptions relate solely to the provision of insurance, they are exempt from VAT. However, if the subscription covers other goods and services, that part of the subscription relating to those other supplies will not be exempt as an insurance transaction. However, other VAT reliefs may be available elsewhere (e.g. under the exemption covering supplies relating to health and welfare).

VAT Notice 701/36/, paragraph 3.2

3.4.1. Medical and welfare funds

Subscriptions to a medical or welfare fund which is not a Friendly Society but provides specified non-discretionary benefits in the event of, for example, illness or accident, are exempt as a supply of insurance.

Where benefits are not specified and the amounts paid out are at the discretion of the persons controlling the fund, then this is not a supply of insurance. However, the subscriptions may qualify as donations and fall outside the scope of VAT.

VAT notice 701/36/, paragraph 3.3

3.5. Insurance intermediary services

An insurance intermediary describes someone who acts between a person seeking insurance and the person providing insurance. It is important to note that VAT exemption is not restricted to traditional insurance brokers or agents; it will apply to any business that provides an insurance-related service as described in **3.5.2** below. For the purposes of VAT, it is what a business does that is key, not the category of business or profession. So, for example, a retailer, solicitor or accountant could be providing an insurance-related service if it is involved in the sale of an insurance product to its customer or client.

It is also quite common for there to be more than one intermediary involved in arranging an insurance transaction. Providing that what each intermediary does meets the criteria outlined in **3.5.2** below, then each intermediary supply will be VAT exempt.

An interesting tribunal case was heard in December 2016 which considered whether an intermediary supplied their services to the insurer or the insured (or the person seeking insurance). In the case of *Unicom Insurance services Ltd [2016] UKFTT 782* (a case which involved insurance provided to UK motor dealers by a Gibraltar insurer, the first tier tribunal ruled that Unicom supplied their services to the insurer, even though they negotiated and arranged insurance on behalf of the motor dealers. The decision was based on the facts and circumstances of this case but it would serve as a good starting point should this question or issue arise. Similar issues arose in the case of *Safestore Ltd [2020] UKUT 0322* where the question was whether or not the appellant was providing insurance as principal to its UK customers (exempt so no input tax recovery) or providing insurance intermediary services to an associated Guernsey based insurer (outside the scope but with recovery. The Upper Tribunal ruled against the appellant (supporting the initial decision of the FTT which found on the facts of the case that the appellant was acting as principal). What these cases show is that this area is complex. There are potentially multiple parties involved and establishing whether a person is acting as agent or principal is not always clear.

In recent years, in addition to the traditional high street broker or insurance agent, it has become common for insurance to be sold online, either on websites run directly by insurers or brokers themselves, or on third-party comparator sites. Consequently, much of the intermediary process has been automated but again, provided it fulfils the criteria in **3.5.2** below, this service should also qualify for exemption (see also **3.5.6**).

The VAT status of insurance intermediary services has also become a key issue with an apparent conflict between the VAT treatment in the UK and the treatment elsewhere in the EU. The way the insurance market operates in the UK is often significantly different from how insurance markets operate elsewhere in Europe. This has become particularly apparent with cases such as that of *Staatssecretaris van Financiën v Arthur Andersen & Co Accountants cs (ECJ Case C-472/03) [2005] STC 508*. See **3.5.4** and **4.10** for more details of the case.

In general terms, the UK (in the Tribunal and the Courts) has probably been more liberal in its acceptance of VAT exemption for intermediary services than the tax authorities and Courts elsewhere in the EU. At the time of writing, an EU review of VAT on insurance and financial services is still ongoing. With the UK's departure from the EU, the outcome of the review may not have any specific bearing on the position within the UK but it could potentially influence future decisions of the UK court when it comes to looking at the scope of VAT exemption for insurance related services.

3.5.1. Legislation

The VAT exemption for insurance-related services is derived from article 135(1)(a) of *Council Directive 2006/112/EC*. It is located in UK legislation in *VATA 94, Sch 9, Group 2, Item 4*. (See **3.1.2** above).

3.5.2. Scope of services

Subject to the uncertainties of the Arthur Andersen case (see **4.10** and also summarised below) the provision by an insurance broker or insurance agent of any of the services of an insurance intermediary are exempt from VAT where those services are:

- related to an insurance transaction or a reinsurance transaction; and
- provided by the broker or agent in the course of acting in an intermediary capacity.

'Acting in an intermediary capacity' means acting as an intermediary or one of the intermediaries between (a) a person providing insurance or reinsurance and (b) a person seeking insurance or reinsurance or an insured person.

'Services of an insurance intermediary' include any of the following:

(a) bringing together, with a view to an insurance transaction, persons seeking and persons providing insurance and/or reinsurance;
(b) carrying out work preparatory to the conclusion of the contract of insurance or reinsurance;
(c) assistance in the administration and performance of insurance contracts, including claims handling; or
(d) the collection of premiums.

With regard to (c) HMRC view 'assistance in the administration and performance of contracts' as covering services intermediaries perform in connection with the day-to-day administration of policies (e.g. maintaining up-to-date details of policyholders and dealing with requests from policyholders for changes to insurance cover).

However, the UK courts have found that the definition of 'assistance in the administration' goes wider than the examples given by HMRC.

In the case of *Century Life plc v C & E Commrs, (CA) [2001] STC 38*, pension review services carried out as a result of an FSA-inspired review of potential pension mis-selling were found to fall within this definition. Similarly in *Winterthur Life UK Ltd (No 3) (2002) (VTD 17572) (TVC 38.13)* services of management of a Self-Administered Personal Pension Scheme were also found to fall within the definition.

However, in the case of *Claims Advisory Group Ltd [2021] UKUT 0199*, services relating to the misselling of payment protection insurance (PPI) were ruled not to be VAT exempt. In this case, the appellant was deemed not to be an insurance agent – it had no relationship with either insurers or persons seeking insurance – nor did it undertake the activity of an insurance agent. Furthermore, the compensation claim was not related to the original supply of insurance.

Telephone helpline services that provide assistance to insured parties in matters such as variations of contracts and in making claims were also found to be VAT exempt (*C & V (Advice Line) Services Ltd (2001) (VTD 17310) (TVC 38.17)*) (see **4.9**).

However, following enquiries from the European Commission, HMRC announced a change to the treatment of both telephone helpline services and pension review services. Consequently, with effect from 1 April 2013, these services were no longer exempt.

Claims handling is a term used to describe a number of services that may be provided by an intermediary following the making of the claim. These may include:

- checking that the documents are correctly completed;
- ensuring that the claim falls within the terms of the policy;
- processing the claim;
- liaising with the insurer regarding their exposure;
- verifying the validity of the claim;
- agreeing the quantum of the claim; and
- arranging settlement of the claim.

VAT Notice 701/36/, para 8.5

3.5.3. Services not regarded as those of an insurance intermediary

UK legislation specifically excludes certain services from the scope of the insurance intermediary exemption. These include:

- market research, product design, advertising, promotion or similar services (or the collection, collation and provision of information used in connection with such activities);
- valuation or inspection services;
- services supplied by loss adjusters, average adjusters, motor assessors, surveyors or other experts unless the services consist of claims handling and the person handling the claim is authorised to act on behalf of the insurer and has written authority to accept or reject the claim and to arrange settlement of any amount agreed to be paid; and
- services supplied under the contract of insurance or instead of financial indemnity.

VATA 94, Sch 9, Group 2, Notes 7 to 10

3.5.3.1 Services of loss adjusters etc

Services provided by loss adjusters, average adjusters, motor assessors, surveyors or other experts (e.g. valuation services provided by jewellers or damage assessments by antique dealers), will normally be standard rated.

However, if they provide insurance claims handling services, those services will be exempt when acting as the agent of the insurer when supplying those services. For the services to qualify for exemption, all of the following conditions must be met:

- they must be providing an insurance claims handling service (see **3.5.2** above);
- they must be authorised when doing so to act on behalf of the insurer or reinsurer;

- they must hold the insurer's written authority to determine whether to accept or reject a claim; and
- where the claim is accepted in whole or in part, they have the insurer's written authority to settle the amount to be paid on the claim.

The written authority should allow claims to be investigated, all services necessary for the claim to be settled to be performed and the power to agree the amount of a claim or cost of repairs or replacement without reference to the insurer. The authority may also include avoiding or repudiating claims. In all circumstances it must bind the insurance company to pay the amount of a claim or meet the cost of repair or replacement as determined by the adjuster or expert.

In many cases delegated authority will be given up to a certain monetary limit or only in respect of specific types of claim. Where full written authority is not held, or the monetary limit for which the adjuster or expert is authorised is exceeded, the service is standard rated.

VAT Notice 701/36 para 9.3

3.5.3.2 *Riskstop Consulting [2015] UKFTT 0469*

Riskstop are a company that provide risk management services to insurers. The insurers then use this information as part of their acceptance procedures. The First Tier Tribunal ruled that Riskstop were not acting as an 'insurance agent' as they played no part in bringing together the person seeking insurance and the insurer providing insurance and consequently these supplies were liable to VAT. It is worth noting that HMRC had previously accepted that these supplies qualified for exemption.

3.5.4. *Staatssecretaris van Financiën v Arthur Andersen & Co Accountants cs (ECJ Case C-472/03) [2005] STC 508* (see also 2.10)

Andersen Consulting Management Consultants (ACMC) provided certain 'back-office' activities in the Netherlands to a Dutch insurer. These activities included the issuing, management and cancellation of policies, the management of claims and, in most cases, taking decisions binding the insurer to enter into insurance contracts.

In this case the ECJ was asked whether these services qualified for exemption under Article 13B(a) (now *Article 135(1)(a) of Directive 2006/112/EC*), as 'related services performed by insurance brokers and insurance agents'. To fall within the exemption Andersen had to qualify as either a broker or an agent.

The ECJ held that the essential characteristic of insurance brokers was that they had complete freedom of choice of insurer for their client. Andersen did not work on behalf of an insured party, but rather for a single insurance company, therefore it could not qualify as a broker.

The Court further held that an insurance agent, while usually tied to a particular insurer, must be instrumental in bringing together the two parties to the insurance contract by finding prospective clients and introducing them to the insurer. Andersen did not perform any type of introductory service and therefore could not qualify as an agent. The fact that they were able to bind the insurer was not a determining factor.

The ECJ judgment was binding on the UK up to the point the UK left the EU and HMRC did state that the UK VAT exemption for insurance-related services is too wide and would require amendment. However, in the light of an EU review of the VAT treatment of financial services and insurance, the UK decided to delay any implementation of this decision. Businesses that are affected should still be entitled to apply the revised VAT liability from current date or make an adjustment retrospectively, should they wish to do so.

Further details can be found in *Business Briefs 11/05* and *23/05*.

3.5.5. Broker networks

The case of *Westinsure Group Limited [2014] UKUT 452* looked at the treatment of supplies made by a broker network to its insurance broker and agent members.

Westinsure provided services to a network of small insurance brokers and agents. It charged a fee to its members based on gross income. It also recruited various partner insurers who would offer favourable terms to its member brokers. Westinsure promoted its partner insurers to its network members. In addition to the introduction services, Westinsure also provided some advice and consultancy services to the network members as well as arranging trade fairs. Westinsure never involved itself in negotiating or arranging specific contracts of insurance, neither did it communicate with individual policyholders. HMRC took the view that these services were taxable and therefore that Westinsure were obliged to register for VAT.

Westinsure argued that fees charged related to an insurance transaction undertaken in their capacity as a broker and therefore should qualify for exemption. The FTT rejected this argument so Westinsure appealed to the Upper Tax Tribunal.

The Upper Tax Tribunal upheld the decision of the FTT ruling that Westinsure was not providing the services of an insurance broker. Specifically, it did not act for clients seeking insurance, negotiate the terms of any particular transaction, assess the needs of clients or find insurance suitable to their needs. As nothing Westinsure did related directly to any insurance transaction, its services were therefore not insurance-related.

Westinsure were granted leave to appeal and a hearing was expected in March 2016. However, the case subsequently disappeared from the listings, suggesting that the appeal had been withdrawn. It is rumoured that Westinsure have amended their arrangements to fall within the exemption.

3.5.6. Web-based intermediaries

In general terms, whether an intermediary provides services electronically or more traditionally by face-to-face meeting or telephone, makes no difference to the VAT treatment. However, where insurance is sold via the web (e.g. via comparative sites) it can be more difficult to distinguish between exempt insurance intermediary services and taxable advertising services.

The case of *InsuranceWide.com Services Ltd v Revenue and Customs Commissioners; Revenue and Customs Commissioners v Trader Media Group Ltd [2010] EWCA Civ 422 STC 1572* considered the VAT treatment of commissions paid by insurers to web-based intermediaries. The two cases were heard together as the facts were very similar, although the original Tribunals came to opposite decisions.

In brief, InsuranceWide operates a price comparison website. Customers who are seeking insurance are offered a choice of insurance contracts, selected via a computer program, which will be suitable for them. InsuranceWide are paid a commission each time a policy is taken up. At the original Tribunal, HMRC were successful in arguing that the commissions were not VAT exempt.

Trader Media is a publishing company which publishes motor vehicle magazines, including Auto Trader. Trader Media operate a website providing access to an 'insurance centre'. Via the insurance centre, users could complete a series of questions which led to the generation of an insurance quotation. The insurance centre was operated by third party, which in turn contracted with motor insurers. Similar to the InsuranceWide Tribunal, HMRC challenged the exempt status of commissions received by Trader Media. However, in this case HMRC were unsuccessful and the Tribunal found in Trader Media's favour.

The question in the High Court boiled down to whether the act of introduction was itself sufficient to qualify the transactions for exemption in accordance with *VATA 94, Sch 9, Group 2, Item 4 and Note 1*. The High Court held that it was.

The decision also made the following points, of relevance to the specific case but also to insurance intermediary services generally:

- It was an essential characteristic of an insurance broker or an insurance agent, that they were engaged in the business of putting insurance companies in touch with potential clients or, more generally, acting as intermediaries between insurance companies and clients or potential clients.
- For VAT exemption to apply, it was not necessary for a person to be carrying out all the functions of an insurance agent or broker.
- An agent or broker can be one of a chain of persons bringing together an insurance company and a potential insured provided that the services that person renders were in themselves characteristic of the services of an insurance agent or broker.
- Whilst there was a need to exercise the characteristic functions of an agent or broker, a direct legal relationship with both or either of the ultimate parties was not required.
- It was immaterial that neither InsuranceWide nor Trader Media had anything to do with the negotiation of the terms of the insurance contract or its preparation or the collection of premiums or the handling of claims.

See also the first tier tribunal decision in *Dollar Financial UK Ltd [2016] UKFTT 0598* which took a similar approach in relation to personal loans.

3.6. Lloyd's

The same VAT rules apply to Lloyd's as apply to insurance and reinsurance companies. However, because of the way Lloyd's operates, special VAT arrangements have been agreed between the Lloyd's market and HMRC.

Lloyd's is not an insurance company but a society of members (corporate and individual names). Policyholders are insured 'at Lloyd's' by a member of Lloyd's rather than by Lloyd's itself. In general, underwriting is done by members (individual names or corporate) trading on their own account.

Members operate through syndicates (generally known by their numbers) which are not partnerships but looser associations which effectively exist for a Lloyd's accounting year (the accounting year runs from 1 January to

31 December) which then 'reinsure to close' (normally into the following year of account of the same syndicate).

Each syndicate has a Managing Agent appointed to manage its affairs. Employees of the Managing Agent carry out the underwriting and insurance functions. Managing Agents are not themselves insurers but the supplies they make are those of an insurance intermediary. Therefore the VAT treatment of their supply follows that of the insurance underwritten by the syndicate or syndicates that they manage.

Names and the majority of smaller corporate members (including Scottish Limited Partnerships) are required to appoint a Members' Agent. Members' Agents ensure that their members meet the Lloyd's entrance criteria and requirements, introduce them to syndicates and provide information on the performance of the syndicates on which they participate.

It was recognised that having individual names registered for VAT would be very difficult practically, particularly where names were members of more than one syndicate. Therefore, up to the end of 1999 the Lloyd's Special Arrangements dealt with VAT accounting through registration of Managing Agents (neither the names nor syndicates to which they belonged were registered for VAT).

However, the arrangements changed from 1 January 2000 with the introduction of the new special arrangements. Whilst individual names will generally not be VAT registered, the position has changed for syndicates. Even though they are not, in law, partnerships they are now treated as the main registrable entity.

A copy of the Lloyd's Special Arrangements can be found at **Appendix B**.

3.6.1. Syndicates

Syndicates will generally have two main activities: underwriting and the generation of investment income. When it comes to partial exemption and VAT recovery, the rules are similar to other insurance entities. Direct attribution is required where possible and appropriate. For the recovery of residual input tax, the underwriting and investment activities are seen as separate business areas or sectors, each with their own recovery calculations.

The calculation in the underwriting sector is based on the value of premiums processed through Xchanging (previously the Lloyd's Policy Signing Office (LPSO)) and elsewhere. At the beginning of the month following the quarter end, Xchanging provide Managing Agents with a premium VAT report detailing the value of EU and non-EU supplies made by the syndicates in that period. These values are then used to calculate the syndicate's VAT recovery rate.

Premiums are coded as:

X = exempt
Z = outside the scope credit
M = mixed (split 50/50 to X and Z).

VAT recovery is then calculated as the percentage of outside the scope with credit premiums (i.e. non-EU premiums) to total premiums. The recoverable percentage is calculated to two decimal points.

The calculation in the investment sector is also dealt with in much the same way as with other insurance companies. Recoverable input tax is calculated as the percentage of outside the scope with credit investments (i.e. non-EU investments) to total investments (although this could be based on either the value or number of transactions). Again the recoverable percentage is calculated to two decimal points.

A syndicate that is wholly owned by a corporate member or Scottish limited partnership is not allowed to register. In these cases, VAT should be accounted for via the VAT registration of the relevant corporate member or Scottish limited partnership.

3.6.2. Managing agents

HMRC accept that fees and or profit commission charged to members are exempt as insurance intermediary services. The outputs of Managing Agents are these fees plus any other supplies. The Managing Agent's partial exemption calculation is effectively made in the same way as for syndicates and in practice will mirror the VAT recovery position of the syndicates managed.

3.6.3. Members' agents and Lloyd's advisers

HMRC's initial view was that services supplied by Members' Agents and Lloyd's advisers were taxable. This was tested in the case of *SOC Private Capital Ltd (2002) (VTD 17747) (TVC 38.15)* where the Tribunal ruled that the supplies of insurance were made by the members rather than the syndicates and therefore a Members' Agent was an insurance agent within *VATA 94, Sch 9, Group 2, Item 4* meaning that its supplies were exempt.

Members' Agents recover VAT on their costs using a Members' Agent rate issued annually by Lloyd's.

3.6.4. Corporate members and Scottish limited partnerships

Unless the corporate member or Scottish limited partnership has 100% of the capacity in a syndicate, then they do not account for any outputs related to underwriting activities in the Lloyd's market.

Corporate members and Scottish limited partnerships may be able to register in their own right to recover VAT on non-insurance activities and recover VAT on insurance related costs that they incur directly (rather than at syndicate level).

Recovery of input tax on insurance-related costs will use a formula based on the premium or investment calculation of the syndicates to which they belong. This can create problems where corporate members or Scottish limited partnerships participate in a number of syndicates. In these cases, subject to the agreement of HMRC, the global market rate can be used.

3.6.5. Lloyd's entrance fees or subscriptions

Lloyd's subscription fees are exempt from VAT. Entrance fees are liable to VAT at the standard rate.

3.6.6. Imported services

A number of fees from overseas suppliers are paid centrally by Lloyd's and then recharged to the syndicates.

Fees charged by LeBoeuf Lamb Green & Macrae are subject to reverse charge with the reverse charge VAT being deemed as residual.

As a result of the *Deutsche Ruck* case, HMRC initially accepted that US legal fees recharged to Lloyd's could be regarded as being directly related to US insurance policies (and therefore the reverse charge VAT would be fully recoverable). However, this view has now changed and they tend to view these services as being more general in nature, and therefore any reverse charge VAT is likely to be residual.

Xchanging provide claims expense data to Managing Agents detailing the value of claims expense that is subject to the reverse charge. They supply a percentage (at the time of writing 0.04%) which should be applied to gross claims expenses which reflects the overseas element of claims costs. The reverse charge is then applied to this element.

3.7. Insurance claims

The payment of an insurance claim by an insurer is not a supply for VAT. The payment is compensation made under an indemnity contract and is therefore not consideration for any supply. What this means in effect is that any VAT on costs incurred in respect of the claim is not input tax for the insurer; any input tax 'belongs' to insured party. As a consequence, if the insured party is VAT registered, they should be entitled to make a claim from HMRC and the insurer should pay the claim on a net of VAT basis.

The case of *WHA Ltd and another v C & E Comrs [2004] EWCA Civ 559 [2004] STC 1081* which involved a complex offshore reinsurance structure introduced primarily to enable VAT on vehicle repair costs to be recovered by an agent of the insurer. In summary, NIG, a UK company, issued motor breakdown insurance (MBI) policies to car buyers. All of NIG's risk under the policies was reinsured with a Gibraltar-based company, Crystal, which in turn retroceded 85% of the risk to another Gibraltar-based company, Viscount. The task of claims handling passed with each of these arrangements with the result that Viscount had responsibility for its own risk and for the risk which rested with Crystal. Viscount contracted with WHA, a UK company, to instruct garages to carry out any works to motor vehicles under policies and to pay for those works. Crystal, Viscount and WHA were part of the same group of companies. On each occasion that such work was carried out by a garage on WHA's instructions, the garage rendered VAT invoice to WHA. The VAT Tribunal ruled that the supply of garage services was made to the insured party rather than the insurer or WHA. However, the Court of Appeal ruled that a garage carrying out works to a motor vehicle under a policy on WHA's instructions made a taxable supply of services to WHA, and that WHA was, in principle, entitled to claim input tax in respect of the VAT payable by it. However, in a second part of the appeal, *WHA Ltd and another v C & E Comrs [2007] EWCA Civ 728 [2007] STC 1695*, the scheme was found to be abusive applying the criteria outlined in *Halifax plc v Customs and Excise Commrs (ECJ Case C-255/02) [2006] STC 919*. WHA subsequently appealed. Finally, after 13 years of litigation, the Supreme Court issued its judgment in early 2013 (*WHA Ltd and another v C & E Comrs [2013] UKSC 24*). They ruled that there was no supply of repair services from the garage to WHA; the consumer of those services was the insured. Hence, there was no need to consider anything further.

A similar decision was reached in the case of *U-Drive v HMRC [2017] UKUT 0112* which involved a self-drive hire company which set up a captive insurance company to provide fleet insurance. To minimise claims, U- Drive sometimes paid for repairs to third party vehicles directly. Consequently, they argued that they should be entitled to recover input tax on the repairs. This argument was rejected by HMRC and after appeal by both the First Tier and Upper Tier Tribunals. The UTT ruled that the fact that U-Drive paid the repairers did not mean that they were the recipient of the supply in these circumstances.

Where there are certain claims-related goods and services that are supplied to the insurer the amount of VAT recoverable is likely to depend on the partial exemption method and or the application of the Deutsche Ruck principles noted in **3.7.2** below.

It is also common for insurers to take title to goods as a result of an insurance claim (and then dispose of those goods) or provide replacement goods as an alternative to financial indemnification.

3.7.1. Legal costs

Where an insurer obtains legal advice in connection with a dispute with the policyholder or for advice on general policy interpretation, the supply of services is made to the insurer.

However, in the case of subrogated claims, where an insurer exercises its right to pursue or defend the claim against a third party on behalf of, or in the name of, the insured party, the supplies of legal services are seen as being made to the insured party rather than the insurer.

3.7.2. Costs on individual claims

Where an insurer incurs costs in respect of an individual claim (for example, legal costs where the insurer is in dispute with the policyholder) VAT on those costs is directly attributable to the underlying of insurance. As a result, the recoverability of any VAT charged will depend on the VAT status of the underlying insurance. This treatment was confirmed in the case of *C&E Commrs v Deutsche Ruck Reinsurance Co Ltd, QB [1995] STC 495*. Therefore, where the claim arises in respect of a policy where the insured belongs outside the EU, the VAT on the cost will be recoverable in full. In all other cases, the VAT is wholly irrecoverable.

3.7.3. Loss adjusters and loss assessors

Loss adjusters act on behalf of the insurer and the supply of their services is made to the insurer. Where the cost can be attributed to an individual claim, then any VAT charged can be recovered as outlined in **3.7.2** above.

Loss assessors are normally appointed by, and act in the interest of, the insured party and therefore supply their services to the insured party rather than the insurer.

For information of claims handling services provided by loss adjusters, loss assessors and other experts, see **3.5.3.1**.

3.7.4. Supply of surrendered goods following an insurance claim

The disposal of:

- works of art, antiques and collectors' items, and
- second-hand goods

by an insurer who has taken possession of them in settlement of a claim under an insurance policy is outside the scope of VAT, subject to certain conditions.

These conditions are:

- That the goods are in the same condition at the time disposal as they were when taken into the insurer's possession. The condition of the goods is deemed to have been changed if any repairs, improvements, replacement parts or general making good of the damage are carried out. The cleaning of goods generally does not affect condition nor does the inclusion of any missing instruction manuals.
- For goods other than motor cars
  - (a) that if the goods had been supplied in the UK by the policyholder, that supply would not have been chargeable with VAT or would been chargeable on less than full value;
  - (b) that if the goods had been imported into the UK, they must have borne VAT that has been neither reclaimed nor refunded; and
  - (c) that the goods must not have been reimported having previously been exported as a zero rated supply.
- In the case of motor cars, the VAT on any previous supply, acquisition or importation must have been wholly excluded from credit.

Cars which have been written off and received by the insurer as scrap metal should be treated the same as any other goods and VAT should be accounted for on the scrap value if the insured party would have been required to account for VAT. This applies whatever salvage category the vehicle falls into.

[SI 1992/3122, Arts 2, 4; SI 1995/1268, Arts 2, 4; SI 1995/1269; SI 1995/1385; SI 1995/1667; SI 1999/3118; SI 1999/3120; SI 2001/3649, Art 432; SI 2004/3084; SI 2004/3085].

VAT Notice 701/36/ para 5.6

Where the above conditions are not met, VAT is chargeable on the full selling price of the item.

The insurer, therefore, needs to be aware of the VAT status of the policyholder and have access to the VAT history of the asset in order that they can establish the correct VAT treatment of the disposal.

3.7.5. Replacement goods and services

Where insurance claims are settled by way of replacement goods or services, the supply position will depend on the terms of the contractual arrangements. Normally, the supply of replacement goods and services by third-party supplier is made to the insured party. However, in some circumstances, subject to the terms of the contract, the supply may be made to the insurer.

Sometimes goods are supplied to an insurer for transfer to the insured party in settlement of a claim. In these circumstances the insurer may choose to recover the VAT charged on the goods as input tax and account for output tax on the cost price when the goods are handed over. Alternatively, the insurer may refrain from claiming the VAT charged and, therefore, not be liable to account for output tax when the goods are transferred to the insured party.

VAT Notice 701/36/ paras 5.1 and 5.4

3.8. Insurers in 'run off'

Insurers in 'run off' are insurers who have ceased accepting new business. However, a liability to deal with claims under contracts already written remains.

The insurer will have to deal with additional premiums (APs) and return premiums (RPs) in respect of these existing contracts, for example where the insurance relates to long term risks or there are changes to the cover required. APs and RPs can cause problems, particularly regarding partial exemption.

It is also common for insurers to appoint third party agents (or TPAs) to

3.8.1. Partial exemption for insurers in run off

If an insurer uses a values-based partial exemption method, the impact of APs and RPs in the calculations can be problematic (if not occasionally perverse as it can result in recovery percentages of more than 100% if significant levels of RP on EU business are processed). As a result, RPs should be excluded from the calculation.

Alternatively, to avoid potentially complex calculations, most insurers in run off will calculate a fixed recovery percentage, based on actual business written in the three years up to the point that the business ceased writing new business. Whilst this is the common methodology used, it is not obligatory.

3.8.2. Administration of run off

Insurers will often appoint third party specialists to administer the run off of insurance business. Where the third party takes on responsibility for the run off business (including administration of premium adjustments and handling and settling of claims) this is not deemed to be exempt as an insurance transaction, because the third party does not have a contractual relationship with the insured. However, the service should qualify for exemption as an insurance-related service provided the services meet the tests outlined in 3.5 above.

Separate supplies of administration services (e.g. accounting, supplies of staff or investment management) will attract VAT at the standard rate.

VAT Notice 701/36/ paras 3.8, 7.6 and 10.6

3.9. Other types of insurance

3.9.1. Guarantees and Warranties

It is quite common for retailers to sell guarantees and warranties alongside goods such as domestic white goods, furniture and motor cars. In addition to standard guarantees and warranties (i.e. where the purchase price includes an amount in consideration of which the manufacturer or retailer agrees to replace or repair defective goods within a specified period) retailers may also sell extended warranty agreements. Under an extended warranty, the provider enters into a distinct contract under which they undertake for a specific consideration to be subject to the same (and possibly some additional) obligations as are covered in the original warranty.

Where a guarantee or warranty is written under a contract of insurance, it will, in principle, fall within the VAT exemption for insurance (but see **3.9.4** below regarding insurance supplied with other goods and services).

In the case of *Mapfre Warranty SpA (Case C-584/13)* the ECJ ruled that insurance-backed vehicle breakdown warranties which have the characteristics of an insurance contract, should be exempt from VAT (and this is regardless of where or how the benefits are provided to the owner or how premiums are calculated). Furthermore, in this case the ECJ considered that the supply of the vehicle and the supply of the warranty were separate supplies.

However, guarantees and warranties provided by the manufacturer or retailer are unlikely to be seen as insurance by the FSA because:

- when provided by the retailer, the guarantee or warranty is seen as an automatic and often statutory consequence of the contract of sale under which the substance of the retailer's obligation is the transfer of risk and property in the goods, not provision of insurance cover; and

- when provided by the manufacturer, the risk of product failure lies within the control of the manufacturer. (Contracts under which the occurrence of an uncertain event lies within the control of either the provider or the recipient are unlikely to be regarded as insurance).

Some extended warranties are unlikely to be seen as contracts and insurance regardless of who provides them. This may be because the provider undertakes to maintain or repair goods at the customer's expense (sometimes at a discounted rate). Alternatively, in some contracts there will be both insurance and non-insurance elements (e.g. such as the provision of regular servicing of equipment) where on balance the provider's obligation is not seen as being one to insure.

The supply of any non-insurance warranty will be liable to VAT at standard rate.

VAT Notice 701/36/ para 3.7

3.9.2. Vehicle breakdown

Subscriptions to motoring organisations will normally include an element of assistance in the event of breakdown which is provided under a contract of insurance. Under these types of insurance contract, the benefits to the policyholder (or the member) are given in kind rather than in the monetary form (i.e. by way of roadside repairs and recovery).

Where vehicle breakdown insurance is provided as an independent supply, that part of the subscription that is attributable to the breakdown cover will be exempt from VAT. Where this is supplied with other services, the normal rules on single or multiple supplies will apply (see **7.4** below and **3.9.4** below).

VAT Notice 701/36/ para 3.6

3.9.3. Funeral plans

Certain funeral plans are written under contracts of insurance so that on death the policy pays out the cost of the funeral. These contracts will be treated as VAT exempt supplies of insurance, even though the contracts themselves are not regulated in the same way as other insurance policies.

Some funeral plans represent prepayments for a funeral and as a consequence do not qualify for exemption as supplies of insurance. However, they may well qualify for exemption under the provisions of *VATA 94, Sch 9, Group 8.*

Management charges in respect of non-insurance or non-prepayment funeral plans (e.g. where the client's money is placed in a trust to be spent on a funeral at his or her death) will be liable to VAT at the standard rate.

VAT Notice 701/36/ paragraph 3.5

3.9.4. Insurance supplied with other goods or services

Where exempt insurance is provided with goods or services that are liable to VAT, the correct VAT treatment will depend on whether there are two or more distinct supplies, independent of each other, each with their own VAT treatment or a principal supply to which the other goods and services are ancillary, with the VAT treatment following the liability of the principal supply.

Tests to determine whether there are single or multiple supplies were laid down in the CPP case (*Card Protection Plan Limited v C&E Commrs, ECJ Case C -349/96, [1999] STC 270*). This is considered in more detail at **7.4.**

Each case will need to be examined and considered on its own merits and no single factor is necessarily determinative of either single or multiple supplies. However, there are some factors which HMRC state could be indicative of separate rather than composite supplies:

- optionality – i.e. whether customers can choose to have the goods or services without the insurance and, if appropriate, vice versa;
- pricing – i.e. if both insurance and the goods or services have their own price and this is reflected in the amount the customers pay should they choose to have one without the other (so that the overall amount a customer pays is reduced by the cost of insurance should they decide to buy the goods or services without insurance); and
- customer awareness – i.e. are customers fully aware that they are receiving more than one supply, as evidenced by the invoicing and contractual arrangements in place.

3.9.4.1 Add-on services

Add-on services are additional services supplied as part of a package with the main supply of insurance. An example would be telephone helplines. The services may be supplied under the contract of insurance itself or under a separate contract and may be provided by the main insurance company, other insurers or by non-insurance third parties.

The VAT treatment of such services will depend on the contractual arrangements in place between the parties and also the nature of the services being supplied.

Add-on services supplied by third parties to the insurer for onward supply to the policyholder under the contract for the main supply of insurance may have different VAT liabilities. Where the add-on service that is supplied by a third party to the insurer for incorporation into an insurance contract is itself insurance, then the premium received by the third party will be exempt from VAT. However, if the add-on service is not insurance (and does not qualify for VAT exemption or zero rating under other provisions) then VAT is chargeable on the supply by the third party to the insurer.

Where the add-on service is supplied directly to the policyholder, then if the add-on service is one of insurance, the whole supply will be exempt from VAT (both the main insurer and the add-on insurer are treated as making an exempt insurance supply, the value of each supply being that element of the premium they have underwritten).

If the add-on service is not one of insurance but supplied by the insurer under the same contract as the insurance, there may be a liability to VAT on the consideration received by the insurer in respect of the add-on service. This will depend on the VAT liability of the add-on service and whether or not it constitutes a single or multiple supply (see above).

Where the add-on service is not insurance and supplied under a contract separate from that of the insurance contract, there may be a liability to VAT dependent on the nature of the add-on service. In such cases, it is unlikely that the add-on service will be seen as ancillary to the main supply of insurance and therefore follow the VAT liability of the insurance but the tests should still be followed.

Where an insurer incurs VAT on an add-on service, it is unlikely that this VAT will be recoverable as it will be seen to directly relate to the exempt supply of insurance.

VAT Notice 701/36/ paras 4.1 – 4.3, 11.1 – 11.3

3.10. Insurance Premium Tax (IPT)

Although IPT is outside the scope of this publication, it is worth mentioning as it is administered by HMRC and it is not uncommon for visiting HMRC officers to deal with both the VAT and IPT together.

3.10.1. General

IPT is a tax on general insurance where the risk is located in the UK (in most cases this means where the insured person belongs in the UK but will also apply to insurance on UK properties, vehicles registered in the UK and short term travel policies taken out in UK).

3.10.2. Rates

The standard rate of IPT is rising from 10% to 12% on 1 June 2017 with a higher rate of 20% applying to certain insurances relating to motor cars (other than normal fully comprehensive, third party, fire and theft or third-party covers) domestic appliances and travel. A higher rate was introduced to prevent the VAT 'value shifting' on supplies of goods with insurance, where suppliers would increase the charge for the VAT exempt insurance element whilst making a corresponding reduction to the charge for the standard rated goods, thus reducing the amount of VAT payable to HMRC whilst charging the customer the same amount.

3.10.3. Exemptions

Reinsurance, life assurance, contracts relating to commercial ships, aircraft and international railway rolling stock, contracts relating to credit and exchange losses in the provision of financial facilities along with contracts relating to risks located outside the UK are exempt from IPT.

3.10.4. Liability to pay

In nearly all cases the insurance company is liable to account for IPT to HMRC.

IPT is calculated on the premium paid by the insured policyholder (which will include commissions administration costs etc., unless these services are provided under a separate contract, separately notifiable to the policyholder. However, note that these rules were tightened following the case of *Homeserve GB Ltd IPT00014* in respect of certain types of insurance cover).

Overseas insurers writing taxable insurance business in the UK are required to account for IPT in the UK. They can do this either by registering directly with HMRC or by appointing an agent. In the last resort, HMRC can recover any IPT due from the policyholder.

3.10.5. Overseas premium taxes

Most countries in the EU (and indeed in many countries around the world) have insurance premium taxes and/or stamp duties. Therefore, UK insurers writing business located overseas may have liabilities to account for tax to the relevant overseas authorities. It should be noted that under the terms of the Mutual Assistance in *Recovery Directive (MARD) (Council Directive 2010/24/EU)* an EU tax authority can request that HMRC recovers premium tax due in that EU country. Whilst this power has not been widely applied it is available and its use is increasing.

3.10.6. IPT and partial exemption

An insurance business can choose either to include or to exclude the value of IPT within the partial exemption calculation. If they choose to include UK IPT in their calculations they should also include any equivalent non-UK premium taxes or other duties chargeable on insurance premiums. If they choose to exclude UK IPT, then similarly they should exclude the value of any non-UK premium taxes or duties.

Further information on Insurance Premium Tax in the UK can be found in *HMRC Notice IPT 1.*

4. Outsourcing

4.1. Introduction

Over recent years, it has become increasingly common for financial institutions and insurance companies to outsource a variety of tasks that in the past would have been provided in-house. The providers of outsourced services may be located elsewhere in the UK or may be located outside the UK (and indeed outside the EU). Common locations for the 'offshoring' of services include India, Sri Lanka, Malaysia and South Africa. The types of services that are outsourced include data processing or data inputting, insurance claims-handling or administration, the provision of telephone help lines, direct sales or general administration.

Clearly, one of the main reasons for outsourcing is likely to be to reduce costs (e.g. in the case of offshoring this may be to benefit from lower labour costs; in the UK, it may be to benefit from economies of scale). Where services are provided in-house by employees VAT is not an issue (as there is no supply). What businesses often fail to recognise, however, is that outsourcing brings VAT into play and getting the VAT treatment wrong could result in adding up to 20% to the budgeted cost of an outsourcing transaction for a partially exempt business.

VAT is a particular issue for financial institutions and insurance companies which outsource processes as they will invariably be looking to achieve exemption or VAT-free treatment for those costs wherever possible. Exemption will be available where the provider is seen to be acting as an intermediary in the provision of financial or insurance transactions. Note that if the outsourced services relate to land or buildings situated overseas then the place of supply will be where the land/buildings are situated, with potential VAT costs there.

The changes to the place of supply of services rules introduced on 1 January 2010 have also had an impact on the treatment of outsourced or offshored services received from providers located outside the UK. Before 1 January 2010, a number of services (such as data inputting and general administration) would have been deemed to be supplied in the country where the supplier was established. Consequently, where a UK business received these services from a supplier established in a country which did not have a VAT system, or allowed a VAT relief for export services, there was no VAT due (either in the supplier's country or the UK). However, with the changes to the place of supply rules, UK finance and insurance businesses receiving such services from outside the UK are now liable to account for VAT under the reverse charge procedure (see **7.10**).

It is not uncommon for the range of services outsourced to an offshore provider to develop or extend over time; often, at the start of the contract a limited number of services are outsourced in order to 'test the water'. As a result, it may be that what were initially purely administrative services develop into something where the provider acts in intermediary capacity and therefore ends up providing a service which would qualify for VAT exemption in the UK.

There are a number of key VAT cases concerning outsourcing and the scope of exemption for intermediary services. These are summarised below.

4.2. *Sparekassernes Datacenter (SDC) v Skatteministeriet (Case C- 2/95) [1997] STC 932*

SDC is a key case and has often been cited in subsequent judgments.

SDC was an association registered for VAT in Denmark. The majority of its members were savings banks. SDC provided to its members, partly by electronic means, services relating to transfers of funds, advice on and trading in securities and the management of deposits, purchase contracts and loans. SDC also offered services relating to its members' administrative affairs.

A typical service consisted of a number of components which together made up the service which a bank or its customers wished to have performed. SDC performed services only at the request of the banks, their customers, and other authorised persons. It undertook no legal obligation in regard to those customers and received remuneration only from the banks. A new company, controlled by the members, later performed all the services, and that company invoiced SDC which in turn invoiced its members.

Initially, the Danish tax authorities took the view that the services provided by SDC were exempt. However, in February 1992, a Danish VAT Tribunal decided otherwise and after an appeal to a higher court in Denmark the following questions were referred to the ECJ for a preliminary ruling.

> (1) Should art 13B(d)(3), (4) and (5) of the Sixth VAT Directive be interpreted as meaning that VAT exemption should be granted for services of a type [SDC provided to its members]. In that connection, is the granting of exemption from VAT under art 13B(d)(3), (4) and (5) precluded where a

transaction within the meaning of that provision is performed, wholly or in part, electronically?

(2) The wording used in art 13B(d)(1) and (2) of the VAT Directive is "by the person granting [the credit]" (ved den person, som har ydet lånene) and "by the person who is granting the credit" (ved den person, de har ydet kreditten). That description is not employed by art 13B(d)(3), (4) and (5). Should any importance be attached to that difference in the interpretation of art 13B(d)(3), (4) and (5)?

(3) (a) Is it significant as far as the application of art 13B(d)(3), (4) and (5) is concerned whether transactions are performed by financial institutions or by others?

(b) Is it significant as far as the application of art 13B(d)(3), (4) and (5) is concerned whether the entire financial service is performed by a financial institution which has links with a customer?

(c) If it is unnecessary for the application of art 13B(d)(3), (4) and (5) that the financial institution itself should perform the entire service, can the financial institution buy in transactions wholly or in part from another person, with the effect that the services performed by that other person are covered by art 13B(d)(3), (4) and (5), or may particular requirements be made of that other person?

(4) How is the wording used in art 13B(d)(3), (4) and (5) "transactions ... concerning" to be interpreted? This question seeks to ascertain whether the words "transactions ... concerning" are to be understood as meaning that VAT exemption should also be granted in cases where a person either performs only a part of the service or performs only some of the transactions within the meaning of the directive which are necessary for supplying the complete financial service.

(5) In the interpretation of art 13B(d)(3), (4) and (5), should significance be attached to the fact that the taxable person who requests tax exemption for transactions within the meaning of the provision performs those transactions on behalf of the financial institution in whose name the service is performed?

(6) Following SDC's reorganisation, is it significant, as far as application of art 13B(d)(3), (4) and (5) is concerned, that the services in question are now provided by a company which supplies the services to the associated financial institutions? It will be noted that the said services are invoiced by the limited company to the plaintiff which in turn invoices its financial institution members.

In answer to these points, the judgment of the ECJ was as follows:

1. Paragraphs (3) and (5) of art 13B(d) of the Sixth Directive were to be interpreted as meaning that the exemption is not subject to the condition that the transactions be effected by a certain type of institution, by a certain type of legal person or wholly or partly by certain electronic means or manually. It was the nature of the services that mattered, not who supplied them.

2. The exemption provided for by paragraphs (3) and (5) of art 13B(d) was not subject to the condition that the service be provided by an institution which has a legal relationship with the end customer. The fact that a transaction covered by those provisions is effected by a third party but appears to the end customer to be a service provided by the bank does not preclude exemption for the transaction.
3. Paragraph (3) of art 13B(d) was to be interpreted as meaning that transactions concerning transfers and payments include operations carried out by a data-handling centre if those operations are distinct in character and are specific to, and essential for, the exempt transactions.
4. Services consisting in making financial information available to banks and other users were not covered by paragraphs (3) and (5) of art 13B(d).
5. The mere fact that operations concerning the management of deposits, purchase contracts and loans are carried out by a data-handling centre did not prevent them from constituting services covered by paragraphs (13) and (15) of Annex F to the Sixth Directive. It was for the national court to determine whether, before 1 January 1991, those operations were separate in character and specific to, and essential for, those services.
6. The mere fact that a service was invoiced by a third party did not prevent the transaction to which it relates from being exempt under paragraphs (3) and (5) of art 13B(d) of the Sixth Directive.

Very soon after the ruling was given, HMRC issued *Business Brief 13/97* commenting on the SDC case. They stated that the judgment gave rise to no change in policy in the UK and that they continued to accept that services provided by outsource providers who themselves directly effect payments and transfers of funds qualify for exemption. However, in other cases, outsourced activities will normally remain liable to VAT at the standard rate.

So, in summary, the key points arising from the SDC case are:

- VAT exemption is not restricted to transactions effected by financial institutions;
- it does not matter whether the supplies are carried out partly or wholly electronically or manually;
- is not necessary for the services to be provided by a person that has a legal relationship with the end customer (the fact that the services are provided by a third party does not prevent the services from falling within the exemption); and
- the services supplied to the financial institution must themselves qualify for exemption.

4.3. *C&E Commrs v Civil Service Motoring Association [1998] STC 111*

CSMA ('the Association') was a non-profit-making, non-charitable voluntary organisation that provided motoring, leisure, financial and related services to its members. One of the benefits offered to its members was a credit card scheme on terms agreed between the Association and a bank. The bank paid commissions to the Association for introducing its members to the bank's credit card scheme. The Association was also granted the right to develop, market and issue an affinity card bearing the CSMA logo. In addition, CSMA worked with the bank under an agreement in respect of marketing, negotiating the provision of benefits, customer handling and providing an arbitration service. The issue was whether or not the commission received fell within the exemption for credit in what was then *VATA 83, Sch 6, Group 5* (and is now *VATA 94, Sch 9, Group 5, Item 5*).

HMRC said that, in their view, the exemption should be narrowly construed and limited to intermediaries bringing together parties seeking credit and those providing credit and arranging for the specific grant of credit. Exemption should not extend to the supply of general preparatory marketing arrangements to develop credit products. As an alternative, HMRC argued that there was sufficient ambiguity within the relevant article in the Sixth VAT directive (*art 13B(d)(1)*) to support a reference to the ECJ.

In dismissing HMRC's appeal the Court of Appeal held that the services of CSMA could reasonably and sensibly be described as negotiation of credit and as making arrangements for a transaction for the granting of any credit, and therefore exempt. The Court of Appeal also rejected the request for a reference to the ECJ and refused leave to appeal to the House of Lords.

Similar decisions were also arrived at in the joint cases of *BAA plc and Institute of Directors [2003] STC 35* and *C&E Commrs v Lloyds TSB Group Limited [1998] STC 528*.

4.4. *C&E Commrs v CSC Financial Services Limited (formerly Continuum (Europe) Limited) (Case C–235/00) [2002] STC 57*

CSC provided a 'call centre' service for financial institutions, including Sun Alliance. Sun Alliance entrusted to CSC all communications and contacts with the public concerning a particular investment product under which investment was made by means of units in a unit trust. CSC operators provided potential investors with information and the relevant investment application forms. CSC processed the forms, checked that they had been properly filled in, that the applicant satisfied eligibility conditions, that the correct payment was enclosed and dealt with cancellation requests. It did not deal with the formalities of issuing and transferring the units in the unit trust. Sun Alliance paid CSC a fee for its services.

HMRC took the view that the services provided by CSC were not exempt under *art 13B(d)(5)* of the *Sixth VAT Directive* (now *art 135(f) of Directive 2006/112/EC*) which exempted transactions, including negotiation, but excluding management and safekeeping, in shares and securities.

CSC appealed to the Tribunal which allowed its appeal, holding that art 13B(d)(5) extended to the necessary preliminary stages of the issue and transfer of securities.

On appeal by the commissioners, the High Court stayed proceedings and sought a preliminary ruling from the ECJ on the meaning, in art *13B(d)(5),* of the words:

(i) 'transactions in securities'; and
(ii) 'negotiation in securities'.

In answer to these two questions, the ECJ ruled:

- 'transactions in securities' means transactions liable to create, alter or extinguish parties rights and obligations in respect of securities;
- 'negotiation in securities' does not cover services limited to providing information about a financial product and, as the case may be, receiving and processing applications for subscription to the relevant securities, without issuing them.

Thus, the ECJ effectively came down on the side of HMRC.

The distinction between SDC (who were successful in their dispute with the Danish tax authorities) and CSC (who were unsuccessful) is that SDC in providing their services altered the legal and financial relationship between the parties to the underlying financial transaction. CSC, in the services it provided to Sun Alliance, did not do this; they were not authorised to provide advice, only information. Although they did check that application forms had been properly filled in etc., they did not undertake the formalities for issuing and transferring the units in the unit trust (these were carried out by an unconnected company).

4.5. *C & E Commrs v FDR Ltd [2000] STC 672*

FDR Ltd acted as a clearing house for payment card transactions for card issuers and acquirers. It claimed that its services were an exempt supply or supplies under *art 13B(d)(3) of the Sixth VAT Directive* (now *art 135(d) of Directive 2006/112/EC*), which exempts:

transactions, including negotiation, concerning deposit and current accounts, payments, transfers, debts, cheques and other negotiable instruments, but excluding debt collecting and factoring.

The Tribunal allowed FDR's appeal.

HMRC's appeal against that decision went directly to the Court of Appeal. The Court of Appeal held that—

- The essential commercial activity consisted in the movement of money between cardholder, merchant, issuer and acquirer, for the convenience of the cardholder and the profit of the other three parties. Under the contractual arrangements, that activity was outsourced to FDR Ltd. So regarded, FDR Ltd's supplies fell within *art 13B(d)(3).*
- There was a single or core supply provided by FDR Ltd which consisted of processing all the card transactions and settling the liabilities and claims under those transactions in accordance with the obligations of the issuers and the acquirers.

Given that the core supply consisted in a number of supplies integral to one another, it was necessary to look at its constituent elements to ascertain what its tax treatment should be. The result of that enquiry was that the making of "transfers" within *art 13B(d)(3)* was at the centre of the core supply, and accordingly it should be treated as exempt.

HMRC consider that the FDR decision has clarified where clearing house type services are exempt, but that it does not affect the fundamental point that services such as credit management by someone other than the credit provider, data preparation, authorisation services and account maintenance services are taxable. (See *Business Brief 10/01*).

4.6. *C & E Commrs v Electronic Data Systems Ltd [2003] STC 688*

EDS provided outsourced services to Lloyds Bank; operating a call centre on behalf of the bank, receiving and processing loan applications, signing loan agreements on behalf of the bank and releasing funds to borrowers.

HMRC took the view that the services supplied by EDS to the bank were taxable, maintaining that the supplies of the grant of negotiation of credit were made by the bank and not by EDS and that the services provided by EDS were purely that of a call centre. EDS did receive some income in relation to the sale of loan protection insurance and whilst HMRC accepted that this was exempt, they argued that these supplies were ancillary to the main standard rated supplies and were therefore included in a single composite taxable supply.

EDS argued that its supplies to the bank were exempt because it granted or negotiated credit within *art 13B(d)(1) of the Sixth VAT Directive* (now *art 135(1)(b) of Directive 2006/112/EC*) or, alternatively it entered into transactions, including negotiation, concerning deposit and current accounts, payments, transfers and debts within the meaning of *art 13B(d)(3) of the Sixth VAT Directive* (now *art 135(1)(d) of Directive 2006/112/EC*). EDS also argued that supplies it made in respect of the insurance agreements were also exempt as they constituted a service performed by an insurance broker or an insurance agent.

At the Tribunal, EDS were successful on all counts. HMRC subsequently appealed to the Court of Appeal but their appeal was rejected.

Following the EDS decision, HMRC now accept that where a business provides a package of outsourced services to a loan provider, the supply is exempt if:

- it consists of services before and after the granting of a loan; and
- the business provides, as a central part of the supply, the services of
  - (a) the operation of bank accounts on behalf of the credit provider;
  - (b) arranging the transfers of funds to the borrower; and
  - (c) the processing of loan repayments and any additional charges or fees by direct debit or cheque.

VAT Notice 701/49/, para 4.11

4.7. *Century Life plc v C&E Commrs [2000] STC 276*

The cases in **4.2** to **4.6** above all dealt with outsourcing in the banking and financial services sector. Similar cases have arisen in the insurance sector, a principal one being *Century Life.*

Century Life was the representative member of a group of companies which included CFS Ltd whose business consisted of administering insurance and pension contracts for third party insurance companies. In October 1994, the regulatory authorities required all insurance companies to review their personal pensions business sold between April 1988 and June 1994 and to provide compensation to policyholders who had been disadvantaged as a result of receiving bad advice.

CFS Ltd was retained by an insurance company, Lincoln, to review its pension policies and determine whether there had been any mis-selling of policies during the relevant period. Under an agreement between CFS Ltd and Lincoln, Lincoln identified cases for review and passed the papers to CFS Ltd. In carrying out the review, CFS Ltd acted in the name of Lincoln at all times. If CFS Ltd concluded that there had been no mis-selling, the case was referred back to Lincoln and, if Lincoln agreed with CFS Ltd's conclusion, the relevant investor was informed. If CFS Ltd considered that there had been mis-selling, it arranged for the loss to be calculated and checked and prepared a compensation offer letter.

HMRC took the view that the services supplied by CFS Ltd were taxable and issued an assessment. Century Life appealed arguing that CFS Ltd was an insurance agent providing the services of an insurance intermediary and that the services were therefore exempt under *VATA 94, Sch 9, Group 2, Item 4* and *art 13B(a) of the Sixth Directive* (now *art 135(1)(a) of Directive 2006/112/EC*), which exempts 'insurance and reinsurance transactions, including related services performed by insurance brokers and insurance agents'.

The Tribunal accepted that CFS Ltd had acted as an insurance agent but it dismissed the appeal on the grounds that the services supplied by CFS Ltd were required to be performed in the regulation of insurance companies and were therefore not the type of services contemplated by art 13B and Item 4 because they were not part of the normal work of an insurance agent.

Century Life appealed. HMRC argued that the exemption was restricted to those services establishing or acting upon the commercial relationship between insurer and insured that arose from the insurance contract and did not apply to services concerned with financial compliance procedures.

Century Life's appeal was allowed on the basis that:

(i) In determining whether a supply of services was of the type contemplated by *art 13B(a)* and *item 4* no distinction should be drawn between the services identified by those provisions and those which arose because of a need for a review of insurance transactions to ensure compliance with the regulations covering such transactions. The transaction of insurance business in compliance with the rules of the regulatory bodies and the relevant legislation was at the very heart of the nature of insurance business and any attempt to distinguish between a commercial transaction and a compliant one was unreal.

(ii) In this case, if these activities had been undertaken by Lincoln, it would have been impossible to say that those activities were not part of the transaction of its insurance business or the administration of its insurance business or were services related to that business performed by an insurance agent within the meaning of *art 13B*.

(iii) The need to see that a contract was compliant was part of the administration and performance of a contract and was therefore a related service performed by an insurance agent falling within *note (1)* to *item 4*, namely the provision of assistance in the administration and performance of contracts of insurance, including the handling of claims.

4.8. *Försäkringsaktiebolaget Skandia (Case C – 240/99) STC 754*

This is a Swedish case which raises some interesting points on outsourcing in the insurance industry and also illustrates some differences between the insurance market in the UK and elsewhere in the EU. It should also be noted that at the time the case was heard in Sweden, VAT grouping was not permitted under Swedish legislation, although this has now been changed.

Skandia was an insurance company with a wholly-owned subsidiary (Livbolaget) engaged in the business of life assurance. Under a restructuring plan it was proposed that Livbolaget's staff and operations would be transferred to Skandia, which would, in effect, conduct all Livbolaget's business, including the sale of insurance, the settlement of claims, the calculation of actuarial forecasts and capital management. In return, Skandia would receive remuneration at market rates from Livbolaget. Skandia would assume no liability in respect of those insurance activities and all risks would lie with Livbolaget which would retain its status of insurer for the purposes of Swedish law.

Skandia requested a preliminary opinion (binding on the Swedish administrative authorities) from the Skatterättsnämnden on whether its assumption of a commitment to run Livbolaget's business activities could be regarded as the supply of insurance services under Swedish law, thus qualifying for exemption from VAT. The preliminary opinion decided that the supply would be of administrative and management services. Skandia challenged the opinion before the Regeringsrätten, which dismissed the appeal.

Skandia appealed on a point of law and the Regeringsrätten referred to the ECJ the question of whether a commitment assumed by an insurance company to carry out, in return for remuneration at market rates, the activities of another insurance company, which was its wholly-owned subsidiary and which would continue to conclude insurance contracts in its own name, would constitute an insurance transaction within the meaning of *art 13B(a) of the Sixth Directive* (now *art 135(1)(a) of Directive 2006/112/EC*) which exempts

> insurance and reinsurance transactions, including related services performed by insurance brokers and insurance agents'.

Skandia contended that:

(i) the interpretation of the term 'insurance' should not differ according to whether it appeared in the Sixth Directive or the Community directives on insurance which provided that insurance companies had to limit their objects to the business of insurance and operations arising directly therefrom to the exclusion of all other commercial business, so that all the transactions that an insurance company might carry out under the insurance directives had, by definition, to be exempt under art 13B(a); and that

(ii) for the purposes of the exemption for insurance transactions it was not necessary for the transaction to be carried out by a company which had a legal relationship with the insurer's end customer so that the services provided by one insurance company to another were exempt and the absence of any legal relationship between Skandia and Livbolaget's clients was not relevant.

The ECJ ruled in the following terms:

> For there to be an "insurance transaction" within art 13B(a), there had to be a contractual relationship between the provider of the insurance service and the insured. Sparekassernes Datacenter v Skatteministeriet (Case C-2/95) was distinguished as that case was concerned with art 13B(d)(3), (5) of the Sixth Directive, which was framed in a less specific way than art 13B(a). In this case, there would be no legal relationship between Skandia and the subsidiary's clients.
>
> Furthermore, it could not be inferred from the fact that under the directives insurance companies had to limit their business to the provision of insurance, so that all transactions carried out by such companies were "insurance" ones for the purposes of art 13B(a). The insurance directives allow insurance companies to carry out not only insurance transactions proper but also "operations arising directly therefrom".
>
> Therefore, a co-operative arrangement under which one insurance company ran the business of another for remuneration, but without concluding the insurance contracts in its own name or assuming the

related liabilities, was not an "insurance transaction" within art 13B(a), but a service effected for consideration that is subject to VAT.

Although this case and decision may appear surprising from a UK perspective, it needs to be borne in mind that it is based both on Swedish domestic law, in particular, the definitions of insurance company and insurance agent under Swedish law and also the fact that the ECJ only answers the specific questions that it is asked.

It is understood that under Swedish law, there is a clear distinction between insurance companies and insurance agents. Both Skandia and Livbolaget considered themselves insurance companies and neither were registered in Sweden as insurance agents. As neither considered themselves as insurance agents, they never sought to argue that the exemption available to the activities of insurance agents would apply to them. As a result, the ECJ was left to answer the narrow question of whether or not the supply was an insurance transaction. If such an arrangement occurred within the UK then, notwithstanding VAT grouping, Skandia would more likely argue that it is acting as an insurance intermediary providing exempt services to Livbolaget in that capacity.

4.9. *C & V (Advice Line) Services Ltd v C & E Comrs (2001) (17310)*

C & V provided a telephone helpline service to customers of an insurance company (Direct Line). The telephone service provided by C & V was the interface between legal expenses policyholders and Direct Line, the insurer.

The helpline service was manned by the C & V's employees, and the services provided included:

- answering questions on legal matters relating to the policy, including the giving of self-help advice (i.e. where a claim was not appropriate), and helping the policyholder to fill in a claim form; and
- advising the policyholder on whether he had a valid claim, and if so, sending a claim form.

C & V treated the service supplied to the insurance company as exempt. HMRC regarded the service as the provision of a standard rated legal service, and assessed C & V for VAT plus interest and a misdeclaration penalty.

Before the Tribunal, C & V argued that its services were exempt under *art 13B(a) of the Sixth Directive* (now *article 135(1)(a) of Directive 2006/112/EC*) and *VATA 94, Sch 9, Group 2, Item 4*.

The Tribunal considered that both provisions contained conditions relating to the nature of the service, and the status of the service provider, which had to be complied with for exemption to apply:

Under the EC legislation the service must relate to insurance and reinsurance transactions.

Under the UK legislation the service must:
(a) be related to the provision of insurance;
(b) be provided by an insurance broker or insurance agent in the course of his acting in an intermediary capacity; and
(c) constitute the provision of assistance in the administration and performance of such contracts, including the handling of claims.

With regards to (a), the Tribunal drew assistance from *Century Life v C & E Comrs [2001] STC 38*. There was an inseparable nexus between the appellant's services to Direct Line and Direct Line's insurance transactions; a closer relationship, in fact, than that in *Century Life*.

In relation to (b), the Tribunal found that the appellant had no activity other than the provision of the helpline service, which amounted to the assistance in the administration and performance of Direct Line's policies. As such, the appellant was acting in the course of an intermediary capacity.

With regards to (c), the Tribunal held that the appellant's services did constitute the provision of assistance. The telephone helpline was the only means through which a policyholder could receive assistance and make a claim.

The Tribunal also commented on *VATA 94, Sch 9, Group 2, Note 9*, which excludes from Item 4 services of "experts", unless those experts have authority to determine whether to accept or reject a claim. The legal consultants, it was held, did not have such authority since they provided advice only (the final decision on the acceptance of a claim being taken by Direct Line). However, the Tribunal held that the legal consultants were not "experts" in the sense intended by Note 9, and hence the exclusion did not apply.

Both EC and UK domestic legislation provided that for exemption to apply the service must be performed by an insurance broker or insurance agent.

It was never suggested that the C & V was an insurance broker, so the question to be decided was whether it was an insurance agent. Under the law as it applies in England and Wales, the appellant would not be regarded as an agent since it had no power to enter into a contract on behalf of its principal. However, the Court of Appeal in *Century Life* recognised that the description of insurance agent within the *Insurance Intermediaries Directive* was applicable to art 13B(a); the concluding words of art 2.1(b) of this directive spread the net wider than UK law, and thus enabled C & V to be described as an insurance agent. The insurance intermediary elements of the C & V's services were sufficiently dominant to create a single exempt supply.

Note, that with effect from 1 April 2013, these services are no longer exempt (see **3.5.2**).

4.10. *Staatssecretaris van Financiën v Arthur Andersen & Co Accountants cs (Case C-472/03) [2005] STC 508*

Arthur Andersen cs group was established in the Netherlands and included a private company, Andersen Consulting Management Consultants (ACMC). ACMC entered into an agreement with a life assurance company to undertake various 'back office' activities. These included the processing of applications, dealing with amendments to contracts and premiums, issuing, managing and rescinding policies, managing claims, setting and paying commission to insurance agents, organisation and management of information technology, supplying information to the life assurance company and to insurance agents and drafting reports for policyholders and others, such as the tax inquiry and inspection service.

Where an application for insurance required a medical examination then the life assurance company would make the decision as to whether to accept the risk; in all other cases ACMC would decide whether the risk should be accepted and the life assurance company was bound by that decision.

ACMC claimed a reimbursement of VAT on the ground that the services it supplied were exempt under *art 13B(a)* of the Sixth Directive (now *art 135 (1)(a) of Directive 2006/112/EC*) as

> insurance and reinsurance transactions, including related services performed by insurance brokers and insurance agents.

In the proceedings which followed, the Hoge Raad der Nederlanden concluded that the activities in question were not exempt insurance transactions. The life assurance company alone bore the risks inherent in the performance of insurance activities and the insurance contracts were underwritten, not in the name of ACMC but in the name of the life assurance company. However, the Court was unsure as to the meaning of 'services performed by ... insurance agents' and therefore it stayed the proceedings and referred the following question to the ECJ for a preliminary ruling:

> whether, where a taxable person had concluded an agreement with a (life) assurance company, such as the agreement at issue in the instant case, under which the taxable person undertook, for a certain remuneration and with the aid of qualified personnel who were expert in the insurance field, most of the actual activities related to insurance, including the taking of decisions that bound the insurance company to enter into insurance contracts and maintaining contact with the agents and, as the occasion arose, with the insured, while the insurance contracts were concluded in the name of the insurance company and the insurance risk was borne by the latter, the activities undertaken by that taxable person in execution of the agreement were *'related services performed by insurance brokers and insurance agents'* within the meaning of art 13B(a).

In its decision, the ECJ rejected Andersen's arguments and ruled that the services of ACMC did not qualify for exemption. The ECJ identified services provided by ACMC that they considered were not activities of an insurance agent (setting and payment of commission for insurance agents, the maintenance of contact with them, the handling of aspects relating to reinsurance and the supply of information to insurance agents and to the tax authorities). Also essential aspects of the work of an insurance agent, such as the finding of prospects and their introduction to the insurer, were not undertaken by ACMC. In effect, ACMC's activities were seen as a division of the life assurer, rather than an insurance transaction in themselves or an insurance agent supply.

In response to the *Andersens* decision HMRC issued *Business Brief 11/05*. HMRC stated that, in their view, the judgment meant that the UK VAT exemption for insurance related services was drawn too widely and that to bring it into line with the judgment, UK legislation would need to be amended. A consultation period was announced to enable discussions take place with the insurance industry. However, in light of the EU review of VAT and financial services, within which the European commission is considering the VAT treatment of insurance related services, the UK has delayed any amendment to UK legislation until the outcome of the review is known. Meanwhile, HMRC have reserved the right to make amendments to the UK legislation at any time. Furthermore, businesses may, if they wish, apply the *Andersen* judgment under the 'direct effect' principle.

The *Andersens* decision was raised in the VAT Tribunal case of *MorganAsh Ltd (VTD 19,777)* which concerned a company involved in the completion of health questionnaires in respect of life assurance policies. In this case both parties recognised that the appellant failed to meet the Andersen interpretation of the relevant EU VAT exemption but the appellant was successful in their appeal under the UK legislation.

4.11. *JCM Beheer BV v Staatssecretaris van Financien (Case C-124/07) [2008] STC 3360*

The case of Beheer looks at the VAT position of sub-agents. Beheer acted as a sub-agent on behalf of a Dutch insurance broker, VDL. VDL acted as an insurance agent (in some cases as an authorised agent) for certain insurance companies, concluding insurance contracts in the name of those insurers. Beheer carried out certain activities in the name of and on behalf of VDL, including the conclusion of insurance contracts, the processing and transfers of policies, issuing policies, the payment of commissions and the provision of information to the insurance company and the policyholders. Under the contract between VDL and Beheer, Beheer received a commission equal to 80% of the commission paid to VDL for the conclusion of the insurance contract. The question referred to the ECJ was whether or not VAT exemption extended to work carried out in the name of another insurance broker or agent.

The ECJ ruled that *article 13B(a)* of the *Sixth Directive* had to be interpreted as meaning that the fact that an insurance broker or agent did not have a direct relationship with the parties to the insurance or reinsurance contract in the conclusion of which he had been instrumental, but merely an indirect relationship with them through the intermediary of another taxable person who was, himself, in a direct relationship with one of those parties, and to whom the insurance broker or agent was contractually bound, did not prevent the service provided by the latter from being exempt under that provision.

Although the ECJ had previously decided that the expression 'related services performed by insurance brokers and insurance agents' in *art 13B(a)* of the *Sixth Directive* referred only to services provided by professionals who had a relationship with both the insurer and the insured party, it was clear that, although Beheer did not have a formal relationship with the insurers on whose behalf VDL acted, it nonetheless had an indirect relationship with those insurers.

Thus, through its contract with VDL, which itself had a contractual relationship with the insurers, Beheer, acting in the name and on behalf of VDL, was indirectly linked with those insurers.

A similar decision was arrived at the ECJ case of *Volker Ludwig (C-453/05)* regarding credit management which found

> the fact that the taxable person has no contractual link with any of the parties....and that he does not establish direct contact with one of those parties does not preclude that taxable person from providing a service of negotiation....which is exempt....

4.12. *Aspiro (formerly BRE Ubezpieczenia Sp. z o.o.) v Minister Finansów (Case C – 40/15)*

Aspiro (formerly BRE) are a claims handling company who provide a full claims handling service to insurance companies. This includes contacting the insured, commissioning expert reports, facilitating repairs and taking all relevant decisions regarding the claim. The question was whether or not this service fell within the insurance exemption.

The ECJ ruled:

(a) This did not constitute an insurance transaction as Aspiro did not undertake to ensure that the insured person had insurance cover, neither was there any contractual relationship with the insured; and,

(b) With regard to the question as to whether Aspiro were an insurance broker or agent, whilst the court accepted that Aspiro had a direct relationship with the insurer and an indirect relationship with the insured, they did not carry out the essential work of a broker or agent (i.e. they did not find prospective clients and introduce them to the insurer).

Consequently, the ECJ gave the following judgment:

> *Article 135(1)(a) Council Directive 2006/112/EC* of 28 November 2006 on the common system of value added tax must be interpreted as meaning that claims settlement services, such as those at issue in the main proceedings, provided by a third party in the name and on behalf of an insurance company, do not fall within the exemption laid down by that provision.

This adds a bit more pressure on tax authorities such as the UK (which has always taken a more expansive view of what constitutes an insurance related service) but I suspect that in the light of the ongoing Brexit negotiations, any immediate change of policy by HMRC is unlikely.

5. Input Tax and VAT recovery

5.1. Introduction

The recovery of VAT incurred on expenditure is probably the key area for businesses in the financial and insurance sectors. The basic concept of VAT is that VAT is charged by each person in the supply chain on the value of the supply that they make. In principle, each person in the chain can recover the VAT charged to them by their supplier. The final consumer (the person at the end of the chain) then incurs the 'sticking' VAT.

This model is fine where each supply in every link of the chain is taxable. However, supplies of financial services and insurance are generally exempt. As a result, VAT incurred wholly on these supplies is irrecoverable. However, financial services and insurance businesses commonly make some taxable supplies and supplies which generate an entitlement to VAT recovery (certain 'specified supplies' - see **5.6** below). As a result, VAT will be partly recoverable, with the level of recoverable VAT calculated by use of a partial exemption method.

Recovery of some types of input tax is always blocked (specifically that relating to the purchase of motor cars and business entertainment, see below) and input tax on certain capital items is subject to an adjustment regime (the 'Capital Goods Scheme') which is intended to enable VAT recovery to reflect the use of those items over a specified period of time.

5.2. Definition of input tax

Broadly, input tax is VAT incurred on business costs.

It is defined in *VATA 94 s24(1)* to mean in relation to a taxable person:

- VAT on the supply to him of any goods or services;
- VAT on the acquisition by him from another member state of any goods; and
- VAT paid or payable by him on the importation of any goods from a place outside the member states.

In each case the goods or services must be used or to be used for the purpose of a business carried on by the taxable person.

5.3. Who can recover input tax

The claim to recover input tax can only to be made by the person to whom the supply was made. In most cases, it is quite clear who the recipient of the services is and therefore who is entitled to seek to recover the related input tax. However, it is not always so straightforward. One example of this was seen in the case of *C&E Commrs v Redrow Group plc, HL 1998,*

[1999] STC 161. In this case, Redrow, the representative member of a group of housebuilding companies, paid the cost of estate agent fees incurred by prospective buyers (this was because Redrow could not sell their houses until the prospective housebuyers had sold their existing properties). HMRC took the view that the VAT on those fees was not Redrow's input tax, as it was the prospective buyers who received the supply. When the case came before the House of Lords, they took a different view and ruled that Redrow were entitled to recover the VAT charged by the estate agents as input tax; the estate agents were doing what Redrow instructed them to do. Redrow were receiving something in respect of the payment (a right to have goods delivered for services rendered to a third party) and Redrow obtained something for value in return for the payment of the fees and what it obtained was for the purposes of its business.

The Redrow principles have been applied or distinguished in a number of cases (see *R&C Commrs v Loyalty Management UK Ltd and Baxi Group Ltd v R&C Commrs, jointly heard cases C-53/09 and C-55/09* (rewards schemes and third party consideration). See also *HMRC v Aimia Coalition Loyalty UK Ltd (formerly known as Loyalty Management UK Ltd) [2013] UKSC 15; HMRC v Airtours Holiday Transport Ltd [2010] UKUT 404 (TCC) [2011] STC 239* (accountants services regarding a company in financial trouble; services supplied to creditors rather than company) and *WHA Ltd and another v HMRC Commrs [2004] STC 1081* (car repair costs in an insurance claim; whether insurer entitled to recover VAT as input tax). See also the case of *Vos Aannemingen BVBA case C-405/19* which would appear to confirm the Redrow principle that incidental benefits accruing to a third party should not restrict the taxable persons right to deduct input tax provided there is a direct and immediate link between the input tax and the economic activity and the benefit to the third party is ancillary to the taxable persons business purposes.

5.4. Blocked input tax

The recovery of VAT on most business entertainment and the purchase of motor cars (unless used exclusively for business purposes) is blocked.

5.4.1. Business entertainment

Business entertainment means entertainment, including hospitality of any kind, provided by a taxable person in connection with the business carried on by him or her. However, it does not include the provision of entertainment to employees or directors. Furthermore, with effect from 1 May 2011, the block does not apply to the entertainment of overseas customers.

For these purposes, an 'overseas customer', in relation to a taxable person, means:

(a) any person who is not ordinarily resident nor carrying on a business in the United Kingdom or the Isle of Man and avails himself or herself, or may be expected to avail himself or herself, in the course of a business carried on by that person outside the United Kingdom and the Isle of Man, of any goods or services the supply of which forms part of the taxable person's business; and

(b) any person who is not ordinarily resident in the United Kingdom or the Isle of Man and is acting, in relation to such goods or services, on behalf of an overseas customer as defined in paragraph (a) above or on behalf of any government or public authority outside the United Kingdom and the Isle of Man.

The entertainment must also be 'of a kind and on a scale which is reasonable, having regard to all the circumstances'.

Value Added Tax (Input Tax) (Amendment) Order 2011, SI 2011/1071

HMRC will also accept claims for costs incurred prior to 1 May 2011, subject to acceptable evidence and the four year cap.

HMRC regard business entertainment as including:

- provision of food and drink;
- provision of accommodation (for example hotels);
- the provision of theatre and concert tickets;
- entry to sporting events and facilities;
- entry to clubs; and
- the use of capital goods such as yachts and aircraft the purpose of entertaining.

(VAT Notice 700/65/02 para 2.2)

With regards to staff entertainment, HMRC accept that when an employer provides entertainment for the benefit of its employees, it does so for a business purpose. As a result VAT incurred is input tax and is not blocked under the business entertainment rules. (See *Ernst & Young [1997] (VTD 15100)*).

Where entertainment is only provided for directors, partners or sole proprietors, the VAT incurred is not input tax as the goods or services are not used for a business purpose. However, where directors/partners attend staff parties together with other employees, HMRC accept that the VAT incurred is input tax and is not blocked under the business entertainment rules.

Where business entertains both employees and non-employees (e.g. at a Christmas party where employees are entitled to bring spouses or guests) the proportion of VAT incurred relating to entertaining non-employees is blocked under the business entertainment rules. (See *KPMG (No 2) [1997] (VTD 14962)*).

5.4.2. Motor cars

Unless a motor car is used exclusively for business purposes (e.g. as a pool car), VAT incurred on its purchase is blocked from recovery. Purchase means not only outright purchase but also purchase under a hire-purchase or other agreement whereby property in the car eventually passes.

Similarly, VAT charged on accessories fitted to a car when purchased cannot be reclaimed, even if they are itemised separately on the sales invoice. However, VAT on accessories subsequently purchased can be treated as input tax provided the vehicle is owned by the business or where it is not owned by the business (e.g. an employee's own car) is used in the business and the accessory has a business use.

5.4.2.1 *Road fuel*

VAT on road fuel bought by the business or by the employee can be recovered provided it relates to the business and subject to certain provisions.

Where a business pays for road fuel that is used for business motoring only, all of the VAT on the road fuel can be treated as input tax and is recoverable subject to normal rules. However, where the fuel purchased is used for both business and private motoring, the business has three options to deal with the VAT incurred:

- treat all the VAT incurred as input tax and apply the fuel scale charge;
- use detailed mileage records to separate business mileage and private mileage and treat only the fuel relating to business mileage as input tax; or
- decide not to claim any input tax on road fuel.

Where road fuel is purchased by an employee of the business, provided:

- the fuel is used in whole or in part in respect of the employer's business; and
- the employer has agreed to reimburse the employee for the cost of the road fuel,

then the employer can treat the VAT charged on the road fuel as input tax subject to holding a VAT invoice.

The fuel scale charge is now based on the CO_2 emissions level of the vehicle and changes each year. For more information, go to www.gov.uk/fuel-scale-charge.

5.5. Purchases from overseas suppliers

Where a business purchases goods or services from an overseas supplier it generally does not incur overseas VAT. However, there is normally a UK VAT consequence.

For further details see **Chapter 7**.

5.6. Partial exemption

5.6.1. Overview

Input tax that is wholly incurred in making taxable supplies (including certain specified supplies) is recoverable in full. Input tax that is wholly incurred in making exempt supplies is wholly irrecoverable. However, businesses in the financial services and insurance sectors tend to make a mix of taxable and exempt supplies and as a result are required to carry out certain calculations to apportion input tax so as to recover only that proportion deemed to be 'used' in making taxable supplies. This apportionment calculation is the partial exemption calculation or partial exemption method.

5.6.2. Direct attribution

The first stage in any partial exemption method is direct attribution. This means any input tax that can be directly attributed to taxable supplies is fully recoverable. Any input tax that can be directly attributable to exempt supplies is wholly irrecoverable. The remaining input tax (commonly referred to as 'residual' or 'pot' input tax) is partially recoverable subject to a calculation reflecting the proportion of use in making taxable supplies. However, be aware of the de minimis tests as outlined in **5.6.4** below.

It is important to be clear what direct attribution means. The legislation (in particular *Regulation 101, Value Added Tax Regulations, 1995 SI 1995/2518*) refers to input tax used, or to be used, exclusively in making taxable or exempt supplies. Therefore it does not mean mainly or almost exclusively. For example, where an insurance company issues 1000 policies and 999 of those policies are issued to policyholders in the UK but one is issued to a policyholder in Jersey, any input tax in respect of that activity is not exclusively used in making exempt supplies and as a consequence any related input tax will be residual (and dealt with as explained in **5.6.3** below).

5.6.2.1 *Direct and immediate link*

There needs to be a direct and immediate link between a particular cost and a specific taxable supply in order to establish direct attribution and therefore establish a right to input tax deduction. A direct and immediate link will exist where the cost incurred directly forms a cost component of a supply or supplies being made.

This requirement was confirmed in the case of *C&E Commrs v Midland Bank plc, ECJ case C98/98, [2000] STC 501* and has been highlighted as a key principle in subsequent cases; see, for example, *BAA Ltd v HMRC [2013] ECWA Civ112*.

A business cannot look through to the ultimate purpose of a transaction when considering input tax recovery. For example, in the case of *BLP Group plc v C&E Commrs, Case C-4/94, [1995] STC 424* a holding company incurred input tax on professional fees in connection with the disposal of shares in a trading subsidiary company which it was selling in order to pay off debts which had been incurred in relation to its taxable activities. The ECJ held that the input tax was not recoverable as it related to the exempt sales of shares, even though the ultimate purpose the sale of the shares was to enable the business to continue to make taxable supplies.

A significant ECJ decision was made in the case of *Sveda UAB, ECJ Case C-126/14*. The case involves a Lithuanian organisation involved in tourism activities. Its business activities included the provision of accommodation, food and beverages, trade fairs and conferences. It constructed a recreational path featuring various aspects and items of Baltic mythology. The path was 90% funded by the Lithuanian Ministry of Agriculture, under an agreement that provided for free public access for five years. The tax authorities took the view that Sveda were not entitled to deduct VAT incurred on the construction of the path as they took the view that there was no direct and immediate link to the business activities. Sveda, took a different view, arguing that the public using the path would, as a result of using the path, pay for supplies of catering etc. Consequently, the Lithuanian court referred the following question to the ECJ for a preliminary ruling:

> May Article 168 [of Directive 2006/112/EC] be interpreted as granting a taxable person the right to deduct the input VAT paid in producing or acquiring capital goods intended for business purposes, such as those in the present case, which (i) are directly intended for use by members of the public free of charge, but (ii) may be recognised as a means of attracting visitors to a location where the taxable person, in carrying out his economic activities, plans to supply goods and/or services?

The Advocate General proposed the following response:

> Article 168 ... must be interpreted as meaning that it confers on a taxable person the right to deduct input tax paid on the acquisition or production of capital goods, which are directly intended for use free of charge by the public, but can be used as a way to encourage visitors to come to a place where the taxable person carrying on his business plans to supply goods and/or services

The ECJ effectively followed the AG's opinion ruling that:

> Article 168... must be interpreted as granting, in circumstances such as those in the main proceedings, a taxable person the right to deduct the input value added tax paid for the acquisition or production of capital goods, for the purposes of a planned economic activity related to rural and recreational tourism, which are (i) directly intended for use by the public free of charge, and may (ii) enable taxed transactions to be carried out, provided that a direct and immediate link is established between the expenses associated with the input transactions and an output transaction or transactions giving rise to the right to deduct or with the taxable person's economic activity as a whole, which is a matter for the referring court to determine on the basis of objective evidence.

The case is important as it seems to confirm some key principles relating to input tax deduction – in particular that input tax can be deducted on an asset that is used free of charge, provided the asset is used for a business purpose, that the cost of the input does not need to be factored into the price of the output and that a restriction on input tax recovery should only occur where there is no link to any economic activity or where partial exemption applies.

The Sveda judgment was applied in the First Tier Tribunal case of *Durham Cathedral v HMRC [2016] UKFTT 750* and in *Associated Newspapers Ltd [2017] EWCA Civ 54*.

In the case of *Royal Opera House [2021] EWCA Civ 910*, the court ruled that there was no direct and immediate link between the costs of producing operatic and ballet performances and catering and ice cream sales – the production costs were not part of the catering costs – and there was effectively a chain breaking exempt supply of admission. In the judgement the Court of Appeal distinguished Sveda on the basis that the recreational path was used free of charge with the intention that users of the path would be attracted to the taxpayers taxable catering facilities – hence there was no chain breaking exempt supply between use of the path and the taxable supplies. Similarly, it distinguished Associated Newpapers Ltd which concerned vouchers freely given away with the intention of increasing newpaper sales because again there was no chain breaking transaction between the cost of acquiring the vouchers and the taxable sale of newpapers.

Other cases of interest (which distinguish or perhaps even depart from BLP) are the Supreme Court decision in *Frank A Smart & Sons Ltd [2019] UKSC 39* and the more recent First Tier Tribunal decision in *Hotel la Tour Ltd [2021] UKFTT 0451*. In Frank Smart, the appellat acquired units under the EU Common Agricultural Policy's Single Farm Payment Scheme (SFP). The court upheld previous court decisions that the appellant was entitled to treat the costs of acquiring SFP units as a general overhead of the business and therefore treat the costs as residual (and in this case fully recoverable). In hotel la Tour, the appellant sold shares in order to fund a new taxable business activity and sought to recover the VAT on related professional fees. In essence the FTT ruled that although the issue of shares was exempt, provided the cost of the fees was not added to the cost of the shares but funded out of the proceeds of the share sale, VAT can be recovered to the extent the new business is taxable. The FTT referred to Frank Smart in it's decision, noting that the Supreme Court had modified the 'direct and immediate' link so that even if the initial transaction was non taxable, where the use of the services was for fundraising and that fundraising was to fund an asset to be used for taxable supplies at a later date, the cost of the services is a component of the later 'downstream' transaction. HMRC have been granted leave to appeal Hotel la Tour to the Upper Tribunal but no hearing date had been given at the time of writing.

5.6.2.2 *Holding Companies and VAT Groups*

The issue of VAT recovery by holding companies has been (and will be going forward) a key issue for VAT groups. The *BAA* case (as noted above) is an important case in this area. In summary, a UK company, Airport Development and Investments Ltd (ADIL), which was owned by an investment consortium, made a bid to acquire the entire issued share capital of BAA plc. ADIL received supplies of services that related to the takeover bid. The bid was successful and, subsequently, ADIL joined the BAA VAT group which then sought to recover the VAT that ADIL had incurred on those services.

The Court stated that there are two conditions for the recovery of VAT:

(a) the tax must be incurred by a taxable person in the course of an 'economic activity' and
(b) the goods/ services on which the VAT is incurred must have a 'direct and immediate link' with taxable supplies made by that person.

The Court held that the BAA VAT group was not entitled to recover the VAT incurred on the costs of acquisition because when ADIL incurred the VAT it was not carrying on an economic activity for VAT purposes (it was intending to takeover BAA plc by acquiring the shares in it) and there was no direct and immediate link between the services received by ADIL and the taxable supplies made by the BAA VAT group.

Consequently, the Court found that ADIL did not make, or have any intention to make, taxable supplies of goods or services at the time the VAT was incurred. Whilst the acquisition of the shares had economic consequences, that did not mean ADIL was engaged in an economic activity for VAT purposes.

Following the decision in BAA Ltd above, HMRC issued *R&C Brief 32/14* covering VAT recovery by holding companies – in effect they said that the decision supported their existing policy and also updated their VAT Input Tax Manuals (VIT 40100). However, they noted that further changes in this area may still be required once the ECJ had issued their rulings in the joined cases of *Laurentia + Minerva mbH & Co KG and Marenave Schiffahrts AG (ECJ Cases C-108/14 and C-109/14)*. The Laurentia + Minerva case looked at the position of 'active' holding companies – i.e. holding companies that do more than just hold shares in their subsidiaries ('passive' holding companies).

The ECJ confirmed that just acquiring and holding shares is not a business activity. However, the also ruled that where a holding company is directly or indirectly involved in the management of its subsidiaries and provides services liable to VAT (e.g. technical, commercial, financial or administrative services) then there is a business activity and the ability to recover related input tax, subject to the normal rules.

Where there is a mixture of 'active' and 'passive' holdings, then an apportionment is required (the methodology to be agreed with the tax authority).

The ECJ also considered the question of VAT grouping and what is of particular interest here is that they rejected the restriction applied in the UK that only corporate bodies under common control can form VAT groups. So in theory, 'natural persons' such as individuals, partnerships and trustees in funds should be able to form VAT groups. Furthermore, the common control requirement may be overly restrictive.

5.6.2.3 HMRC guidance

Early in 2016, HMRC issued *R&C Brief 3/16* announcing a consultation on VAT grouping in the light of both the Laurentia + Minerva and Skandia cases. Further guidance on holding companies was issued in April 2017 and can be found in HMRC Manual VIT40600. The relevant extract on VAT recovery reads as follows:

> **When a shareholding is used as part of an economic activity?**
> VAT may only be recovered if incurred in the course of an economic activity.
>
> Simply holding shares in order to receive dividends and perhaps to sell them for a capital gain is an investment activity and not an economic activity for VAT purposes. Therefore the VAT on the costs of acquiring and holding shares for either of these purposes is not recoverable. For the VAT to be potentially recoverable the entity acquiring the shares must do so, for some other purpose which is economic.
>
> For example
> - Shares may be acquired and held temporarily as part of an activity of trading in securities. Trading in securities differs from investment in securities because the aim is to profit from short term movements in the price rather than the long term growth. A profit can be made regardless of whether the shares are increasing or decreasing in price. Trading in securities is an economic activity.
> - A company may acquire and hold shares in subsidiaries to which it intends to provide management services for consideration. The provision of services for consideration is an economic activity.
>
> Following the CJEU decision in the joint cases Larentia+Minerva and Marenave (L+M) HMRC reviewed its existing policy in respect of holding companies and deduction of VAT incurred on acquisition costs. Prior to L+M our policy was that VAT incurred on costs of acquiring shares by a holding company was only deductible where it was directly attributable to the provision of taxable management or technical services. VAT incurred had to be apportioned between non-economic activity of shareholdings and economic activity. Additionally, VAT on costs incurred by a holding company was only recoverable if the intention was to recoup the expenditure from the income resulting from taxable services provided to subsidiaries within a reasonable time.
>
> In L+M the CJEU held that VAT incurred by a holding company on the costs of acquiring shareholdings in subsidiaries, to which it also intends to provide taxable management services, must be regarded as belonging to the Holding company's general expenditure and is deductible subject to any Partial Exemption restriction in place.

In order to be able to deduct VAT incurred on costs of acquiring shareholdings in subsidiaries the following conditions must be satisfied:

- the holding company making the claim must be the recipient of the supply
- the holding company must be undertaking economic activity for VAT purposes
- that economic activity must involve the making of taxable supplies.
- If the holding company is VAT grouped with its subsidiaries, it makes taxable supplies or loans for which it earns interest and the loans support the making of taxable supplies by the VAT group.

If the holding company is not the recipient of the supply, or is not undertaking economic activity, it will not be able to recover VAT.

Is the Holding Company the recipient of the supply

HMRC consider that a holding company is the recipient of the supply where it has contracted for the supply, including by novation and it has made use of the supply, been invoiced and paid for the supply.

Is the Holding Company undertaking economic activity for VAT Purposes

In addition to an activity which any other business may undertake (supplies of goods and services more generally), the holding company is undertaking economic activity for VAT purposes where it makes or intends to make supplies of management services for consideration, to its subsidiaries.

It is important to note that the management services must be genuine and provided for consideration which is more than nominal.

Where the Holding company is passive with no economic activity of its own, any VAT incurred on the costs of acquiring subsidiaries is not recoverable, and this will still be the case if the holding company joins a VAT group with the acquired companies.

For VAT to be recoverable, the costs on which it is incurred (including acquisition costs) must have a direct and immediate link to taxable supplies conducted as part of the economic activity. VAT will only be recoverable to the extent that those costs are used for the taxable activity. For more on the meaning of the term direct and immediate link see VIT21000

If a holding company provides taxable management services, to all its subsidiaries, then any VAT incurred on acquisition costs relating to the holding in those subsidiaries will be deductible. The receipt of dividends does not affect the deduction.

However, if a holding company incurs costs on acquiring shares in subsidiaries intending to make taxable supplies to some of them, but not others, the acquisition of the latter subsidiaries is an investment activity and not an economic activity for VAT Purposes. Accordingly, the VAT incurred should be apportioned between the economic activities and the investment activities.

Alternatively a holding company may incur costs on acquiring shares in a subsidiary to which it both provides management services and makes a loan in respect of which it earns exempt interest. In those circumstances any VAT incurred on costs relating to the holding must be apportioned between the taxable and exempt supplies in line with the company's partial exemption method.

Shareholding acquired as a direct, continuous and necessary extension

If the shareholding is acquired as a direct, continuous and necessary extension of a taxable economic activity of the holding company, the VAT incurred may also have a direct and immediate link to taxable supplies and be recoverable.

For example

- A retail company incurs costs acquiring a subsidiary whose main asset is a property from which the retail company intends to trade. In these circumstances the acquisition of the shares may be an extension of the retail business rather than an investment.If this is the case, the costs of acquisition are likely to be cost components of the retail supplies to be made from the property. The shares were acquired in order to obtain the property for the retail business. The VAT incurred will be recoverable to the extent that the retail supplies are taxable.
- A business acquires a direct competitor, a similar and complementary business or a key supplier/customer with a view (as the case may be) to increasing market share, achieving economies of scale, or achieving efficiencies through greater integration of its supply chain.

In the above examples the shareholding is a direct, continuous and necessary extension of the existing business activity. There is no need for a specific supply (e.g. management services provided to the acquired business) to link the VAT costs to the existing economic activity.

This is to be contrasted with:

- A company which purchases a business as a free-standing enterprise with a view to making money on dividends or an eventual sale.

In the first two examples the buyer is buying to strengthen its business, but by contrast in the above example there is no direct link between the acquisition and its own business and the acquired business does not itself benefit by being part of a larger, similar operation.

The VAT on costs incurred by the target of an acquisition, such as vendor due diligence costs, may also be deductible provided it can be shown that the target is the recipient of the supplies in question and those supplies were received for the purposes of the business carried out by the target.

Intention to make taxable supplies
If a holding company recovers VAT on acquisition costs because it intends to make taxable supplies to the subsidiary, it should retain evidence to demonstrate that this was the intended business model.

Where a holding company can evidence a genuine intention to make taxable supplies to its subsidiaries but those services are not actually made then the normal input tax rules regarding intention to make supplies will apply. See VIT22000

Contingent consideration for management services
Where a holding company incurs input tax on costs in providing or intending to provide management services to subsidiaries on terms whereby any payment will be contingent upon the profitability of those subsidiaries, then the holding company is not engaged in economic activity. This is because where services are supplied for no consideration or there is no contractual expectation that consideration will be received there is no supply for VAT purposes.

The supplies in question are not being provided for a consideration because the essential direct link and reciprocity between the obligations on the one hand of the holding company to provide the management services and the obligations on the other of the subsidiaries to make a payment for those services, is absent.

The issue of what constitutes a supply for a consideration has been the subject of a substantial body of case law. Most recently we have the decision of the Upper Tribunal in the case of Norseman Gold see VIT64050

Both the FTT and the Upper Tribunal on appeal considered the adequacy for the purpose of making taxable supplies of an intention to charge at some time in the future for services being provided. The FTT concluded that this would be insufficient in the absence of evidence of any agreement about the amount to be charged, the frequency with which invoices would be sent and the details of the services to be provided in exchange for the charge. It decided that it was important that the price or consideration is stipulated rather than there being 'a rather vague intention to levy an unspecified charge, at some undefined time in the future'.

The recent CJEU decision in the Hungarian case of MVM see VIT64050 reinforces the above decisions. It also supports HMRC policy following L+M in that the holding company has economic activity only if it provides genuine management charges under an agreement to charge for those services and does actually charge fees and receive consideration for those services.

The effect of a holding company joining a VAT Group
Joining a VAT group does not, of itself give rise automatically to an entitlement to recover VAT. It cannot change a non-economic (i.e. out of

the scope) activity into an economic activity. Nor does it automatically create a direct and immediate link between all input costs of a holding company and the taxable outputs of other VAT group members unless such a link can be traced through the intra group supplies, or the input costs are such that they are properly and naturally attributable to the VAT group's taxable outputs.

VAT grouping has the effect that all supplies are treated for VAT purposes as made to and by the representative member and imposes joint and several liability on all the members. It doesn't have any other effect. If a member of a VAT group incurs costs which it uses for non-economic activities, then the VAT on those costs still relates to the non-economic activities and VAT grouping does not change that. The supplies are treated as being used by the representative member for non-economic purposes.

In Commission v Ireland C-85/11, the court accepted the opinion of the Advocate General in its entirety. The Advocate General commented at para 43:

"the right of the persons belonging to the VAT group to deduct VAT for purchases is not expanded. This right continues to be applicable only to those supplies that are made for the activities subject to VAT by the VAT group. Nor are the members of a VAT group entitled to deduct VAT on supplies made for VAT exempted activities"

It does not make a difference whether the acquirer was already part of the VAT group or VAT groups on acquisition of the target; the right to deduct VAT on the costs cannot be different.

If the cost is received by the VAT group for the purposes of the holding company and the holding company doesn't undertake economic activity, then it won't be able to recover the related VAT.

If costs incurred have a direct and immediate link to taxable supplies made by the holding company outside the VAT group, the related VAT will be recoverable to the extent those costs are used for that purpose.

If the holding company provides management services or loans in respect of which it earns interest (see VIT64050 EDM C-77/01) to the companies acquired in the VAT group and these can be seen to support the making of taxable supplies by the VAT group (identifiable by 'looking through' the supply chain within the group), the related VAT will be recoverable to the extent that the costs support taxable supplies made. This is the case whether the transactions within the group would be taxable or exempt supplies, were they not disregarded because of the VAT grouping.

It is use that determines whether input tax is deductible and the existence of a direct and immediate link between the cost and the taxable supply. The question to ask is 'has the VAT group incurred the costs for use in its economic activity?'.

Stewardship Costs

It is important to determine whether the supplies are received by the group for the purposes of the holding company's activities, or for the purposes of the VAT group as a whole. Some supplies may be invoiced to the holding company for convenience (generally referred to as stewardship costs), even though they are for the purposes of the group as a whole. The most common examples are the general audit fees of the group, regulatory compliance, brand defence, bid defence and group legal costs. In those circumstances any input tax incurred should be treated as a cost of the group as a whole, rather than as a cost of the holding company.

Mixed economic and non-economic activities

A holding company may be involved in carrying out both economic and non-economic activities. In such cases VAT recovery is only allowable to the extent that the costs on which the VAT is incurred are attributable to taxable supplies which are intended to be made in the course of an economic activity.

L+M endorsed the court's decision in Securenta C-437/06 that where the holding company holds shares in subsidiaries in which it has no involvement (which does not constitute an economic activity) and also has shares in subsidiaries to which it provides management services for consideration (and which therefore does constitute economic activity) the costs should be apportioned according to use.

5.6.3. Residual input tax

Any input tax which is not directly attributable becomes residual VAT and will need to be apportioned to determine how much can be recovered. The method of recovery can either be by using the standard method or by applying a partial exemption special method (PESM). Each has their own advantages and disadvantages and these are explored below.

Before 1 April 2009, a newly partly exempt business was required to use the standard method (see **6.6.5** below) to calculate recoverable input tax. If this did not produce a fair recovery of input tax it would either have to wait until the year-end to calculate a standard method override adjustment (see 6.6.7 below) or seek approval for a special method.

From 1 April 2009, a new partly exempt business can recover input tax on the basis of use in the following situations:

- during its 'registration period', the period running from the date a business is first registered for VAT to the day before the start of its first tax year;
- during its first tax year provided it did not incur input tax relating to exempt supplies during its registration period; or

- during any tax year, provided it did not incur input tax relating to exempt supplies in its previous tax year.

VAT Information Sheet 04/09, para 4

In order to prevent unfair results, certain 'override' provisions exist for both standard and special methods which in effect give HMRC (and indeed with standard methods, the taxpayer) the ability to reject a method if it does not fairly reflect how input tax is used. The override provisions are covered in more detail below.

5.6.4. De minimis limits

Regardless of what method is used, some businesses with relatively small amounts of exempt input tax (input tax attributable to exempt supplies) are deemed to be fully taxable and therefore able to recover all the input tax that they incur. Businesses are deemed fully taxable provided their levels exempt input tax fall within the de minimis limits.

This means that where 'relevant input tax' in any VAT period (or any longer period) is not more than:

- £625 per month on average; and
- 50% of all input tax in the period concerned,

all such input tax in that period is treated as attributable to taxable supplies.

'Relevant input tax' means input tax attributable to exempt supplies or to supplies made outside the UK which would have been exempt if made in the UK, calculated under either a standard or special method.

6.6.4.1 Simplified de minimis tests

For VAT periods starting on or after 1 April 2010, HMRC introduced simplified tests to save some businesses the need to carry out a full partial exemption calculation to confirm their de minimis status.

If, in a VAT period, a business passes Test One or Test Two set out below, the business can treat itself as de minimis and provisionally recover input tax relating to exempt supplies. There is still a requirement to review the de minimis status at the year-end and account for any under/over recovery of input tax as part of your annual adjustment.

The simplified tests are:

- **Test One:** total input tax incurred is no more than £625 per month on average and the value of exempt supplies is no more than 50% of the value of all supplies.

- **Test Two:** total input tax incurred less input tax directly attributable to taxable supplies is no more than £625 per month on average and the value of exempt supplies is no more than 50% of the value of all supplies.

'Total input tax' excludes blocked input tax (e.g. VAT on business entertainment).

'The value of all supplies' includes taxable supplies made in the UK, supplies made outside the UK which confer a right of recovery and exempt supplies.

'Input tax directly attributable to taxable supplies' is input tax on costs that are used or to be used exclusively in making taxable supplies.

5.6.5. Outside the scope supplies

In the case of *C&E Commrs v Liverpool Institute for Performing Arts, HL [2001] STC 891* the court agreed with HMRC's view that two separate regimes are in existence for determining VAT recovery in respect of UK and non-UK supplies. *Regulation 101, Value Added Tax Regulations, 1995 SI 1995/2518* which deals with the standard method only determines recovery of input VAT relating to supplies made within the UK; Regulation 103(1) deals with VAT incurred on foreign (non-UK) supplies.

As a consequence, where a business makes both UK and foreign supplies (e.g. financial or insurance supplies where the recipient belongs outside the UK), there is a two-step procedure in determining recovery of VAT:

1. determine the amount of VAT incurred that relates to foreign supplies on the basis of use (it is up to the business to decide how best to do this); and then
2. any remaining VAT incurred, which relates to UK supplies, is recoverable subject to the standard or special method.

In practice, most businesses will have an agreed special method that adequately deals with foreign supplies (and HMRC allow combined methods which mix UK and foreign and specified supplies in a single method). However, when this is not the case, the procedure set out above will need to be applied.

With regard to businesses using a standard method, changes introduced with effect from 1 April 2009, allow a standard method to deal with input tax on all supplies (including foreign supplies) other than those dealt with separately under *Regulation 103A, Value Added Tax Regulations, 1995 SI 1995/2518* (supplies of investment gold). Before this date, the standard method only applied to UK supplies, so a two-step calculation was required as above.

VAT Information Sheet 04/09, para 5

5.6.5.1 *Supplies by overseas branches*

The *Value Added Tax (Amendment) Regulations 2015, SI 2015/1978* amended the regulations so that with effect from 1 January 2016, supplies made by foreign branches of UK entities can no longer be taken into account when determining VAT recovery on overheads. This in effect implements the ECJ decision in *Credit Lyonnais, ECJ Case C-388/11.*

5.6.6. Standard method

A standard partial exemption method does not require HMRC approval. Under a standard method the recoverable percentage of residual input tax is the percentage calculated as follows:

value of taxable supplies in the period (excluding VAT) x 100 value of all supplies the period (excluding VAT)

If the resulting percentage is not a whole number, it can be rounded up to the next whole number unless the amount of residual input tax to which it is applied is £400,000 per month on average or greater, in which case it should be rounded up to two decimal places.

The legislation requires the following supplies to be excluded from the calculation:

(a) any sum receivable in respect of a supply of capital goods used for the purposes of business;
(b) any sum receivable in respect of a supply of finance that is incidental to the business;
(c) any sum receivable in respect of a real estate transaction that is incidental to the business;
(d) that part of the value of any supply of goods on which output tax is not chargeable by virtue of a Treasury order under *VATA 94, s25(7)*;
(e) the value of any supply which the business makes to itself (e.g. supplies subject to the reverse charge under *VATA 94, s8(1))*;
(f) the value of any business transaction which is not a supply for VAT purposes (e.g. the transfer of a business as a going concern or the issue by a company of new shares in the company to raise capital); and
(g) from 1 April 2009, supplies of financial instruments and supplies from establishments located outside the UK.

The recoverable proportion of residual input tax claimed in each periodic VAT return is provisional and subject to adjustment at the year-end (see **5.6.9** below).

For tax years commencing from 1 April 2009, a business can use the previous year's recovery percentage (as calculated at the annual adjustment) as the provisional quarterly recovery percentage and adjust at the subsequent annual adjustment. The new annual adjustment percentage can then be used provisionally in the following four quarters.

For example, if a business with a 31 March year end, submitting calendar quarterly VAT returns and using the standard method, had an annual adjustment recovery percentage of 10% in the year to 31 March 2010 then that recovery percentage can be used in VAT periods 06/10, 09/10, 12/10 and 03/11. The business then carries out an annual adjustment calculation and finds its annual recovery percentage is 12%. It then adjusts its provisional recoveries (in effect an additional 2% recovery of residual VAT). The new 12% rate can then be used provisionally for VAT periods 06/11 to 03/12 and is adjusted on the next annual adjustment.

VAT Information Sheet 04/09, para 2

5.6.7. Standard method override

Whilst the standard method is a simple way of calculating recoverable residual input tax and in most cases provides a fair and reasonable method of recovery, there have been examples of larger businesses exploiting the standard method provisions to enable recovery of significant amounts of input tax on purchases used to make exempt supplies. In other cases not involving any 'abuse', similar results had been seen to occur and there were other cases where use of the standard method had unfairly penalised businesses that found they were unable to recover input tax used to make taxable supplies.

To address these problems, with effect from 18 April 2002, the standard method override provisions were introduced.

There are two situations where the standard method override can apply:

(1) Where
  (a) for a VAT period (i.e. the period in respect of which a VAT return is made) a taxable person has used the standard method to calculate residual input tax;
  (b) that VAT period does not form part of a longer period (see **5.6.9** Annual Adjustments below);

(c) the attribution which results from using the standard method 'differs substantially' from one which represents the extent to which the goods or services are used or to be used by the taxable person (or 'successor' of his) in making taxable supplies; and

(d) the residual input tax incurred in the VAT period is more than £50,000 p.a. (£25,000 p.a. for group undertakings, as defined in Companies Act 2006, which are not members of the same VAT group) adjusted pro rata for the length of the VAT period concerned,

a taxable person must calculate the difference between the standard method and the 'use' method and account for the difference on the return for the VAT period immediately following the VAT period in question.

(2) Where

(a) for a 'longer period' (see **5.6.9** Annual Adjustments) a taxable person has used the standard method to calculate residual input tax;

(b) the attribution which results from using the standard method 'differs substantially' from one which represents the extent to which the goods and services are used to be used by the taxable person (or a 'successor' of his) in making taxable supplies; and

(c) the residual input tax incurred in the VAT period is more than £50,000 p.a. (£25,000 p.a. for group undertakings, as defined in Companies Act 2006, which are not members of the same VAT group) adjusted pro rata for the length of the VAT period concerned,

the taxable person must calculate the difference and with the addition of any amount required to be included as an over- or under-deduction in respect of the normal annual adjustments, account for it on the return for the VAT period immediately following the annual adjustment period.

For these purposes a difference is substantial if it exceeds:

- £50,000, or
- 50% of the residual input tax incurred in the VAT period or longer period, but is not less than £25,000.

A person is a 'successor' of another if he has received assets from the other person by way of a transfer of a business as a going concern.

In order to calculate the extent of use, any method is acceptable providing it produces a fair and reasonable attribution of input tax according to the use or intended use of goods or services.

Regulations 107A – 107D, Value Added Tax Regulations, 1995 SI 1995/2518
VAT Notice 706, para 5

5.6.8. Special methods

HMRC may approve or direct the use of a method other than the standard method. A taxable person may apply to HMRC to use a special method where it is considered that the standard method does not provide a fair and reasonable result. HMRC will require full details of how the proposed method will work and are almost certain to want to discuss the proposals in some detail before approving them.

5.6.8.1 Declarations

With effect from 1 April 2007, HMRC will not approve the use of a special method unless the taxable person has made a declaration to the effect that to the best of their knowledge and belief the method fairly and reasonably represents the extent to which goods or services are used (or to be used) in making taxable supplies. The declaration must be made in writing and must be signed by the taxable person or a person authorised to sign on his behalf. A declaration is required each time a new method is applied for and must relate to the whole business.

The following can be used as a template for the declaration:

Name of Business:

Address:

VAT Registration Number:

This Declaration is in accordance with paragraphs (9) and (10) of regulation 102 of the VAT Regulations 1995.

As [the taxable person (i.e. where the signatory is a sole proprietor) / the person authorised by the taxable person to sign this declaration on its behalf],

I hereby declare that to the best of my knowledge and belief, the proposed special method [state precisely where the method is set out] fairly andreasonably represents the extent to which goods or services are used or tobe used in making taxable supplies.

> I also confirm that I have taken reasonable steps to ensure that I am inpossession of all relevant information before making this declaration.
>
> Name (print):
>
> Signed:
>
> Position:
>
> Date

If HMRC think that the declaration is incorrect, in that the method applied for is not fair and reasonable and that the person signing the declaration either knew or should reasonably have known that this was the case at the time the declaration was made, they may serve a notice on the person to that effect. Any such notice must set out HMRC's reasoning and can only be served if HMRC are satisfied that the result of the application of the new method is an over deduction of input tax.

Where a notice is served by HMRC, then in relation to VAT periods commencing on or after the effective date of the method, the taxable person must calculate the difference between deductible input tax using the special method and deductible input tax calculated based on use. The difference must then be accounted for on the return for that VAT period. This process then continues until the method is terminated.

5.6.8.2 Gaps in special methods

A special method may have a 'gap' if it fails to specify how to deal with certain types of residual input tax, possibly because the business has changed or possibly because of poor drafting.

Where this happens, VAT recovery should be calculated based on use (i.e. the relevant input tax should be attributed to taxable supplies to the extent that the goods and services are used in making taxable supplies expressed as a proportion of the whole use).

Once a gap has arisen, HMRC will expect the taxpayer to make proposals for a new method.

5.6.8.3 Types of special methods

A partial exemption special method can be any method agreed by the business and HMRC that is designed to reflect the activities of the business in question. Whereas the standard method bases the VAT recovery calculation on the value of the supplies made, under a special method other calculations are possible. These could include:

- use of transaction counts; calculating VAT recovery based on the number (rather than value) of taxable transactions as a proportion of all transactions;
- use of headcounts or staff time; calculating VAT recovery based on the number of staff making taxable supplies as a proportion of all staff, or of staff time spent making taxable supplies as a proportion of all staff time;
- inputs based or input tax based methods; calculating VAT recovery based on the ratio or value of taxable inputs or input tax directly attributable to taxable supplies as a proportion of total inputs or input tax;
- use of floor space apportionments; calculating VAT recovery using the ratio of floor space occupied by staff exclusively generating taxable supplies as a proportion of total floor space; and
- using cost allocations or management accounts information as the basis for apportionments.
- The value of supplies can also be used (as per the standard method) and a special method could use a combination of different calculations for different parts or sectors of the business.

This list is not exhaustive and other calculations are possible provided both business and HMRC can agree them as resulting in a fair and reasonable recovery. One decision worth noting is the Upper Tribunal decision in *Lok'nStore Group Plc [2014] UKUT 0288* where the appellant was successful in arguing for a floor space method. See also *R&C Brief 35/14* where HMRC accept the decision but look to limit the impact of the decision to the facts of this particular case!

It is also worth noting the ECJ decision in *Banco Mais, ECJ Case C-183/13* and the Court of Appeal decision in *Volkswagen Financial Services Ltd [2015] EWCA Civ 832*. Which clarified the principles for the recovery of VAT on overhead costs (the Volkswagen case considered the position of HP transactions and held that overhead costs had a direct and immediate link to the taxpayers outputs even though, in this case, the profit was made from the exempt finance element). HMRC appealed the Volkswagen decision to the Supreme Court, who in April 2017 decided that a referral to the ECJ would be required. The ECJ decided that HP involves two supplies (taxable goods and exempt finance) and that consequently residual input tax recovery should be available using an appropriate pro rata calculation. HMRC subsequently issued *Revenue & Customs Brief 8 (2020)*.

HMRC accept the decision and with regard to the partial exemption method comment:

An output values-based method of apportionment therefore needs to be applied which includes the value of the asset in order to reach a proper apportionment of the residual input tax. HMRC's position is that the calculation should be as set out as:

Value of the asset plus any taxable additional charges or fees. Divided by value of the asset plus value of the credit granted* (should correspond to the value of the asset) plus consideration for the credit as per the credit agreement and any additional charges, related commission or other fees received. This is then multiplied by 100.

*Where the amount of credit is less than the total value of the asset then both the amount shown as value of the asset and value of the exempt credit would be reduced.

Any businesses undertaking HP supplies that have underrecovered overhead VAT were invited to contact HMRC.

5.6.8.4 *Sectors*

It is also common for larger businesses to subdivide the partial exemption special method into 'sectors'. For example, a VAT group registration is likely to have a separate sector for each VAT group member; similarly an individual company may have sectors reflecting different activities or income streams; geographic areas or distinct products or projects. Each sector will then have its own recovery calculation to reflect taxable use as outlined above.

Each sector may incur its own input tax directly but it is also quite likely that costs used by one sector will initially be incurred by another. For example, a group of companies may have a service company which employs the staff and meets all overhead costs. Therefore, the special method will need to include a methodology for allocating an appropriate proportion of the general overhead input tax to the sector that uses or consumes it. This methodology may be based on floor space, headcounts or management accounts information or a mixture of different allocation methodologies appropriate to the type of costs (e.g. premises costs will often be allocated based on a floor space calculation).

Partial exemption special methods must be approved in writing. HMRC approval letters now follow standard templates and there are examples of the templates in **Appendix C**.

On the issue of sectorisation, with effect from 1 January 2016, HMRC amended the provisions of *paragraph 1A of Regulation 102* (use of other methods) of the VAT Regulations to:

(i) provide that, where an approved or directed method is based on sectors, the method must reflect the use of goods and services and each sector must reflect the use of goods or services in that sector, the structure of the business and the type of activity undertaken by that sector and

(ii) prohibit a taxable person from taking into account the value of supplies made from an establishment situated outside the UK unless that person is authorised or required to use a method based on sectors.

Value Added Tax (Amendment) Regulations 2015, SI 2015/1978

5.6.8.5 *Special method override*

As circumstances change, a special method agreed with HMRC will commonly no longer provide a fair and reasonable result. As a consequence, a new method is required. As agreeing this is often a fairly lengthy procedure and, in general, special methods cannot be backdated, this can lead to either HMRC or the business suffering a loss of tax.

Special rules are in place to enable either HMRC or the business to introduce an override with immediate effect which enables an unfair method to be corrected and ensure that VAT recovery properly reflects the extent to which recoverable input tax is used in making taxable supplies. This is intended to be a temporary measure until such time as a new special method is agreed.

In respect of a special method override, either HMRC or the taxable person can serve a notice on the other party specifying their reasons in support of the override.

Where a notice is served by HMRC (or served by the business with the approval of HMRC) then in relation to VAT periods commencing on or after the date of the notice, and longer periods to the extent of that part of a longer period that falls on or after the date of the notice, the taxable person must calculate the difference between the VAT recoverable using the current special method and the VAT recoverable based on use. Any difference should then be accounted for on the return for that VAT period or on the return on which the longer period of adjustment is required to be made.

This procedure will then continue until HMRC either approve a new method or direct the termination of the current special method.

HMRC should only issue or approve a notice where there is clear evidence that the current special method does not fairly and reasonably reflect the principle of use and it is clear that agreeing a replacement method will not conclude quickly.

A business can appeal to a VAT Tribunal (normally First-tier Tribunal but could be Upper Tribunal if complex) against either HMRC's decision to issue a notice or a decision not to approve a notice and also any VAT assessments made under a notice.

VAT Notice 706, para 8 and HMRC Business Brief 27/03

5.6.9. Annual adjustments

Regardless of the method used, the business is required to carry out a longer period or annual adjustment.

Where a business incurs exempt input tax during any tax year, the longer period corresponds with the tax year unless it did not incur exempt input tax during the immediately preceding tax year or during its registration period (i.e. the period commencing on the effective date of registration and ending on the day before the commencement of the first tax year). In this latter case, the longer period commences on the first day of the first VAT period in which it incurs exempt input tax and ends on the last day of the tax year, unless the only exempt input tax of the business is incurred in the last VAT period of the tax year, in which case there is no longer accounting period applied in respect of that tax year.

The tax year is the 12 months ending on 31 March, 30 April or 31 May according to the VAT periods within which VAT returns are submitted. HMRC may approve a different tax year or may direct or approve a tax year for other than 12 months.

The annual adjustment calculation follows the same methodology as the periodic calculation but uses values relevant to the whole tax year. Any difference between VAT recovery calculated on the annual adjustments and VAT recovery made on the periodic VAT returns (either an over- or under-recovery) is normally accounted for on the VAT return following the year-end although HMRC will allow the results of the annual adjustments to be declared on an early return.

VAT Notice 706, para 12

5.6.10. Change in use adjustments

As noted above, attribution of input tax is based on use or intended use of the relevant goods or services. However, occasionally that intended or actual use of the goods or services may change. Therefore, to deal with situations where the business either changes its intention before using the goods or services or actually uses the goods or services for a different purpose, there are clawback and payback provisions in place.

5.6.10.1 Clawback provisions

The clawback provisions apply where a taxable person has:

- deducted input tax as attributable to making taxable supplies because he intended to use the goods and services to make either taxable supplies or a mix of both taxable and exempt supplies; and
- during a period of six years commencing on the first day of the VAT period in which the attribution was determined and before that intention was fulfilled has used or forms an intention to use the goods or services in making exempt supplies.

In these cases, the taxable person must account for an amount equal to the input tax that ceased to be attributable to taxable supplies, in accordance with the method used at the time of the initial attribution. This is done on the VAT return for the period in which the use occurs or the revised intention is formed.

Regulation 108, Value Added Tax Regulations, 1995 SI 1995/2518 VAT Notice 706, paras 13.6 and 13.7

However, the following cases are worth noting.

In the case of *Belgium v Ghent Coal Terminal NV, Case C-37/95, [1998] STC 260*, a company purchased land, had work carried out on that land and reclaimed input tax on the supplies as it intended to use the land for taxable purposes. The local council then required the company to exchange the land for other land before the original land had been used for any taxable purpose. In this case the ECJ held that the right to deduction arose immediately the input tax was incurred and that right remained even if, by reason of circumstances beyond the taxpayer' control, the goods and services were never used to make taxable supplies.

On a slightly different point, the jointly heard cases of *C&E Commrs v Briararch Ltd and Curtis Henderson Ltd, QB [1992] STC 732* considered situations where there was an interim use different from the original intention. Both cases related to properties where the businesses had recovered input tax in full on the basis that the properties would be the subject of a taxable supply. However, because of the commercial circumstances at the time, the companies supplied the properties on short term leases, which were VAT exempt. In cases such as these, where goods and services are put to an interim use which is different to the original intention, provided the original intention is still retained, input tax must be apportioned on a fair and reasonable basis. In the case of Briararch, the company let the property on a four-year exempt lease whilst the intention to make a taxable supply of a 25 year lease remained. Therefore, the High Court ruled that 4/29 of the original claim was subject to the clawback provisions.

Also, note the Tribunal decision in *Pembridge Estates (VTD 9606)*. In this case, a company refurbished a flat with the declared intention of letting it out for holiday accommodation (taxable). It subsequently sold the flat, after two weeks of holiday letting, to one of the directors of the company for his personal use (exempt). The Tribunal found that at the time that the first supply of holiday letting was made, there was no intention by the company to sell the flat. The business was entitled to the input tax on the refurbishment in full. When the input tax was initially deducted, the business had an intention to make taxable supplies. This intention was fulfilled. The taxpayer subsequently made another supply of a different liability but since it had already fulfilled its intention, no adjustment was required.

5.6.10.2 The payback provisions

The payback provisions apply where a taxable person has:

- incurred input tax which is treated as not being attributed taxable supplies because of an intention to use the goods or services in making
- either exempt supplies or a mix of both taxable and exempt supplies; and
- during a period of six years commencing on the first day of the VAT period in which the attribution was determined and before the intention was fulfilled, the goods or services were used in making taxable supplies.

In such cases, HMRC must on application by the taxable person, repay to the taxable person an amount equal to the input tax which has become attributable to taxable supplies, subject to the method used at the time of the initial attribution.

Regulation 109, Value Added Tax Regulations, 1995 SI 1995/2518 VAT Notice

5.6.11. Other issues

5.6.11.1 Retrospection

In general terms, HMRC will not allow a method to be agreed retrospectively. However, taxpayers can request that a special method takes effect on the first day of the tax year within which the application and declaration that the methods are fair and reasonable is submitted.

5.6.11.2 Share issues and input tax recovery

In the case of *Kretztechnik AG v Finanzamt Linz, Case C-465/03, [2005] STC 1118,* the ECJ held that the issue of shares by a public limited company is not a supply for VAT purposes and that any relating input tax may be deducted subject to the taxable activity of the company.

HMRC accepted that this decision applies to companies making first issues of shares in circumstances identical to those in *Kretztechnik* and that as a consequence fully taxable companies can recover relevant input tax in full, whereas partially exempt companies can recover a proportion of the input tax subject to their partial exemption method.

HMRC have issued further guidance on the VAT treatment of share transactions in circumstances different from those in *Kretztechnik* in *Business Brief 21/05*:

> **Transactions involving issues of other types of shares**
> Businesses may issue shares of different types. For example, there may be an issue of preference shares, a special rights issue, a bonus issue or issue of scrip dividends. Kretztechnik principles are applicable to all such share issues and these are now to be regarded as non-supplies for VAT purposes.
>
> **Transactions involving issues by different types of companies**
> Kretztechnik was a public limited company but the body issuing shares could be another type of company, a private company for example. Provided that
>
> the issuer's motivation is, like Kretztechnik's, the raising of capital, issues of shares by these other types of company will also be non-supplies for VAT purposes.
>
> **Transactions involving the issue of financial instruments or securities other than shares**
> The issue of other types of security, such as bonds, debentures or loan notes, should also be treated as non-supplies when the purpose of the issue is to raise capital for the issuer's business. The Input tax consequences will be the same as for an issue of shares. Similarly, the issue of shares or units in collective investment funds such as open-ended investment companies or authorised unit trusts will not be supplies for VAT purposes.
>
> **Shares and other securities issued in other situations**
> An issue of shares or other securities may be one of several transactions that take place in the context of wider arrangements. For example, they may be issued in order to effect a company takeover or as part of a company restructuring through merger or demerger. When the issue does take place as part of such wider arrangements, it should still be regarded as a non-supply for VAT purposes.

Although the above transactions are no longer supplies for VAT purposes, related supplies (such as intermediary and underwriting services) remain VAT exempt.

5.7. Capital goods scheme

Special provisions apply to the recovery of VAT incurred on the purchase of certain capital items which were acquired or brought into use after 31 March 1990 and are not used wholly for making taxable supplies. It also applies to certain ships and aircraft obtained on after 1 January 2011. The scheme recognises that certain items of capital expenditure can be used by a business over a number of years and provides a mechanism for adjusting VAT recovery to reflect taxable use over that period.

The CGS applies to capital expenditure on land and buildings with a value of £250,000 or more (exclusive of VAT) which was subject to VAT at the standard or reduced rate. The purchases in question are:

- an interest supplied to an owner in land, a building or part of a building or a civil engineering work. Civil engineering work should be given its everyday meaning. It includes such items as roads, bridges, golf courses, running tracks and installation of pipes for connection to mains services;
- expenditure incurred in the construction of a building, part of a building or a civil engineering work;
- alterations, extensions and annexes to buildings which increase the existing floor space by 10 per cent or more (for input tax incurred on or after 1 January 2011 the CGS definition relating to expenditure in this category has been simplified by removing the floor space element of the definition);
- for input tax incurred on or after 1 January 2011, the CGS has been extended to include alterations, extensions and annexes to civil engineering works;
- capital expenditure on services, and goods affixed to the building in the course of refurbishing or fitting out a building (for input tax incurred on or after 1 January 2011 it no longer matters whether goods are affixed to a structure or not, only whether the expenditure has been capitalised); and
- for input tax incurred on or after 1 January 2011 the CGS has been extended to include refurbishments of civil engineering works.

The CGS also applies to:

- any computer with a VAT exclusive value of £50,000 or more. 'Computer' means a single item of equipment rather than a complete network. Computer software and computerised equipment, such as a computerised phone exchange or computer-controlled blast furnace, are not included.

With effect from 1 January 2011 the CGS has been extended to apply to capital expenditure on aircraft, ships, boats and other vessels with a VAT exclusive value of £50,000 or more. As well as VAT incurred in respect of the purchase of such assets, the scheme also includes VAT incurred in the course of their manufacture, refurbishment, fitting out, alteration or extension.

VAT Notice 706/2/11, para 3

5.7.1. Definition of capital expenditure

When considering whether or not expenditure constitutes capital expenditure, HMRC will normally accept the accounting treatment adopted by the business. Therefore, if the expenditure is treated as a cost used to determine the profit and loss of business, the expenditure will not be capital expenditure. However if the expenditure is added to the cost of assets for accounting purposes, it will be treated as capital expenditure. The costs relating to refurbishments, these will include all costs in making the building ready for occupation.

5.7.2. The adjustment period

Under the terms of the Capital Goods Scheme, businesses are required to adjust the level of VAT recovery over a period of time to reflect any changes in use of the item in making taxable supplies. The adjustment period is either:

- 10 successive intervals in the case of land, buildings or civil engineering works; or
- five successive intervals for computers, aircraft, ships, boats and other vessels.

With effect from 1 January 2011, where the period of time that the business has an interest in an asset is less than the normal period of adjustment under the Capital Goods Scheme, the adjustment period is aligned with the period during which the business has an interest in the asset. Where the number of intervals comprising the normal period of adjustment (five or 10 intervals) exceeds the number of complete years that the business has an interest in the asset by more than one, the period of adjustment is reduced to a number of intervals equal to the number of complete years + 1, down to a minimum of three intervals.

The period of adjustment is reduced to a number of whole years + 1 to cater for any residual interest in the item.

For example, if a business acquired a seven-year interest in a building that was subject to the Capital Goods Scheme the calculation would run as follows. The normal period of adjustment is 10 intervals. The business only has a seven-year interest in the asset. As 10 exceeds 7 by more than 1, the period of adjustment for the building is reduced to the number of complete years +1, i.e. 8 intervals.

If an interest in an asset is for a period of fewer than three intervals, it does not fall within the Capital Goods Scheme.

Generally, intervals will equate to tax years.

VAT Notice 706/2/11, para 6.3

5.7.3. First interval

In most cases, the first interval commences on the day on which the owner first uses the item and ends on the day before the start of his next tax year.

For capital items for which the period of adjustment (under the old rules) had started before 1 January 2011 the first interval is a period of time that starts on:

- the date of purchase, importation or acquisition;
- the date the owner first uses the item where the item is constructed, altered, extended, refurbished or fitted out; or
- the date of registration (or inclusion into an existing VAT group), where the owner is not a registered person when they first use the item.

With effect from 3 July 1997, if there is no change of use between the first and the second interval and the length of the two intervals combined is less than 12 months, the two intervals are rolled together and treated as the first interval.

VAT Notice 706/2/11, para 6.4 and 6.5

5.7.4. Adjustment method

Each year, the business is required to calculate the change in use (increase or decrease) of the capital item in making taxable supplies. This is calculated by applying the following formula:

$$\frac{\text{Total input tax on the capital item}}{\text{Number of intervals}} \times \text{adjustment \%}$$

With effect from 1 January 2011, total input tax on the capital item means all VAT incurred by the owner on the capital expenditure on that item including any non-business VAT and where a person is treated as making a supply to himself under *VATA 94, Sch 10, para 37(1)* (change in use of relevant residential or charitable buildings), the VAT charged on that supply.

The adjustment percentage is the difference between the recovery percentage calculated at the time the item was acquired or first used and the recovery percentage calculated in each subsequent interval.

The result of the calculation (i.e. a payment due to or due from HMRC) is accounted for in the VAT return for the VAT period immediately after the one in which the result of the partial exemption annual adjustment declared. For example, for a business with a year end of 31 March which submits quarterly returns, the partial exemption annual adjustment is accounted for in the VAT return for the quarter ending 30 June. The result of the Capital Goods Scheme adjustment is accounted for in the VAT return for the quarter ending 30 September.

5.7.5. Disposals during the adjustment period

If the capital item is sold without ever being used, HMRC do not regard it as a capital item for the purposes of the Capital Goods Scheme. However, in cases where a capital item has been used but is either sold or deemed to be supplied (e.g. by deregistration) before the last interval, and this supply is a taxable supply, the owner is treated as having used the item in each of the remaining complete intervals wholly in making taxable supplies. However, if the supply is exempt supply, the owner is deemed to be using the item in each of the remaining complete intervals in making no taxable supplies.

There is a disposal test which applies in certain circumstances. The test compares the total input tax recovered in relation to the capital item with the output tax chargeable on its disposal. The total input tax recovered is the aggregate of:

- the input tax initially recovered on the capital item;
- any adjustments already made under the Capital Goods Scheme; and
- any final adjustment that is required as a result of the sale of the item.

If the total input tax exceeds the output tax due on the disposal of the item then, in principle, HMRC may require an adjustment to the amount of input tax recovered in relation to the capital item.

The disposal test is an anti-avoidance measure designed to ensure that exempt businesses such as banks, insurance companies, educational establishments, providers of private healthcare etc. do not obtain an unjustified tax advantage by, for example, making a substantial exempt supply of a long lease of a property followed immediately by the taxable disposal of the freehold for a low consideration.

HMRC do not intend that it should be applied to normal commercial arrangements and they have stated that it will not apply in the following circumstances:

- to sales of computer equipment;
- where an owner disposes of an item at a loss due to market conditions (such as a general downturn in property prices);
- where the value of the item has depreciated;
- where the value of the item is reduced for other legitimate reasons (such as accepting a lower price to effect a quick sale);
- where the amount of output tax on disposal is less than the total input tax claimed due to a reduction in the VAT rate; and
- where the item is used only for taxable (including zero rated) purposes throughout the adjustment period (which includes the final disposal).

However, where there is an unjustified tax advantage, a business will be required to calculate the net tax advantage and then work out how much of that net tax advantage is unjustified.

VAT Notice 706/2/11, paras 11.1-11.3

5.7.6. Records

In respect of each capital item, a business is required to keep records to enable them to carry out the Capital Goods Scheme adjustment for each interval in the adjustment period. These should include:

- the description of the capital item;
- its value;
- the amount of input tax incurred on it;
- the amount of input tax reclaimed on it;
- the start and end date of each interval, including the first;
- when adjustments are due; and
- the date and value of disposal if the item is sold before the end of the adjustment period.

Although businesses are not required to keep VAT records longer than six years, because some Capital Goods Scheme adjustments will be required for up to 10 years, it is recommended that records are kept for as long as is required to carry out any adjustments.

5.8. Recovery of VAT incurred in the EU

VAT periods up to 31 December 2020 (for businesses established in the EU)

An electronic cross-border refund system is in place to enable a business that incurs VAT on expenditure in a member state where it is not established and makes no supplies, to recover that VAT directly from that member state (the member state of refund) subject to certain conditions. The previous system, known as the Eighth VAT Directive refund system, was a lengthy, burdensome, paper-based system.

The electronic system applies to all claims submitted on or after 1 January 2010.

Requests for refunds continue to be dealt with by the member state of refund. The amount refundable will also continue to be determined under the deduction rules of the member state of refund and the relevant repayment will be made directly by that member state to the business. There are specified timescales for refunds and interest payable if these are not met.

5.8.1. The Refund Scheme – general rules

Electronic claims are completed and submitted via the competent authorities in the member state in which the claimant is established.

The applicant must be a taxable person established in a member state other than the member state of refund, or an authorised agent. They must not be registered, liable or eligible to be registered in the member state from which they are claiming the refund or have any fixed establishment, seat of economic activity, place of business or other residence there.

During the refund period the applicant must not have supplied any goods or services in the member state of refund with the exception of:

(i) transport services and related ancillary; or
(ii) supplies of goods or services where VAT is payable by the person to whom the supply is made.

The member state of establishment makes certain checks before the application is forwarded electronically to the member state from which the refund is being claimed. If the member state of establishment decides not to forward the application it must notify the applicant of this decision.

A separate application must be completed for each member state. Applications can be commenced and stored in an incomplete state on the system and may be recalled and finalised to be submitted at a later date.

5.8.2. Refund periods

The refund period must not be more than one calendar year or less than three calendar months unless the period covered represents the remainder of a calendar year (e.g. where interim applications have already been submitted earlier in the year, or if the applicant has recently become VAT registered).

If the refund application relates to a period of less than a calendar year, but not less than three months the minimum amount claimable is EUR 400 or the equivalent in national currency.

If the refund application relates to a period of a calendar year or the remainder of a calendar year the minimum amount claimable is EUR 50 or the equivalent in national currency.

5.8.3. Time limits

Properly completed applications must be submitted to the member state of establishment at the latest on 30 September of the calendar year following the refund year. If a business deregisters during the refund year any application should be submitted as soon as possible following deregistration.

5.8.4. Partly exempt applicants

A restriction to the amount of VAT claimable will be applied to applicants who make taxable and exempt supplies.

5.8.5. Notification

The member state of refund must notify the applicant of the decision to approve or refuse the application within four months of the date they first received the application.

If the member state of refund requires additional information in order to process the application, it can request this from the applicant, the applicant's tax authority, or a third party before the expiry of the four month period.

The additional information must be provided by the person to whom the request is made within one month of receiving the request.

Once the member state of refund has received the additional information, it has two further months in which to notify its decision.

If further additional information is requested by the member state of refund, the final deadline for making a decision can be extended up to a maximum of eight months from the date they received the application.

Payment must be made within 10 working days following expiry of the appropriate decision deadline.

If the member state of refund refuses an application fully or partly they must also notify the applicant of the reasons for refusal.

If this happens the applicant can appeal against the decision using the appeals procedure of that member state. This means that the normal VAT appeals rules of that member state on time limits, form of appeal etc., will apply.

If the member state of refund has not notified its decision within the appropriate decision deadline the applicant should consider that the application has been rejected unless any alternative procedures apply in that member state.

Interest may be payable by the member state of refund to the applicant if payment is made after the final payment deadline set out above.

For further information see Notice 723A.

5.8.6. System for UK (and other non EU) businesses from 1 January 2021

For claims made from 1 January 2021, the EU VAT refund system is only available for businesses established in Northern Ireland or businesses that have an establishment in Northern Ireland and make supplies of goods in or from Northern Ireland or EU intra community acquisitions of goods. Please note, this is the position at the time of writing but as these arrangements fall under the contentious Northern Ireland protocol, this may change.

For other UK businesses, claims should be made via the EU Thirteenth Directive mechanism. This requires separate claims to be made from the relevant tax authority in each member state where VAT has been incurred. Full details of the process can be found on the Europa website.

6. Legislation, Case Law and Appeals

6.1. Introduction

In order to interpret how VAT applies to their activities, businesses will need to be aware of the relevant legislation, which includes both domestic UK provisions and EU law which even post Brexit has an effect and ongoing influence on UK legislation (see *6.3* below).

The legislation consists of various Directives, Acts, and Statutory Instruments (SIs). In addition, there are various publications, Public Notices and Leaflets issued by HMRC, some of which have the force of law (for example, *sections 8 to 13 of Notice 709/05/09, The Tour Operators Margin Scheme*). HMRC also publish regular Business Briefs which generally comment on and provide HMRC's interpretation of legislative changes, often as a result of case law.

In addition to legislation, there is an ever increasing raft of case law, both European and domestic, which can assist in the interpretation of the legislation (and somewhat cynically, maybe on occasions confuse!).

6.2. EU legislation

EU legislation is based on a graded set of Regulations, Directives, Decisions and Recommendations and Opinions.

These are described and defined in *Article 288 of the Treaty of the Functioning of the European Union.*

> **Article 288**
> To exercise the Union's competences, the institutions shall adopt regulations, directives, decisions, recommendations and opinions.
>
> **A regulation** shall have general application. It shall be binding in its entirety and directly applicable in all member states.
>
> **A directive** shall be binding, as to the result to be achieved, upon each member state to which it is addressed, but shall leave to the national authorities the choice of form and methods.
>
> **A decision** shall be binding in its entirety upon those to whom it is addressed.
>
> **Recommendations and opinions** shall have no binding force. (my emphasis)

6.3. Primacy of EU Directives over national legislation and European Union (Withdrawal) Act 2018

The overriding law on VAT throughout the EU is found in various EU Directives. The main Directive affecting VAT is now *Directive 2006/112/EC*, often referred to as the Principal VAT Directive, which replaced the *Sixth VAT Directive 77/388/EEC*.

Until 31 December 2020, the *Principal VAT Directive 2006/112* was the ultimate source of UK VAT legislation. Since 1 January 2021, when the UK's withdrawal from the EU was completed, this has now changed. EU legislation is no longer primary but many of the Principal Directives propositions remain as they were effectively transferred into UK legislation by way of the *European Union (Withdrawal)Act 2018*. In effect this mean that any right or obligation which was in place on 31 December 2020 and was recognized by the Court of Justice or by the UK tribunal or courts in litigation commenced before 31 December 2020, continued in UK law from 1 January 2021. I guess what this means in practice will only develop over time but a knowledge of EU legislation and case law will remain essential in understanding and applying UK VAT.

Whilst compliance issues are generally left to the member states, where any provisions are mandatory, EU law can take precedence over domestic legislation. One example of this having an effect in the UK can be found in the case of *EC Commission v United Kingdom, Case C-416/85, [1988] STC 456*, where the ECJ ruled that the UK had contravened the provisions of the Sixth VAT Directive by zero rating certain supplies of sewerage and water, news services, supplies of fuel and power and the construction of commercial buildings. The European Commission also took action against the UK (and some other member states) because the UK allows 'non-taxable persons' to be included in VAT groups (e.g. holding companies that do not make management charges to their subsidiaries or indeed make any other type of supply). The UK's failure to amend its legislation in the light of an Opinion from the European Commission led to a referral to the ECJ. However, in this case, the ECJ ultimately ruled in favour of the UK (*ECJ Case C-86/11*).

If the UK VAT legislation is unclear or ambiguous on any point, a VAT Tribunal is entitled to refer to the EU Directives to resolve any ambiguity (see *English-Speaking Union of the Commonwealth (VTD 1023)*).

Where a member state has failed to implement a Directive or its national law is contrary to EU law, that member state may be liable to pay damages to any individuals affected by that failure (*Francovich v Italian State, Case C-6/90, [1991] 1 ECR 5357; [1993] 2 CMLR 66*).

6.4. UK legislation

VAT was introduced into UK on 1 April 1973, and VAT was introduced into UK legislation in the *Finance Act 1972*. The UK. VAT legislation was consolidated in the *Value Added Tax Act 1983* and subsequently in the *Value Added Tax Act 1994 (VATA 94)*. The VATA 94 has been amended by subsequent Finance Acts.

Whilst VATA 94 provides the framework for how VAT operates in the UK, much of the detail is found in Statutory Instruments (SIs) which come in the form of Orders made by the Treasury or Regulations made by HMRC. SIs can both create new law and amend existing law. The main VAT regulations made by HMRC can be found in the *Value Added Tax Regulations 1995 (SI 1995/2518)*.

HMRC publish VAT Notices and Leaflets along with VAT Information Sheets, VAT Notes and Business Briefs which explain how they interpret and apply the legislation. Other than in certain exceptional circumstances (and this is indicated in the relevant text) Notices and Leaflets do not have the force of law. The fact that these publications are simply HMRC's interpretation of the law should always be borne in mind when reading them and indeed when reading those parts of this publication that are referenced to HMRC publications.

6.5. Appeals

If a business disagrees with HMRC's interpretation of the law it will generally have the right of appeal to a Tribunal, normally the First-tier Tribunal (Tax Chamber).

The First-tier Tribunal deals with the majority of appeals (although a small number of the most complex appeals may be transferred immediately to the Upper Tribunal). Decisions of the First-tier Tribunal (other than excluded decisions) can be appealed to the Upper Tribunal on a point of law. So most of the Upper Tribunal's time is spent dealing with appeals against decisions of the First-tier Tribunal.

In England and Wales, either party can appeal a decision of the Upper Tribunal with leave, to the Court of Appeal and the Supreme Court. In Scotland, appeals go to the Court of Session and, with leave, directly to the Supreme Court. A Tribunal or Court can also refer a question to the ECJ.

Further information on the operations of both the First-tier and Upper Tribunals can be found in *Tribunal Procedure (First-tier Tribunal) (Tax Chamber) Rules 2009 (SI 2009/273)* and *Tribunal Procedure (Upper Tribunal) Rules 2008 (SI 2008/2698).*

6.6. Legislation relevant to the financial services and insurance sectors

The following are the main legislative references relating to the topics in this publication are:

6.6.1. Directive 2006/112/EC

- Exemptions for financial and insurance transactions – *article 135*
- supply of services – *articles 24 to 29*
- place of supply of services – *articles 43 to 59*
- right to deduct VAT (recovery of input tax) – *articles 167 to 192*
- special scheme for investment gold – *articles 344 to 356*

6.6.2. VATA 94 and SIs

- Exemptions for financial and insurance transactions – *VATA 94, Sch 9, Groups 2 and 5*
- supply of services – *VATA 94, s 5(2)(b)*
- place of supply of services – *VATA 94, s7A; Sch 4A; Finance Act 2009, Sch 36*
- right to deduct VAT (recovery of input tax) – *VATA 94, s24(1); s26; SI 1995/2518, Regs 101 to 111*
- special scheme for investment gold – *SI 1973/173, arts 4-7 and SI 1999/3117*

7. VAT supply and liabilities

7.1. Meaning of supply

VAT is a tax on transactions. In order for UK VAT to apply there needs to be a supply of goods or services, made in the UK, by a taxable person, in the course of furtherance of any business carried on by the taxable person. (*VATA 94, s4*).

In order for there to be a supply for VAT purposes, there needs to be consideration for that supply. There are some exceptions where even in the absence of consideration there is a deemed supply for VAT purposes (e.g. some gifts of goods, use of assets for non-business purposes and self supply of goods or services). So, unless these exceptions apply, where there is no consideration for the supply, there is no supply for VAT purposes.

In addition, there are specific exclusions in the VAT legislation for business gifts costing £50 or less (or a series of gifts to the same person in one year not exceeding in total £50), samples and some transactions specifically deemed to be neither a supply of goods nor services (see **7.4** below).

UK VAT legislation does not specifically define 'supply' other than to say that 'supply' includes all forms of supply but not anything done otherwise than for a consideration and that anything done for consideration that is not a supply of goods, is a supply of services (*s5*).

What constitutes a supply of goods is given wide interpretation. For example, in the case of *C&E Commrs v Oliver, QB 1979, [1990] STC 73*, which involved the sale at auction of stolen cars, it was held that the transaction at the auction was still a supply within the meaning of the VAT Act. As a result, VAT was due on the sale proceeds. Supply was defined as meaning the

> passing [of] the possession in goods pursuant to an agreement whereunder the supplier agreed to part and the recipient agreed to take possession, and 'possession' in that context meant the control over the goods in the sense of having the immediate facility for their use.

As illustrated by Oliver, a transaction may still constitute a supply despite the fact that it is carried out unlawfully. For other examples, see Criminal proceedings against *Goodwin, Case C-3/97 [1998] STC 699*, (concerning sale of counterfeit perfume infringing third party's rights); *Fischer v Finanzamt Donaueschingen Case C-283/95 [1998] STC 708*, (lawful game of chance carried out unlawfully); *R v Citrone [1999] STC 29*, (anabolic steroids supplied without a licence); *Staatssecretaris van Financiën v Coffeeshop*

"Siberië" vof (Case C-158/98) [1999] STC 742, (space in cafe for sale of narcotic drugs); *C & E Comrs v Polok [2002] EWHC 156(Ch), [2002] STC 361* (supplies by an escort agency).

However, no supply takes place if the subject matter of the supply itself is unlawful (e.g. is harmful in itself or cannot be lawfully traded). For example, see *Vereniging Happy Family Rustenburgerstraat v Inspecteur der Omzetbelasting Case 289/86), Mol v Inspecteur der Invoerrechten en Accijnzen Case 269/86[1989] 3 CMLR 729,* (drugs); *Witzemann v Hauptzollamt-München-Mitte Case C-343/89 [1994] STC 108,* (importation of counterfeit currency).

Another key case in helping define the meaning of supply is *Tolsma v Inspecteur der Omzetbelasting Leeuwarden, Case C–16/93, [1994] STC 509.* Mr Tolsma played a barrel organ on the public highway in the Netherlands. During performances he solicited donations from passers-by by rattling a collection tin and occasionally by knocking on the doors of houses and shops adjacent to where he performed. The tax authorities in the Netherlands assessed Mr Tolsma for VAT on the basis that there was a direct link between the service he provided and the sums of money he received. Mr Tolsma challenged the assessment on the basis he was not providing a service for consideration as there was no agreement between the parties – the donations were voluntary and the passers-by were not requesting that music was played to them. The Dutch court referred two questions to the ECJ. The questions were whether the service of playing music on the public highway without stipulating that it was for payment but nevertheless receiving payment should be regarded as a supply of services effected for consideration; and, whether it was relevant that the payments were solicited and might, in view of customary usage, be expected even though their amounts were neither quantified nor quantifiable.

The ECJ held that a supply of services was effected 'for consideration' (and therefore was taxable) only if there was a legal relationship between the provider of the service and the recipient with the remuneration received by the provider of the service constituting the value actually given in return for the service supplied to the recipient. There was no such agreement between the parties and no link between the musical service and the payment in the case of Mr Tolsma.

7.2. Supply of goods

The Treasury can by order determine whether the transaction is treated as a supply of goods or supply of services or as neither a supply of goods nor supply of services. *VATA 94, Sch 4* specifies transactions to be treated as supply of goods or services. The following are treated as supplies of goods:

- any transfer of the whole property in goods;
- the transfer in possession of goods under an agreement for the sale of the goods or under agreements which expressly contemplate that the property in the goods will pass at sometime in the future (determined by, or ascertainable from, the agreements but in any case not later than when the goods are fully paid for);
- the supply of any form of power, heat, refrigeration or ventilation;
- the grant, assignment or surrender of a major interest in land;
- the disposal of business assets so that they no longer business assets;
- the transfer of own goods between EU member states;
- goods sold in satisfaction of a debt; and
- a deemed supply of assets on deregistration.

7.3. Supply of services

Under UK legislation, anything done for a consideration which is not a supply of goods is a supply of services.

VATA 94 Sch 4 states that the transfer of any undivided share of the property in goods or of the possession of goods is a supply of services.

The undivided share of property in goods refers to situations where title to goods is shared. If all shares in goods are simultaneously sold to the same person there will be a supply of goods. However, where only a part share is sold there will be no transfer of title in the goods to the new owner. Therefore, this is a supply of services. An example of this is sale of a share in a racehorse.

There is, however, an exception applying to certain goods relieved from VAT under the fiscal warehousing rules. Transfers of undivided shares in these cases remain supplies of goods.

The transfer of the possession of goods refers to situations where title to the goods does not change hands, e.g. the lease or rental of goods.

7.4. Supply of neither goods nor services

The following transactions are treated as neither a supply of goods nor a supply of services:

- the transfer of a business as a going concern;
- the sale of repossessed goods;
- the assignment of rights under a hire-purchase or conditional sale agreement by the owner to a bank or financial institution;

- supplies between members of a VAT group or by divisions of the same corporate body; and
- supplies by pawnbrokers.

7.4.1. The transfer of a business as a going concern

To be treated as a transfer of a business as a going concern (or TOGC) certain conditions need to be met and it should also be noted that these provisions are obligatory (i.e. if the conditions are met, the sale of the business must be treated as neither supply of goods nor supply of services and therefore not a supply for VAT purposes).

The conditions for a transfer to be treated as neither supply of goods nor services are as follows:

1. The effect of the transfer must be to put the purchaser (or transferee) in possession of a business which can be operated as such (whether or not as part of any existing business).
2. The business, or part of business, transferred must be a 'going concern' at the time of time transfer.
3. Where the transfer relates to part of the business, that part must be capable of separate operation.
4. The assets must be used by the transferee in carrying on the same kind of business (whether or not as part of an existing business) as that carried on by the seller (or transferor) in relation to the whole or part transferred. If the transferee uses the assets to carry on a different kind of business, VAT must be charged.
5. There must not be a series of immediately consecutive transfers business. For example, if A sells its assets to B who then immediately sells those assets on to C, B has not carried on the business so the TOGC provisions do not apply in this case.
6. Where the transferor is a taxable person (i.e. VAT registered or registrable) the transferee must already be a taxable person or immediately become a taxable person as a result of the transfer.
7. There must be no significant break in the normal trading pattern before or immediately after the transfer. However, any break in trade must be considered in the context of the type of business concerned (e.g. if the business is seasonal).

Where, as is common, the transfer involves land and buildings there are additional conditions to be met.

Where the transfer involves the following assets:

- a grant of land or buildings which would be exempt from VAT but where the transferor has opted to tax; or

- a grant of the fee simple in a new or uncompleted building which would be liable to VAT at the standard rate,

the transaction will not be deemed a TOGC unless the following conditions are met no later than the 'relevant date'. The 'relevant date' is the date upon which the grant would have been treated as having been made or, if there is more than one such date, the earliest of them. The conditions are that:

- the transferee must have opted to tax the land and buildings concerned and provided written notification to HMRC; or
- the transferee must have notified the transferor that the option to tax will not be disapplied by virtue of the anti-avoidance rules in *VATA 94, Sch 10, para 12*.

As it is the responsibility of the transferor to apply the correct VAT treatment, it is generally advisable for the transferor to ask the transferee to provide written evidence of his option to tax (e.g. a copy of the notification letter to HMRC) and confirmation that the option to tax will not be disapplied before the relevant date.

VAT Notice 700/9/08

Value Added Tax (Special Provisions) Order 1995, article 5

7.5. Place of supply

Establishing the place of supply is key to determining whether or not that supply is liable to VAT in the UK or indeed liable to VAT elsewhere. There are different place of supply rules for goods and services and these are outlined below. As the transactions involved in financial services and insurance are generally supplies of services rather than goods, the rules relating to the place of supply of goods are not set out in detail. More emphasis is placed on the rules relating to the place of supply of services particularly with regard to the changes that took place from 1 January 2010.

7.5.1. Place of supply of goods

The rules relating to the place of supply of goods are outlined in *VATA 94, s7*. As a general rule, providing the supply of goods does not involve the removal from or to the UK, they are treated as being supplied in the UK if the goods are located in the UK and treated as supplied outside the UK in all other cases. Where goods are located outside the UK at the time they are supplied, they may well be liable to VAT in the country of their location or the country to which they are removed, if this is relevant.

New rules regarding importations of goods were introduced from 1 January 2021, coinciding with the UK's withdrawal from the EU (although these rules are largely mirrored in the EU). The changes also created a special status for Northern Ireland which effectively keeps them within the single market. However, the arrangements affecting Northern Ireland are politically contentious so may well change by the time this edition is published.

Broadly, any goods valued at £135 sold from outside the UK directly to customers in Great Britain and not sold via an online marketplace are liable to UK VAT at the point of sale, so in effect treated as a domestic sale. For Northern Ireland these goods will be liable to import VAT if they are sold directly from outside the UK and EU. For supplies to GB customers, if the customer has a UK VAT number, they will use this to account for the VAT, otherwise the seller is likely to have a liability to register in the UK. For sales above £135, normal importation rules apply and import VAT will be due. HMRC have introduced a postponed accounting system to eable import VAT to be declared and recovered on the same VAT return.

Goods are also treated as supplied in the UK if the supply involves their installation or assembly at a place in the UK. However, there is a concession that in certain circumstances allows for one-off supplies of imported goods installed or assembled in the UK that would normally be deemed to be supplied in UK to be deemed to be supplied outside the UK (see *Business Brief 1/98* for further details).

7.5.2. Place of supply of services

Significant changes took place to the rules affecting the place of supply of services on 1 January 2010 as part of the VAT Package of legislation adopted in 2008. The 1 January 2010 changes introduced a new 'general rule' for the place of supply of services for business to business (B2B) and business to consumer (B2C) transactions.

The new general rule for the place of supply of B2B services is the place where the customer is established and no longer the place where the supplier is established.

For B2C transactions the general rule for the place of supply continues to be the place where the supplier is established.

There are exceptions to the general rule for certain services where the aim is to achieve taxation in the place of consumption.

7.5.2.1 Place of supply of services before 1 January 2010

Under the old rules, the general rule was that services were supplied where the supplier belonged. This was subject to a number of exceptions:

- supplies of services relating to land were deemed take place where the land was situated;
- a number of services were deemed to take place where they were physically carried out (regardless of where the customer belongs). These services included cultural, artistic, sporting, scientific, educational or entertainment services and any ancillary services; services relating to exhibitions, conferences or meetings and any ancillary services; valuation of, or work carried out on, any goods; ancillary transport services;
- services falling within *VATA 94, Sch 5, paras 1-8*. These services included services of consultants, engineers, lawyers, accountants etc.; advertising services; transfers and assignments of copyrights, patents, licenses etc.; banking, financial and insurance services; supply staff; the letting on hire of goods of the means of transport; telecommunications, broadcasting and electronically supplied services. These services were deemed to take place where the recipient belonged (or 'supplied where received');
- transport services which were effectively deemed to be supplied in the country in which the transportation took place (and only to the extent that the transportation took place in that country). Special rules applied for intra-EU freight transport services, where transport services were treated as supplied in the EU country in which transportation began and ancillary freight transport services treated as made where physically performed;
- the hiring of means of transport took place where the supplier belonged with the exception that if the supplier belonged in the UK but the effective use and enjoyment of the letting on hire took place outside the EU, the place of supply was deemed to be outside the UK (and indeed the EU); if the supplier belonged outside the EU but the effective use and enjoyment of the letting on hire took place in the UK, the place of supply would be the UK; and
- certain intermediary services (e.g. estate agents arranging supplies of land or property, agents arranging for a supply of intra-EU freight transport and making arrangements for any of the supplies within *VATA 94, Sch 5,.paras 1-8*) would have the same place of supply as the supply being arranged except that where the intermediary services were supplied to a customer registered for VAT in an EU country other than that in which the service would otherwise be treated as supplied and who provided the supplier with a valid VAT registration number, the place of supply would be the country in which the customer was registered.

7.5.2.2 *Place of supply of services from 1 January 2010*

New general rules for the place of supply of services came into effect from 1 January 2010. For business to business (B2B) supplies of services, the place of supply is where the customer is established. For business to consumer (B2C) supplies of services, the general rule remains the place where the supplier is established.

With effect from 1 January 2011, supplies of cultural, artistic, sporting, scientific, educational, entertainment and similar services are also deemed to be supplied where the customer is established. However, supplies of admission to cultural, artistic, sporting, scientific, educational and entertainment events retain the previous treatment of being supplied where performed. The EU are introducing changes to the Principal VAT Directive which will exclude admissions to 'virtual' events from the 'supplied where performed' rule. EU members have until 31 December 2024 to introduce this change.

With regard to hire of means of transport, with effect from 1 January 2010, there is a distinction between short term hire (no more than 30 days or 90 days for vessels) and long term hire. For short term hire, place of supply is where the vehicle is put at the disposal of the customer. For long term hire (B2B) the place of supply falls under the new general rule. From 1 January 2013, the place of supply of long term hire for B2C supplies will be where the customer is established, with the exception of long term hire of pleasure boats which will be deemed to be supplied where the boat is put at the customer's disposal provided the supplier has an establishment there.

With effect from 1 January 2015, the place of supply of Broadcasting, Telecommunication and Electronic (BTE) services to private consumers located outside the UK moves to where the supply is effectively consumed (in most cases where the consumer is resident). This covers sales of electronic books, computer apps and other similar services supplied direct to consumers with the result that these supplies are subject to VAT at the rate applicable in the consumer's member state. Where the consumer in located in the EU, a UK supplier has the option of registering in each relevant member state or using a simplification (now known as the Non Union Mini One Stop Shop or MOSS in an EU member state) to report all VAT.

For land-related services, the place of supply remains unchanged as being where the land is situated.

VAT Notice 741A para 2.4.3

7.5.3. Place of belonging and establishment

The concept of place of belonging is important in determining where VAT may be due. The rules are outlined in *VATA 94, s9* as amended by *FA 2009, Sch 36.*

A 'relevant business person' belongs in the 'relevant country'. The relevant country means:

- if the person has a business establishment or some other fixed establishment in only one country, that country; or
- if the person has a business establishment or some other fixed establishment in more than one country, the country in which the relevant establishment is, otherwise, in the person's usual place of residence.

'Relevant establishment' means whichever of the person's business establishments or other fixed establishments, is the one most directly concerned with the supply.

Where a person is not a 'relevant business person', they are deemed to belong in the country of their 'usual place of residence'. A body corporate has its usual place of residence where it is legally constituted. Whilst the usual place of residence of individuals is not defined in the legislation, HMRC regard this as meaning the place where they have set up home with their family and/or are in full-time employment.

The legislation does not define business establishment, but HMRC will take this to mean the principal place of business, normally the office or place from which the business is run. Similarly, fixed establishment is not defined in legislation but HMRC take this to mean an establishment (other than the business establishment) which has both the technical and human resources necessary for providing and receiving services on a permanent basis. Hence, whilst there can only be one business establishment, a business may have several fixed establishments.

Where a business has more than one establishment, the supplies made from or received at each establishment are considered separately. For a supply of services, the business is regarded as belonging in the country where the establishment most directly connected with the particular supply is located. In order to decide which establishment is most directly connected with the supply all relevant facts should be considered. For example, consideration should be given to the establishment from which the services are supplied, the establishment which appears on invoices or is named in contracts, or the location where decision-makers are based and for receipt of services, the establishment which consumes, effectively uses or enjoys the services.

VAT Notice 741A, paras 3.3 to 3.6

7.6. Time of supply

The time of supply (or tax point) determines when VAT becomes due on the supply of goods or services. VAT is then normally accounted for on the return for the period within which the tax point falls. HMRC do have power to alter the tax point, at the request of taxpayer, and these are known as 'accommodation' tax points.

7.6.1. Time of supply of goods

With regard to supplies of goods, subject to any accommodation tax points or other rules applying to specific services, the time of supply is either at the basic or actual tax point. The basic tax point occurs when goods are removed (delivered or collected) or made available to the customer. An actual tax point occurs either at the time of payment or invoicing if this takes place before the basic tax point, or at the date of invoice provided the invoice is issued within 14 days of the basic tax point. The taxable person may request an extension to the 14 day rule and a number of extensions have been agreed centrally (e.g. all government contracts, local authorities and businesses within the scrap metal industry).

7.6.2. Time of supply of services

With regard to supplies of services, again subject to any accommodation tax points, the time of supply is at either the basic or actual tax point. The basic tax point for services is the time that the services are performed (usually taken to be the date when all work has been completed). The actual tax point occurs either at the time of payment or invoicing if this takes place before the basic tax point, or the date of invoice, provided the invoice is issued within 14 days of the basic tax point. Again as with supplies of goods, the taxable person may request an extension to the 14 day rule.

7.6.3. Time of supply for continuous supplies of services

With regard to continuous supplies of services, subject to special provisions on advance invoicing, where the services are supplied in any period for consideration the whole or part of which is determined payable periodically, the services are treated as separately and successively supplied each time payment is received or a VAT invoice issued, whichever is the earlier.

Where continuous supplies of services are provided for periods of up to one year, the supplier can issue an advance invoice specifying the dates that the successive payments become due and these services are then treated as separately and successively supplied each time payment becomes due or is received, whichever is the earlier.

The provisions relating to continuous supplies of services have in the past enabled some suppliers to delay, potentially indefinitely, the time at which they have to account for VAT. To prevent this, anti-avoidance provisions were introduced which apply periodic tax points (normally annual) for certain supplies between connected persons where the recipient of the supply is unable to recover all the VAT on the supply. (*Value Added Tax Regulations 1995/2518, reg 94B*)

7.6.4. Time of supply for exempt supplies

The time of supply for exempt supplies is determined using the normal tax point rules outlined above. However, because you cannot issue a valid VAT invoice for exempt supplies, the references to invoice date have no effect. Consequently, the time of supply for an exempt supply will be the earlier of receipt of payment or performance of the service.

The time of supply for an exempt supply is important in determining when supplies are made for the purposes of a business's partial exemption calculation etc.

7.6.5. Single and multiple supplies

One of the most difficult areas in VAT is establishing the correct VAT treatment of transactions which involve separately identifiable goods or services, in particular where those goods or services have different VAT liabilities (e.g. standard rated training services supplied with zero rated books or standard rated car hire supplied with exempt insurance). The question is whether these elements should be taxed separately or whether in reality there is a single supply.

There is very little assistance on this matter within either UK or EU legislation and guidance has been developed on the back of case law. The key case that provides guidance on this matter is the case of *Card Protection Plan Ltd v C&E Commrs, Case C-349/96, [1999] STC 270*. Card Protection Plan (CPP) provided an assistance package to customers in case of the loss of personal items – mainly credit cards, but also including keys, passports or insurance documents. They also provided an insurance-backed indemnity for fraudulent use of the cards and other forms of assistance, such as medical, where the loss occurred away from the customer's home. The insurance provider was the Continental Assurance Company.

The question was about whether this was a single or multiple supply and whether the package was an exempt supply of insurance or a taxable supply of card registration services – the customers would be paying for someone else to cancel their cards/order new cards etc.

With regards to the single and multiple supply issue, the House of Lords referred the following questions to the ECJ:

> (1) Having regard to the provisions of the Sixth Directive and in particular to art 2(1) thereof, what is the proper test to be applied in deciding whether a transaction consists for VAT purposes of a single composite supply or of two or more independent supplies?
>
> (2) Does the supply by an undertaking of a service or services of the kind provided by CPP through the card protection plan operated by them constitute for VAT purposes a single composite supply or two or more independent supplies? Are there any particular features of the present case, such as the payment of a single price by the customer or the involvement of Continental as well as CPP, that affect the answer to that question?

It is worth reproducing the ECJ's answers to these questions in full:

> 26. By its first two questions, which should be taken together, the national court essentially asks, with reference to a plan such as that offered by CPP to its customers, what the appropriate criteria are for deciding, for VAT purposes, whether a transaction which comprises several elements is to be regarded as a single supply or as two or more distinct supplies to be assessed separately.
>
> 27. It must be borne in mind that the question of the extent of a transaction is of particular importance, for VAT purposes, both for identifying the place where the services are provided and for applying the rate of tax or, as in the present case, the exemption provisions in the Sixth Directive. In addition, having regard to the diversity of commercial operations, it is not possible to give exhaustive guidance on how to approach the problem correctly in all cases.
>
> 28. However, as the court held in *Faaborg-Gelting Linien A/S v Finanzamt Flensburg (Case C-231/94) [1996] STC 774 at 783, [1996] ECR I-2395 at 2411– 2412, paras 12 to 14*, concerning the classification of restaurant transactions, where the transaction in question comprises a bundle of features and acts, regard must first be had to all the circumstances in which that transaction takes place.
>
> 29. In this respect, taking into account, first, that it follows from art 2(1) of the Sixth Directive that every supply of a service must normally be regarded as distinct and independent and, second, that a supply which comprises a single service from an economic point of view should not be

artificially split, so as not to distort the functioning of the VAT system, the essential features of the transaction must be ascertained in order to determine whether the taxable person is supplying the customer, being a typical consumer, with several distinct principal services or with a single service.

30. There is a single supply in particular in cases where one or more elements are to be regarded as constituting the principal service, whilst one or more elements are to be regarded, by contrast, as ancillary services which share the tax treatment of the principal service. A service must be regarded as ancillary to a principal service if it does not constitute for customers an aim in itself, but a means of better enjoying the principal service supplied (see *Customs and Excise Comrs v Madgett and Baldwin (trading as Howden Court Hotel) (Joined cases C-308/96 and C-94/97) [1998] STC 1189 at 1206, para 24*).
31. In those circumstances, the fact that a single price is charged is not decisive. Admittedly, if the service provided to customers consists of several elements for a single price, the single price may suggest that there is a single service. However, notwithstanding the single price, if circumstances such as those described in paras 7 to 10 above indicated that the customers intended to purchase two distinct services, namely an insurance supply and a card registration service, then it would be necessary to identify the part of the single price which related to the insurance supply, which would remain exempt in any event. The simplest possible method of calculation or assessment should be used for this (see, to that effect, *Madgett and Baldwin (at 1208, paras 45 and 46)*).
32. The answer to the first two questions must therefore be that it is for the national court to determine, in the light of the above criteria, whether transactions such as those performed by CPP are to be regarded for VAT purposes as comprising two independent supplies, namely an exempt insurance supply and a taxable card registration service, or whether one of those two supplies is the principal supply to which the other is ancillary, so that it receives the same tax treatment as the principal supply.

It is important to note the comment in paragraph 27 that 'it is not possible to give exhaustive guidance on how to approach the problem correctly in all cases'. So, although the CPP decision provides more certainty in many cases, it is not a universal solution and problem cases can and do still arise. Very often determining whether a transaction is a single or multiple supply will be a matter of impression and it is not unusual for HMRC and the tax payer to arrive at different conclusions looking at the same facts.

The following post-CPP cases are of interest:

Cases where a single supply was found:

- *Levob Verzekeringen BV, OB Bank NV and Others, ECJ Case C-41/04*

- *Peugeot Motor Co plc and Another v C & E Commrs, Ch D [2003] STC 1438*
- *Manchester United plc (VTD 17234)*
- *Tumble Tots (UK) Ltd v HMRC, Ch D [2007] STC 1171*
- *HMRC v Weight Watchers UK Ltd, CA [2008] STC 2313*
- *HMRC v David Baxendale Ltd, CA [2009] EWCA Civ 831*
- *Purple Parking Ltd, Airparks Services Ltd, ECJ Case C-117/11*
- *The Honourable Society of Middle Temple [2013] UKUT 0250 (TC)*

Cases where a multiple supply was found:

- *Sea Containers Services Ltd v C & E Commrs, QB 1999, [2000] STC 82*
- *Telewest Communications plc v C & E Commrs; Telewest Communications (Publications) Ltd v C & E Commrs, CA [2005] STC 481*
- *Cairngorm Mountain (VTD 17679)*
- *Dr Beynon & Partners v C & E Commrs, HL 2004, [2005] STC 55*
- *Church of Scientology Religious Education College Inc [2014] UKFTT 1064 (TC)*

Where a single supply is established, the whole supply will be liable to VAT at the same rate – generally by reference to the liability of the predominant element.

Where a multiple supply is established, where all elements have the same VAT liability, there is no issue. However, where different liabilities apply, an apportionment is required and each part taxed accordingly.

7.7. Taxable supplies

Taxable supplies are supplies made in the UK that are liable to VAT at the standard rate, the reduced rate or the zero rate. There is no list of standard rated supplies and VAT works on the basis that all supplies are liable to VAT at the standard rate unless they are specifically exempted, zero-rated or taxable at the reduced rate.

The current standard rate (effective from 4 January 2011) is 20%. The current reduced rate (effective from 1 September 1997) is 5%.

The full list of supplies liable to tax at the reduced rate can be found in

VATA 94, Sch 7A.

The full list of supplies liable to tax at the zero rate can be found in VATA 94, Sch 8 and includes the issue by a bank of note payable to bearer on demand (i.e. English, Scottish and Northern Irish banknotes). *VATA94, Sch 8 Group 11.*

As standard rated, reduced rate and zero-rated supplies are all taxable, related input tax can be recovered in full (see **Chapter 5**).

7.8. Exempt supplies

Exempt supplies are supplies whose place of supply is within the UK but are exempt from VAT. The full list of exempt supplies is found in *VATA 94, Sch 9* and include supplies of financial services, insurance, land, education and health and welfare.

As exempt supplies are not taxable, related input tax cannot be recovered (see **Chapter 5**).

The value of exempt supplies made does not count towards the threshold for VAT registration. Only the value of taxable supplies needs to be considered when establishing whether VAT registration is compulsory.

7.9. Outside the scope supplies

Supplies may be outside the scope of UK VAT either because they are deemed as such (e.g. non business supplies, donations and statutory fees, such as MOTs and tolls) or because the place of supply rules places the supply outside the UK (e.g. a supply of land situated overseas or insurance where the policyholder is resident overseas). In the latter cases, subject to the type of supply, VAT may need to be accounted for to the overseas tax authority (but see **7.10** below).

With regard to outside the scope supplies made within the UK, no input tax recovery is available. With regard to outside the scope supplies made outside the UK, the recovery of input tax incurred within the UK will be available in the following circumstances:

- where the supply would have been a taxable supply if it was made in the UK; or
- where it is a supply of services which is
  (a) supplied to a person belonging outside the UK (EU prior to 1 January 2021); or
  (b) directly linked to the export of goods to a place outside the UK (EU prior to 1 January 2021); or
  (c) consists of the provision of intermediary services in relation to any transaction within (a) or (b),

provided that the supply is exempt (or would have been exempt if made in the UK) under *VATA 94, Sch 2 or Sch 5* (i.e. as an insurance or finance transaction).

For further details on input tax recovery see **Chapter 5**.

VATA 94, s26 and Value Added Tax (Input Tax) (Specified Supplies) Order 1999 (SI 1999/3121)

7.10. Reverse charge

As noted above, it is quite common for UK businesses to make supplies whose place of supply is outside the UK; similarly many non-UK businesses will be making supplies where the place of supply rules places them in the UK. Normally, it is the supplier of the service who is the person that must account for the VAT. Where that person is not resident in the place of supply, that creates an obvious problem. Either that person would need to register for VAT in all those countries in which he makes supplies or there would be a loss of tax revenue. In order to manage this issue the UK, along with other EU member states and indeed many other countries around the world with VAT systems, have introduced an arrangement whereby it is the customer that must account for any VAT due. This is known as the reverse charge procedure.

The reverse charge applies to virtually all business to business (B2B) supplies except those which fall within the exemption schedule (*VATA 94, Sch 9*). So, as an example, if a UK bank buys in legal services from France they are required to self assess VAT on the full value of the supply received. This VAT is accounted for as output tax.

However, as the supply is also an expense, the self-assessed VAT is also input tax and can be recovered subject to the normal rules. Therefore, for a bank, insurance company or any other partially exempt company there is a cost in acquiring the service from overseas, effectively equivalent to acquiring the same service in the UK.

The value of reverse charge services received from abroad counts towards taxable turnover when determining whether or not VAT registration is compulsory. This has been an issue for businesses such as smaller insurance brokers who only make exempt supplies in the UK (e.g. when they only arrange motor insurance) but acquire services from abroad, through the internet for example, and may not realise that payments made to the overseas supplier may make them liable to register for VAT.

Appendix A – Contracts of Insurance

Extract from the Financial Services and Markets Act 2000 (Regulated Activities) Order 2001

PART I - CONTRACTS OF GENERAL INSURANCE

Accident

1. Contracts of insurance providing fixed pecuniary benefits or benefits in the nature of indemnity (or a combination of both) against risks of the person insured or, in the case of a contract made by virtue of section 140, 140A or 140B of the Local Government Act 1972(a) (or, in Scotland, section 86(1) of the Local Government (Scotland) Act 1973(b)), a person for whose benefit the contract is made—
   (a) sustaining injury as the result of an accident or of an accident of a specified class; or
   (b) dying as a result of an accident or of an accident of a specified class; or
   (c) becoming incapacitated in consequence of disease or of disease of a specified class,

including contracts relating to industrial injury and occupational disease but excluding contracts falling within paragraph 2 of Part I of, or paragraph IV of Part II of, this Schedule.

Sickness

2. Contracts of insurance providing fixed pecuniary benefits or benefits in the nature of indemnity (or a combination of both) against risks of loss to the persons insured attributable to sickness or infirmity but excluding contracts falling within paragraph IV of Part II of this Schedule.

Land vehicles

3. Contracts of insurance against loss of or damage to vehicles used on land, including motor vehicles but excluding railway rolling stock.

Railway rolling stock

4. Contract of insurance against loss of or damage to railway rolling stock.

Aircraft

5. Contracts of insurance upon aircraft or upon the machinery, tackle, furniture or equipment of aircraft.

Ships

6. Contracts of insurance upon vessels used on the sea or on inland water, or upon the machinery, tackle, furniture or equipment of such vessels.

Goods in transit

7. Contracts of insurance against loss of or damage to merchandise, baggage and all other goods in transit, irrespective of the form of transport.

Fire and natural forces

8. Contracts of insurance against loss of or damage to property (other than property to which paragraphs 3 to 7 relate) due to fire, explosion, storm, natural forces other than storm, nuclear energy or land subsidence.

Damage to property

9. Contracts of insurance against loss of or damage to property (other than property to which paragraphs 3 to 7 relate) due to hail or frost or any other event (such as theft) other than those mentioned in paragraph 8.

Motor vehicle liability

10. Contracts of insurance against damage arising out of or in connection with the use of motor vehicles on land, including third-party risks and carrier's liability.

Aircraft liability

11. Contracts of insurance against damage arising out of or in connection with the use of aircraft, including third-party risks and carrier's liability.

Liability of ships

12. Contracts of insurance against damage arising out of or in connection with the use of vessels on the sea or on inland water, including third party risks and carrier's liability.

General liability

13. Contracts of insurance against risks of the persons insured incurring liabilities to third parties, the risks in question not being risks to which paragraph 10, 11 or 12 relates.

Credit

14. Contracts of insurance against risks of loss to the persons insured arising from the insolvency of debtors of theirs or from the failure (otherwise than through insolvency) of debtors of theirs to pay their debts when due.

Suretyship

15.

(1) Contracts of insurance against the risks of loss to the persons insured arising from their having to perform contracts of guarantee entered into by them.

(2) Fidelity bonds, performance bonds, administration bonds, bail bonds or customs bonds or similar contracts of guarantee, where these are—

(a) effected or carried out by a person not carrying on a banking business;

(b) not effected merely incidentally to some other business carried on by the person effecting them; and

(c) effected in return for the payment of one or more premiums.

Miscellaneous financial loss

16. Contracts of insurance against any of the following risks, namely—

(a) risks of loss to the persons insured attributable to interruptions of the carrying on of business carried on by them or to reduction of the scope of business so carried on;

(b) risks of loss to the persons insured attributable to their incurring unforeseen expense (other than loss such as is covered by contracts falling within paragraph 18);

(c) risks which do not fall within sub-paragraph (a) or (b) and which are not of a kind such that contracts of insurance against them fall within any other provision of this Schedule.

Legal expenses

17. Contracts of insurance against risks of loss to the persons insured attributable to their incurring legal expenses (including costs of litigation).

Assistance

18. Contracts of insurance providing either or both of the following benefits, namely—

(a) assistance (whether in cash or in kind) for persons who get into difficulties while travelling, while away from home or while away from their permanent residence; or

(b) assistance (whether in cash or in kind) for persons who get into difficulties otherwise than as mentioned in sub-paragraph (a).

PART II - CONTRACTS OF LONG-TERM INSURANCE

Life and annuity

I. Contracts of insurance on human life or contracts to pay annuities on human life, but excluding (in each case) contracts within paragraph III.

Marriage and birth

II. Contract of insurance to provide a sum on marriage or on the birth of a child, being contracts expressed to be in effect for a period of more than one year.

Linked long term

III. Contracts of insurance on human life or contracts to pay annuities on human life where the benefits are wholly or partly to be determined by references to the value of, or the income from, property of any description (whether or not specified in the contracts) or by reference to fluctuations in, or in an index of, the value of property of any description (whether or not so specified).

Permanent health

IV. Contracts of insurance providing specified benefits against risks of persons becoming incapacitated in consequence of sustaining injury as a result of an accident or of an accident of a specified class or of sickness or infirmity, being contracts that—

(a) are expressed to be in effect for a period of not less than five years, or until the normal retirement age for the persons concerned, or without limit of time; and

(b) either are not expressed to be terminable by the insurer, or are expressed to be so terminable only in special circumstances mentioned in the contract.

Tontines

V. Tontines.

Capital redemption contracts

VI. Capital redemption contracts, where effected or carried out by a person who does not carry on a banking business, and otherwise carries on a regulated activity of the kind specified by article 10(1) or (2).

Pension fund management

VII. (a) Pension fund management contracts, and

(b) pension fund management contracts which are combined with contracts of insurance covering either conservation of capital or payment of a minimum interest, where effected or carried out by a person who does not carry on a banking business, and otherwise carries on a regulated activity of the kind specified by article 10(1) or (2).

Collective insurance etc.

VIII. Contracts of a kind referred to in article 1(2)(e) of the first life insurance directive.

Social insurance

IX. Contracts of a kind referred to in article 1(3) of the first life insurance directive.

Appendix B – Lloyd's VAT Arrangements

Arrangements effective from 1 January 2000

(Revised version incorporating amendments made on 6 January 2004 and 27 November 2006)

CONTENTS

6.5 Lloyd's advisors
6.6 Mixed agents
6.7 Corporate members
6.8 Natural members

7. PARTIAL EXEMPTION
7.1 Registrations making taxable and/or specified supplies
7.2 Input tax
7.3 Investment activities agreed as a separate sector
7.4 Syndicates
7.5 Managing agents
7.6 Members' agents
7.7 Lloyd's advisors
7.8 Mixed agents
7.9 Corporate members
7.10 Natural members

8. GLOBAL MARKET RATE (GMR)
8.1 Calculation of GMR
8.2 Method of calculation

9. MEMBERS' AGENTS RATE (MAR)
9.1 Calculation of MAR
9.2 Method of calculation

10. INPUT TAX- ALTERNATIVE EVIDENCE
10.1 Input tax- claims expenses
10.2 Information contained within the Underwriters Signing Message
10.3 Invoices

11. IMPORTED SERVICES
11.1 LeBoeuf Lamb Greene & MacRae
11.2 Gross net claims
11.3 Claims services subject to reverse charge procedure
11.4 Syndicates to apply percentage gross net claims figures
11.5 Tax point

12. GENERAL

1. INTRODUCTION

This document sets out administrative arrangements for operating VAT within the Lloyd's market. It was drawn up following an extensive review of the previous Lloyd's VAT Arrangements, which dated back to 1985 and a period of review and consultation with the Lloyd's market.

The Lloyd's VAT Arrangements set out in this document provide guidelines on the VAT registration and recovery treatment of entities operating within the Lloyd's market. They are intended to set out a minimum framework that HM Revenue & Customs expect to be adopted, together with some methodology for the supporting evidence. However, the VAT methodology that is contained in these arrangements is not intended to be prescriptive or exhaustive, and so each VAT registered entity will have to formulate and agree with HM Revenue & Customs a VAT recovery method that is suitable for its own specific circumstances and activities.

This document records arrangements that came into effect on 1 January 2000, and which have already been communicated to entities in the Lloyd's market by way of meetings and bulletins. It also records subsequent amendments to those arrangements.

In signing this agreement, HM Revenue & Customs and the Corporation of Lloyd's underline the desirability and the benefit of the Lloyd's market's having a cohesive approach to VAT. However, these arrangements are subject to prevailing VAT law and are therefore without prejudice to the right of any entity to take an appeal to the VAT and Duties Tribunal on a matter of law.

2. SCOPE OF THE ARRANGEMENTS

2.1 The arrangements are for the use of the following entities within the Lloyd's market:

- Syndicates
- Managing agents
- Members' agents
- Lloyd's advisors
- Mixed agents
- Corporate members of Lloyd's
- Natural members of Lloyd's.

2.2 "Corporate members of Lloyd's" means the following entities which are members of Lloyd's:

- Limited liability companies
- Scottish Limited Partnerships (SLPs)

- Limited Liability Partnerships (LLPs)

2.3 The arrangements exclude all other entities.

3. REGISTRATION

3.1 The following entities may register in their own right to account for VAT on their Lloyd's insurance market activities, subject to a requirement or entitlement to register:

- Syndicates (a syndicate is an unincorporated association of the participating members)
- Managing agents
- Members' agents
- Lloyd's advisors
- Mixed agents
- Corporate members (to the extent that para 3.4 applies)

3.2 The following members may register in their own right to account for VAT on activities other than insurance underwriting, subject to a requirement or entitlement to register for VAT:

- Corporate members
- Natural members.

But see also paragraph 3.5 in relation to corporate members that are part of a group of companies.

3.3 Unless HM Revenue & Customs have approved an application to render monthly returns, all registrations covered by these arrangements will render VAT returns on calendar quarters (stagger 1), that is March/June/Sept/Dec.

3.4 A corporate member that has 100% of the underwriting capacity of a syndicate will be required to cancel the VAT registration of the syndicate as all the economic activities, including underwriting activities, are to be accounted for under the VAT registration of the corporate member. However, see also paragraph 3.5 in relation to corporate members that are part of groups of companies.

3.5 Whether or not a corporate member is required or permitted to register in its own right, a corporate member is eligible for membership of a VAT group, subject to the normal VAT grouping requirements being met. In the case where a corporate member has 100% of the underwriting capacity of a syndicate, and the VAT registration of the syndicate must be cancelled, the syndicate activities may be accounted for either under a single registration for the corporate member or under the registration of a VAT group of which it is a member.

3.6 Syndicates that are underwriting in the year 2000 or future years of account are entitled to register for VAT provided they do not write wholly EU business.

3.7 Syndicates that do not have a successor year of account at 31 December 1999 (that will not be underwriting for the 2000 year of account) will continue to be dealt with via the VAT registration of the managing agents. Subsequent to the 1999 year of account, syndicates that do not have a successor year of account can continue to be registered and will recover input tax at an average recovery rate calculated from the previous 3 years' underwriting premiums. For example, a syndicate that does not have a successor year of account to 2000 will have an average recovery rate based on the aggregate value of all premiums for the period from 1 January 1998 to 31 December 2000.

4. OUTPUTS

4.1 The outputs that will be declared by the entities within the scope of these arrangements for their activities at Lloyd's are described below. This is in addition to outputs that are derived from other activities.

4.2 Outputs value

The value to be declared for a supply is the total consideration for that supply. The consideration for a supply of insurance is the gross premium, including Insurance Premium Tax (IPT) and any other fiscal charges or levies, that is payable by the insured, without any deductions. The consideration for a supply of reinsurance is the gross reinsurance premium less reinsurance commission and profit commission.

4.3 The value of insurance and reinsurance premiums processed through LPSO Limited (LPSO) and notified to managing agents and syndicates will be calculated through a procedure agreed by LPSO, to reflect the full consideration.

4.4 Syndicates

The outputs to be declared are the total of the insurance and reinsurance premiums processed through LPSO and notified by them, plus any premiums not processed through LPSO, such as UK motor business. LPSO notification is evidence of the outputs processed through LPSO.

4.5 Managing Agents

The outputs to be declared are the value of supplies (fees charged for services under the managing agents' contract) by the managing agents to the syndicates that they are authorised to manage plus any other supplies made by the agent. Throughout these arrangements the term "fees" includes profit commission.

4.6 Members' Agents

The outputs to be declared are the value of supplies (fees charged to members under the Lloyd's members' agents' agreement) made to members, plus any other supplies made by the members' agent.

4.7 Lloyd's Advisors

The outputs to be declared are the value of supplies made to corporate members, plus any other supplies made by the advisor.

4.8 Mixed Agents

The outputs to be declared will be a combination of the managing agent supplies and the members' agent supplies, plus any other supplies made.

4.9 Corporate Members

No outputs will be declared from the underwriting of insurance in the Lloyd's market as these are to be declared by the syndicate. The outputs to be declared will be those from other activities. Where, however, the corporate member has 100% of a syndicate, the outputs to be declared will include the underwriting of insurance in relation to the wholly-owned syndicate.

4.10 Natural members

No outputs will be declared from the underwriting of insurance in the Lloyd's market as these are to be declared by the syndicates. The outputs to be declared will be those from other activities.

5. LIABILITY OF SUPPLIES

5.1 The liability of any supply will be determined by the VAT legislation in force at the time.

6. ENTITLEMENT TO INPUT TAX RECOVERY

(underwriting related activities only, all other supplies subject to the normal rules)

6.1 Syndicates

Recovery will be based on the value of supplies made by the individual syndicates.

6.2 Managing Agents

Recovery will be based on the value of services supplied to the syndicates they manage.

6.3 Members' Agents (to 31 December 2000)
Recovery will be based on the Global Market Rate.

6.4 Members' Agents (from 1 January 2001)
Recovery will be based on the Members' Agents Rate.

6.5 Lloyd's Advisors
Recovery will be based on the value of services supplied to corporate members.

6.6 Mixed Agents
Recovery will be based on the Members' Agents Rate (for the members' agent activities) and the value of the managing agent services (for the managing agent activities).

6.7 Corporate members
Whilst the primary purpose of the corporate member registration is to account for their activities other than syndicate underwriting, corporate members will also incur input tax directly in relation to their syndicate underwriting. Recovery of this underwriting related input tax will be based on the supplies made by them on the syndicates on which they participate.

6.8 Natural members
Whilst the primary purpose of the member registration is to account for activities other than syndicate underwriting, natural members will incur input tax directly in relation to their syndicate underwriting. Please refer to section 7.10 for details of the possible methods of recovery of input tax.

7. PARTIAL EXEMPTION

7.1 Each registration making taxable and/or specified supplies (under the *Specified Supplies Order 1999 [SI 1999/3121]*) in addition to exempt supplies will agree a partial exemption method with HM Revenue & Customs. The method will reflect their business activities, in relation to which they will calculate the amount of recoverable input tax. The partial exemption methods will conform to the legislation that prevails.

7.2 Input tax will be directly attributed to supplies made and recovered as appropriate.

Input tax that cannot be directly attributed to supplies made will be recovered via the agreed partial exemption calculations.

7.3 The treatment of investment activities undertaken by registrations will be agreed as a separate sector within each individual partial exemption method. Input tax recovery on other activities, e.g. share issues, will be subject to the normal rules and may constitute a separate sector.

7.4 Syndicates- Partial Exemption Method

The tax year will be 1 January to 31 December with the annual adjustment declared in the December quarter of that tax year.

The partial exemption agreement will comprise at least the following components:

SECTOR 1- UNDERWRITING

The calculation will be based on premiums processed, both through LPSO and elsewhere. Premiums processed by LPSO will be notified on summary reports.

Premiums will be coded by LPSO as follows,

- X = exempt and outside the scope with no input tax credit
- Z =outside the scope (O/S) with input tax (liT) credit
- M = mixed, this will be split 50/50 to X and Z

The sector recovery calculation will be,

$$\frac{\text{Value of premiums O/S with liT credit}}{\text{Value of total premiums}} = \text{recoverable \% to 2 decimal places}$$

SECTOR 2 - INVESTMENTS

The calculation will be based on either the number or the value of securities sales. The sector recovery calculation will be,

$$\frac{\text{Number or value of O/S with liT credit sales of securities}}{\text{Number or value of total sales of securities}} = \text{recoverable \% to 2 decimal places}$$

7.5 Managing Agents- Partial Exemption Method

The annual adjustment will be declared in the first quarter following the end of their VAT tax year.

The partial exemption agreement will comprise at least the following components:

SECTOR 1 - MANAGING AGENT

The calculation will be based upon the value of fees charged to syndicates which the managing agent is authorised to manage by Lloyd's. Where the fees relate to services supplied under the Managing Agent's Agreement (General) and Managing Agent's Agreement (Corporate Member) the liability split of the fees will be determined by the insurance business underwritten by the syndicates managed.

The sector recovery calculation will be,

Value of O/S with liT credit fees	=	recoverable %
Total value of fees		to 2 decimal places

SECTOR 2 - INVESTMENTS

The calculation will be based on either the number or value of securities sales. The sector recovery calculation will be,

Number or value of O/S with liT credit sales of securities	=	recoverable %
Number or value of total sales of securities		to 2 decimal places

OTHER SUPPLIES

Recovery of input tax in relation to supplies not made under the Managing Agent's Agreement (General) and Managing Agent's Agreement (Corporate Member) will be subject to the normal rules and may constitute a separate sector.

7.6 Members' Agents- Partial Exemption Method

The annual adjustment will be declared in the first quarter following the end of their VAT tax year.

The partial exemption agreement will comprise at least the following components:

SECTOR 1 - MEMBERS' AGENT

This sector relates to the services provided to members under the terms of the Lloyd's Members' Agent's Agreement

The sector recovery calculation will be,

Non-attributable input VAT multiplied by the Members' Agents Rate =
input VAT recoverable to the nearest penny

SECTOR 2- INVESTMENTS

The calculation will be based on either the number or the value of securities sales. The sector recovery calculation will be,

Number or value of O/S with IiT credit sales of securities	=	recoverable %
Number or value of total sales of securities		to 2 decimal places

OTHER SUPPLIES

Recovery of input tax in relation to supplies that are outside the terms of the Lloyd's Members' Agent's Agreement will be subject to the normal rules and may constitute a separate sector.

7.7 Lloyd's Advisors- Partial Exemption Method

The annual adjustment will be declared in the first quarter following the end of their VAT tax year.

APPENDIX B

The partial exemption agreement will comprise at least the following components:

SECTOR 1 - LLOYD'S ADVISOR

The calculation will be based upon the value of fees charged to individual corporate members which the advisor is authorised by Lloyd's to advise.

The sector recovery calculation will be,

<u>Value of taxable supplies and other supplies with liT credit</u>	=	recoverable %
Total value of supplies		to 2 decimal places

Input tax recovery on supplies that are outside the terms of the advisor's agreement may comprise a separate sector.

SECTOR 2 - INVESTMENTS

The calculation will be based on either the number or value of securities sales.

The sector recovery calculation will be,

<u>Number or value of O/S with liT credit sales of securities</u>	=	recoverable %
Number or value of total sales of securities		to 2 decimal places

7.8 Mixed Agents- Partial Exemption Method

The annual adjustment will be declared in the first quarter following the end of their VAT tax year.

The partial exemption agreement will comprise at least the following components:

SECTOR 1 -MANAGING AGENT

The calculation will be based upon the value of fees charged to syndicates which the managing agent is authorised to manage by Lloyd's. Where the fees relate to services supplied under the Managing Agent's Agreement (General) and Managing Agent's Agreement (Corporate Member) the liability split of the fees will be determined by the insurance business underwritten by the syndicates managed.

The sector recovery calculation will be,

<u>Value of O/S with liT credit fees</u>	=	recoverable %
Total value of fees		to 2 decimal places

SECTOR 2- MEMBERS' AGENT

This sector relates to the services provided to members under the terms of the Lloyd's Members' Agent's Agreement

The sector recovery calculation will be,

Non-attributable input VAT multiplied by the Members' Agents Rate = input VAT recoverable to the nearest penny

SECTOR 3 - INVESTMENTS

The calculation will be based on either the number or value of securities sales. The sector recovery calculation will be,

Number or value of O/S with liT credit sales of securities	=	recoverable %
Number or value of total sales of securities		to 2 decimal places

OTHER SUPPLIES

Input tax recovery on supplies that are outside the terms of the Managing Agent's Agreement (General), Managing Agent's Agreement (Corporate Member) or the Members' Agent's Agreement will be subject to the normal rules and may comprise additional separate sectors.

7.9 Corporate Members

The annual adjustment will be declared in the first quarter following the end of their VAT tax year.

The partial exemption agreement will comprise at least the following components:

SECTOR 1 - INVESTMENTS

The calculation will be based on either the number or value of securities sales. The sector recovery calculation will be,

Number or value of O/S with VT credit sales of securities	=	recoverable %
Number or value of total sales of securities		to 2 decimal places

SECTOR 2- SYNDICATE UNDERWRITING

The calculation will be based on the premiums processed through LPSO and elsewhere.

The sector recovery calculation will be,

Value of premiums O/S with VT credit	=	recoverable%
Total value of premiums		to 2 decimal places

Where the corporate member participates on a number of syndicates which makes the above calculation difficult, the Global Market Rate may be used in its place for this sector subject to agreement with HM Revenue & Customs. However, those members that participate solely on syndicates which write only EU business will not be permitted to use the Global Market Rate or recover input tax in relation to these supplies.

Where a corporate member owns 100% of the capacity on a syndicate consideration will need to be given to establishing a further sector for this activity.

.7.10 Natural members- Partial Exemption Method

Input tax arising from underwriting activities incurred by natural members who are registered for VAT as sole proprietors by virtue of business activities other than underwriting at Lloyd's may be recovered subject to the normal rules. The Global Market Rate will normally be used to calculate the recoverable amount. The exception to this will be any members who participate solely on syndicates that write only EU business. These members will be unable to recover any underwriting related input tax as they have only written insurance in respect of which there is no right to recover input tax.

Natural members who are VAT registered other than as sole proprietors are not entitled to recover input tax arising from their underwriting activities by virtue of that registration.

8. GLOBAL MARKET RATE (GMR)

8.1 The Global Market Recovery rate (GMR) will be calculated on an annual basis for each VAT tax year. During the current VAT tax year, the recoverable amount of non-attributable input VAT incurred in each quarter will be determined by reference to the GMR for the previous tax year. The actual GMR for the current year will be used to determine the annual adjustment for that year.

8.2 The GMR will be calculated using the value of all insurance business written in the Lloyd's market to include:

- the LPSO calculated gross premium VAT figures, including small pool business and IPT,
- gross premiums (including IPT) not processed through LPSO for the previous year of account,
- Records and Amendments section adjustments.

The method of calculating the GMR will be through a procedure agreed between Lloyd's and HM Revenue & Customs and will be subject to review.

9. MEMBERS' AGENTS RATE (MAR)

9.1 The Members' Agents Recovery Rate (MAR) will be calculated on an annual basis for each VAT tax year. During the current VAT tax year, the recoverable amount of non-attributable input VAT incurred in each quarter will be determined by reference to the MAR for the previous year. The actual MAR for the current year will be used in determining the annual adjustment.

9.2 The MAR will be calculated using the value of all insurance business written in the Lloyd's market except for business written by those syndicates all of whose capacity is provided by a single corporate member or by a number of corporate members that belong to the same group. It will include:

- the LPSO calculated gross premium VAT figures, including small pool business and IPT,
- gross premiums (including IPT) not processed through LPSO for the previous year of account,
- Records and Amendments section adjustments.

The method of calculating the MAR will be through a procedure agreed between Lloyd's and HM Revenue & Customs and will be subject to review.

10. INPUT TAX- ALTERNATIVE EVIDENCE

Input Tax - Claims expenses ("tabulation figures")

10.1 The input tax on services supplied from within the UK in relation to claims will only be regarded as recoverable by the syndicate if the supply is to the syndicate and if the insured in relation to the claim belongs outside the EU. Such input tax is directly attributable to outside the scope supplies with input tax recovery under the terms of the Specified Supplies Order 1999. The evidence to substantiate input tax claims by syndicates is the Underwriters' Signing Message (USM).

10.2 The information contained within the USMs will be substantiated by LPSO upon requests made by HM Revenue & Customs to Lloyd's via procedures agreed with Lloyd's.

10.3 LPSO will retain the original invoices or their scanned images for the period required under prevailing VAT legislation and make them available upon request.

11. IMPORTED SERVICES

11.1 LeBoeuf Lamb Greene & MacRae

Fees charged by the US firm of LeBoeuf Lamb Green & MacRae are paid centrally by Lloyd's and recharged to the syndicates. The invoices produced by Lloyd's may be treated as invoices for the purposes of calculating the VAT charges under the reverse charge procedure. The fees charged to syndicates relate to a number of supplies and cannot at this time be directly attributed to specific supplies of insurance. Therefore the fees are regarded as residual and input tax may be recovered at the appropriate syndicate rate.

Gross net claims

11.2 Monthly summaries will be made of the values of claims costs processed by LPSO on behalf of syndicates.

11.3 A proportion of the services received in dealing with claims are supplied from overseas and are subject to the reverse charge procedure. To arrive at the value of the international services a survey is to be conducted periodically. The procedure and intervals will be as agreed with Lloyd's. Lloyd's will advise syndicates of the prevailing percentage figure.

11.4 Syndicates will apply the percentage to the gross net claims figures to arrive at the notional net value of reverse charge services. The VAT rate will be applied to the calculated figure to arrive at the output tax to be declared. The associated input tax will be recovered at the syndicate recovery rate.

Tax point

11.5 The tax point is taken as the last working day of the relevant month.

12. GENERAL

These arrangements are agreed as guidelines setting out a minimum framework for the operation of VAT in the Lloyd's market from 1 January 2000 onwards as amended by further agreements on 6 January 2004 and 27 November 2006. Except as otherwise specifically stated, everything in these arrangements is to be governed by the VAT legislation in force at the time.

Signed.......................... (Corporation of Lloyd's)

Date..................................

Signed......................... (HM Revenue & Customs)

Date ....

Appendix C – Extract from 'HMRC ABI Partial Exemption Guidance for the Insurance Sector'

These templates and the accompanying aide memoir are used by HMRC officers when drafting PESMs that have been proposed by customers.

This template is a suggested format for a PESM and is in no way binding

a3.1 Example 1 – Single pot Values Method

Dear

VAT REGISTRATION NO.

PARTIAL EXEMPTION SPECIAL METHOD FOR THE RECOVERY OF INPUT TAX

1. Approval

Consideration has been given to your request dated [ ] in which you seek approval for the use of a partial exemption special method to determine recoverable input tax and your declaration dated [ ] that to the best of your knowledge and belief your proposals are fair and reasonable. The method is set out in this letter and the Commissioners approve that method (and hereby record their approval of it) subject to the conditions below.

This method has been approved under Regulation 102 of the Value Added Tax Regulations 1995. It incorporates input tax attributable to foreign and specified supplies as defined in Regulation 103 Value Added Tax Regulations 1995.

2. Use of the method

You must use this method to calculate your recoverable input tax for all periods with effect from and must continue to use it until such time as the Commissioners approve or direct the termination of its use.

You should make proposals to this office for a new method if this one no longer results in a fair and reasonable recovery of input tax.

3. Change in business/trading patterns

WORDING FOR NON VAT GROUPS

This approval is given in the context of your current business structure and trading patterns as advised by you to this office. Should there be any changes in the structure of your business and/or trading patterns, which prevent this method from giving a fair and reasonable recovery of input tax, you must notify this office in writing at once. Planned changes in the above mentioned matters should, wherever practicable, be notified to this office at least 30 days in advance of implementation and in any event, no later than upon implementation.

WORDING FOR VAT GROUPS

This approval is given in the context of your current business structure and trading patterns as and is based on information [name of VAT group] has provided to the Commissioners. Should there be any changes in the structure of your business and/or trading patterns, which prevent this method from giving a fair and reasonable recovery of input tax, you must notify this office in writing promptly. I would ask you to inform this office of the change or changes in writing should:

- there be any material change in the structure of your business;
- any member of XXX VAT group cease, commence, or re-commence trading, or commence a new type of business activity;
- there be any changes in the trading patterns of any member of the VAT group, or any other changes affecting the VAT group, that might reasonably be considered to create a risk that the approved method will no longer produce a fair and reasonable recovery of input tax;
- any group undertaking commence or recommence trading with the VAT group. For the purpose of this letter group undertakings shall have the same meaning as in section 1161, Companies Act 2006.

Planned changes in the above mentioned matters should, wherever practicable, be notified to this office at least 30 days in advance of implementation and in any event, within 30 days of implementation.

4. Definitions

For the purpose of this method the words used shall have the meanings defined in this letter, or if not defined here, their meaning as defined in the VAT Act 1994, or if not defined there, their normal everyday meaning.

Where this method refers to taxable supplies it should also be taken to include:

(a) any supply made outside the UK that would be a taxable supply if made within the UK; and

(b) any supply specified in an Order made under section 26(2)(c) of the Value Added Tax Act 1994.

Where this method refers to exempt supplies it should also be taken to include:

(a) any supply made outside the UK which would be exempt if made in the UK, other than any supply specified in an Order made under section 26(2)(c) of the Value Added Tax Act 1994.

5. Tax year

Your tax year begins on and ends on [ ].

6. Attribution

In each prescribed accounting period you shall:

- identify all supplies, acquisitions and imports you receive which are used, or to be used, in whole by you exclusively in making taxable supplies; the input tax thereon is recoverable;
- identify all supplies, acquisitions and imports you receive which are used, or to be used, in whole by you exclusively in making exempt supplies or in carrying on any activity other than the making of taxable supplies; the input tax thereon is not recoverable;
- determine the recoverable amount of any remaining, non-attributable input tax by multiplying that input tax by the formula below:

Value of taxable supplies in the period Value of total supplies in the period

7. Exclusions

You must exclude from the calculations the value of any supplies specifically excluded by regulation 101(3) of the VAT Regulations 1995. You must also exclude the value of supplies in the following categories:

(a) any supply made from branches situated outside the UK;

(b) any supply of any goods or services sold on in the same state connected to the making of an advance or the granting of any credit, including for example, goods sold on by a finance house under a hire-purchase agreement;

(c) any supply of goods or services made to connected persons, where the supply is acquired for the purposes of your business and supplied to the connected person without material alteration or further processing;

(d) supplies made where it is intended that the same, or equivalent, goods or services will be subsequently used by the business including for example, goods or services forming part of a sale and leaseback transaction.

[Amend, exclude or add any other supplies that are likely to cause a distortion to the calculation as appropriate to the particular business]

8. Supplies to connected persons

Where the value of a supply made to a connected person is either significantly less than, or significantly greater than, its open market value, then the value of the supply shall be taken to be its open market value for the purposes of this method.

Any question as to whether a person is connected shall be determined in accordance with section 1122 of the Corporation Tax Act 2010.

9. Percentages to be used

All ratios are to be expressed as percentages. They shall be rounded up to two decimal places in each tax period and in the longer period adjustment.

10. Annual adjustments

A longer period adjustment must be carried out and declared in accordance with regulation 107, Value Added Tax Regulations 1995. This adjustment should be included in the first period following the end of your tax year.

11. Requirements

(a) You are required to keep records to show how you have calculated your deductible input tax and enable an Officer of HM Revenue and Customs to verify the amount claimed.

(b) When you have calculated the value of your non-recoverable input tax refer to the "de minimis" limits currently in force.

12. Contact officer

Should you wish to discuss this letter please contact [ ] at the above address.

Yours

a.3.2 Example 2 Single Pot Transactions Method

This Example a suggested format for a PESM and is in no way binding

Dear

VAT REGISTRATION NO.

PARTIAL EXEMPTION SPECIAL METHOD FOR THE RECOVERY OF INPUT TAX

1. Approval

Consideration has been given to your request dated [ ] in which you seek approval for the use of a partial exemption special method to determine recoverable input tax and your declaration dated [ ] that to the best of your knowledge and belief your proposals are fair and reasonable. The method is set out in this letter and the Commissioners approve that method (and hereby record their approval of it) subject to the conditions below.

This method has been approved under Regulation 102 of the Value Added Tax Regulations 1995. It incorporates input tax attributable to foreign and specified supplies as defined in Regulation 103 Value Added Tax Regulations 1995.

2. Use of the method

You must use this method to calculate your recoverable input tax for all periods with effect from and must continue to use it until such time as the Commissioners approve or direct the termination of its use.

You should make proposals to this office for a new method if this one no longer results in a fair and reasonable recovery of input tax.

3. Change in business/trading patterns

WORDING FOR NON VAT GROUPS

This approval is given in the context of your current business structure and trading patterns as advised by you to this office. Should there be any changes in the structure of your business and/or trading patterns, which prevent this method from giving a fair and reasonable recovery of input tax, you must notify this office in writing at once. Planned changes in the above mentioned matters should, wherever practicable, be notified to this office at least 30 days in advance of implementation and in any event, no later than upon implementation.

WORDING FOR VAT GROUPS

This approval is given in the context of your current business structure and trading patterns as and is based on information [name of VAT group] has provided to the Commissioners. Should there be any changes in the structure of your business and/or trading patterns, which prevent this method from giving a fair and reasonable recovery of input tax, you must notify this office in writing promptly. I would ask you to inform this office of the change or changes in writing should:

- there be any material change in the structure of your business;
- any member of XXX VAT group cease, commence, or re-commence trading, or commence a new type of business activity;
- there be any changes in the trading patterns of any member of the VAT group, or any other changes affecting the VAT group, that might reasonably be considered to create a risk that the approved method will no longer produce a fair and reasonable recovery of input tax;
- any group undertaking commence or recommence trading with the VAT group. For the purpose of this letter group undertakings shall have the same meaning as in section 1161, Companies Act 2006.

Planned changes in the above-mentioned matters should, wherever practicable, be notified to this office at least 30 days in advance of implementation and in any event, within 30 days of implementation.

4. Definitions

For the purpose of this method the words used shall have the meanings defined in this letter, or if not defined here, their meaning as defined in the VAT Act 1994, or if not defined there, their normal everyday meaning.

Where this method refers to taxable supplies it should also be taken to include:

(a) any supply made outside the UK that would be a taxable supply if made within the UK; and

(b) any supply specified in an Order made under section 26(2)(c) of the Value Added Tax Act 1994.

Where this method refers to exempt supplies it should also be taken to include:

(a) any supply made outside the UK which would be exempt if made in the UK, other than any supply specified in an Order made under section 26(2)(c) of the Value Added Tax Act 1994.

A transaction is the issue of a document calling for payment for services or goods supplied or, in the absence of such a document, the receipt of any such payment.

[Or other such definition that is appropriate to the business and the method]

5. Tax year

Your tax year begins on [ ] and ends on [ ].

6. Attribution

In each prescribed accounting period you shall:

(a) identify all supplies, acquisitions and imports you receive which are used, or to be used, in whole by you exclusively in making taxable supplies; the input tax thereon is recoverable;

(b) identify all supplies, acquisitions and imports you receive which are used, or to be used, in whole by you exclusively in making exempt supplies or in carrying on any activity other than the making of taxable supplies; the input tax thereon is not recoverable;

(c) determine the recoverable amount of any remaining, non- attributable input tax by multiplying that input tax by the formula below:

Number of taxable transactions in the period Total number of transactions in the period

7. Exclusions

You must exclude from the calculations:

[insert any transactions that are likely to cause a distortion to the calculation as appropriate to the particular business]

8. Percentages to be used

All ratios are to be expressed as percentages. They shall be rounded up to two decimal places in each tax period and in the longer period adjustment.

9. Annual adjustments

A longer period adjustment must be carried out and declared in accordance with regulation 107, Value Added Tax Regulations 1995. This adjustment should be included in the first period following the end of your tax year.

10. Requirements

(a) You are required to keep records to show how you have calculated your deductible input tax and enable an Officer of HM Revenue and Customs to verify the amount claimed.

(b) When you have calculated the value of your non-recoverable input tax refer to the "de minimis" limits currently in force.

11. Contact officer

Should you wish to discuss this letter please contact [ ] at the above address.

Yours

a.3.3 Example 3 Single Pot 'other' Method

This Example a suggested format for a PESM and is in no way binding

Dear

VAT REGISTRATION NO.

PARTIAL EXEMPTION SPECIAL METHOD FOR THE RECOVERY OF INPUT TAX

1. Approval

Consideration has been given to your request dated [ ] in which you seek approval for the use of a partial exemption special method to determine recoverable input tax and your declaration dated [ ] that to the best of your knowledge and belief your proposals are fair and reasonable. The method is set out in this letter and the Commissioners approve that method (and hereby record their approval of it) subject to the conditions below.

This method has been approved under Regulation 102 of the Value Added Tax Regulations1995. It incorporates input tax attributable to foreign and specified supplies as defined in Regulation 103 Value Added Tax Regulations 1995.

2. Use of the method

You must use this method to calculate your recoverable input tax for all periods with effect from and must continue to use it until such time as the Commissioners approve or direct the termination of its use.

You should make proposals to this office for a new method if this one no longer results in a fair and reasonable recovery of input tax.

3. Change in business/trading patterns

WORDING FOR NON VAT GROUPS

This approval is given in the context of your current business structure and trading patterns as advised by you to this office. Should there be any changes in the structure of your business and/or trading patterns, which prevent this method from giving a fair and reasonable recovery of input tax, you must notify this office in writing at once. Planned changes in the above mentioned matters should, wherever practicable, be notified to this office at least 30 days in advance of implementation and in any event, no later than upon implementation.

WORDING FOR VAT GROUPS

This approval is given in the context of your current business structure and trading patterns as and is based on information [name of VAT group] has provided to the Commissioners. Should there be any changes in the structure of your business and/or trading patterns, which prevent this method from giving a fair and reasonable recovery of input tax, you must notify this office in writing promptly. I would ask you to inform this office of the change or changes in writing should:

- there be any material change in the structure of your business;
- any member of XXX VAT group cease, commence, or re-commence trading, or commence a new type of business activity;
- there be any changes in the trading patterns of any member of the VAT group, or any other changes affecting the VAT group, that might reasonably be considered to create a risk that the approved method will no longer produce a fair and reasonable recovery of input tax;
- any group undertaking commence or recommence trading with the VAT group. For the purpose of this letter group undertakings shall have the same meaning as in section 1161, Companies Act 2006.

Planned changes in the above mentioned matters should, wherever practicable, be notified to this office at least 30 days in advance of implementation and in any event, within 30 days of implementation.

4. Definitions

For the purpose of this method the words used shall have the meanings defined in this letter, or if not defined here, their meaning as defined in the VAT Act 1994, or if not defined there, their normal everyday meaning.

Where this method refers to taxable supplies it should also be taken to include:

(a) any supply made outside the UK that would be a taxable supply if made within the UK; and
(b) any supply specified in an Order made under section 26(2)(c) of the Value Added Tax Act 1994.

Where this method refers to exempt supplies it should also be taken to include:

(a) any supply made outside the UK which would be exempt if made in the UK, other than any supply specified in an Order made under section 26(2)(c) of the Value Added Tax Act 1994.

[Include such definitions that are appropriate to the business and the method]

5. Tax year

Your tax year begins on and ends on [ ].

6. Attribution

In each prescribed accounting period you shall:

(a) identify all supplies, acquisitions and imports you receive which are used, or to be used, in whole by you exclusively in making taxable supplies; the input tax thereon is recoverable;

(b) identify all supplies, acquisitions and imports you receive which are used, or to be used, in whole by you exclusively in making exempt supplies or in carrying on any activity other than the making of taxable supplies; the input tax thereon is not recoverable;

(c) determine the recoverable amount of any remaining, non-attributable input tax by multiplying that input tax by the formula below:

[Insert method of apportionment]

7. Exclusions

You must exclude from the calculations:

[Insert appropriate exclusions, based on the method to be used, that are likely to cause a distortion to the calculation as appropriate to the particular business]

8. Supplies to connected persons

Where the value of a supply made to a connected person is either significantly less than, or significantly greater than, its open market value, then the value of the supply shall be taken to be its open market value for the purposes of this method.

Any question as to whether a person is connected shall be determined in accordance with section 1122 of the Corporation Tax Act 2010.

9. Percentages to be used

All ratios are to be expressed as percentages. They shall be rounded up to two decimal places in each tax period and in the longer period adjustment.

10. Annual adjustments

A longer period adjustment must be carried out and declared in accordance with regulation 107, Value Added Tax Regulations 1995. This adjustment should be included in the first period following the end of your tax year.

11. Requirements

(a) You are required to keep records to show how you have calculated your deductible input tax and enable an Officer of HM Revenue and Customs to verify the amount claimed.

(b) When you have calculated the value of your non-recoverable input tax refer to the "de minimis" limits currently in force.

12. Contact officer

Should you wish to discuss this letter please contact [ ] at the above address.

Yours

a.3.4 Example 4 Multi Pot Method

This Example a suggested format for a PESM and is in no way binding

Dear

VAT REGISTRATION NO.

PARTIAL EXEMPTION SPECIAL METHOD FOR THE RECOVERY OF INPUT TAX

1. Approval

Consideration has been given to your request dated [ ] in which you seek approval for the use of a partial exemption special method to determine recoverable input tax and your declaration dated [ ] that to the best of your knowledge and belief your proposals are fair and reasonable. The method is set out in this letter and the Commissioners approve it (and hereby record their approval of it) subject to the conditions below.

This method has been approved under Regulation 102 of the Value Added Tax Regulations 1995. It incorporates input tax attributable to foreign and specified supplies as defined in Regulation 103 Value Added Tax Regulations 1995.

2. Use of the method

You must use this method to calculate your recoverable input tax for all periods with effect from and must continue to use it until such time as the Commissioners approve or direct the termination of its use.

You should make proposals to this office for a new method if this one no longer results in a fair and reasonable recovery of input tax.

3. Change in business/trading patterns

WORDING FOR NON VAT GROUPS

This approval is given in the context of your current business structure and trading patterns as advised by you to this office. Should there be any changes in the structure of your business and/or trading patterns, which prevent this method from giving a fair and reasonable recovery of input tax, you must notify this office in writing at once. Planned changes in the above mentioned matters should, wherever practicable, be notified to this office at least 30 days in advance of implementation and in any event, no later than upon implementation.

WORDING FOR VAT GROUPS

This approval is given in the context of your current business structure and trading patterns as and is based on information [name of VAT group] has provided to the Commissioners. Should there be any changes in the structure of your business and/or trading patterns, which prevent this method from giving a fair and reasonable recovery of input tax, you must notify this office in writing promptly. I would ask you to inform this office of the change or changes in writing should:

(a) there be any material change in the structure of your business;
(b) any member of XXX VAT group cease, commence, or re-commence trading, or commence a new type of business activity;
(c) there be any changes in the trading patterns of any member of the VAT group, or any other changes affecting the VAT group, that might reasonably be considered to create a risk that the approved method will no longer produce a fair and reasonable recovery of input tax;
(d) any group undertaking commence or recommence trading with the VAT group. For the purpose of this letter group undertakings shall have the same meaning as in section 1161, Companies Act 2006.

Planned changes in the above mentioned matters should, wherever practicable, be notified to this office at least 30 days in advance of implementation and in any event, within 30 days of implementation.

4. Sectors

Your operations are to be defined as the following sectors: -

[Insert the sectors, which must include a description of the activities undertaken in each area]

As you are authorised to split your business into sectors for the purpose of determining input tax recoverability, you should make a separate calculation for the apportionment of non-attributable tax in each sector which reflects the use of the goods or services on which input tax has been incurred.

5. Definitions

For the purpose of this method the words used shall have the meanings defined in this letter, or if not defined here, their meaning as defined in the VAT Act 1994, or if not defined there, their normal everyday meaning.

Where this method refers to taxable supplies it should also be taken to include:

(a) any supply made outside the UK that would be a taxable supply if made within the UK; and
(b) any supply specified in an Order made under section 26(2)(c) of the Value Added Tax Act 1994.

Where this method refers to exempt supplies it should also be taken to include:

(a) any supply made outside the UK which would be exempt if made in the UK, other than any supply specified in an Order made under section 26(2)(c) of the Value Added Tax Act 1994.

Allocated and/or sub-allocated will relate to that residual input tax in any cost centre or income generating area after direct attribution has been made and the fully recoverable and non-recoverable amounts of input tax have been extracted.

Allocation is defined as the act of assigning a share of the non-attributed input tax to a sector. Re-allocation is defined as the act of assigning a share of the previously allocated, or reallocated, input tax to another sector.

A transaction is the issue of a document calling for payment for services or goods supplied or, in the absence of such a document, the receipt of any such payment.

[Or insert other such definition that is appropriate to the business and the method]
[Other definitions to be inserted where appropriate]

6. Tax year

Your tax year begins on [ ] and ends on .

7. Attribution

In each prescribed accounting period you shall:

(a) identify all supplies, acquisitions and imports you receive which are used, or to be used, in whole by you exclusively in making taxable supplies; the input tax thereon is recoverable;
(b) identify all supplies, acquisitions and imports you receive which are used, or to be used, in whole by you exclusively in making exempt supplies or in carrying on any activity other than the making of taxable supplies; the input tax thereon is not recoverable;
(c) identify all supplies, acquisitions and imports you receive which are used, or to be used, both in making taxable and exempt supplies and which are used, or to be used, exclusively within a single sector; the input tax thereon shall be allocated to that sector;
(d) identify all supplies, acquisitions and imports you receive which are used, or to be used, both in making taxable and exempt supplies and which are not used, or to be used, exclusively within a single sector; the input tax thereon should be allocated to the fullest extent possible between the sectors on whose behalf the expense was incurred in the following manner:-

[Insert the method to be used]

The input tax allocated under c) and d) above to the nominated sectors shall be recovered in the following manner:-

[Insert the method to be used]

Non-attributable input tax incurred in respect of activities not covered elsewhere in this method is deductible to the extent that it is incurred on goods or services which are used or to be used to make taxable supplies, expressed as a proportion of the whole use or intended use.

8. Exclusions

You must exclude from the calculations.

[Insert appropriate exclusions, based on the method(s) to be used that are likely to cause a distortion to the calculation, as applicable to the particular business].

[Include the following if there are any values-based calculations]:

You must exclude from the calculations the value of any supplies specifically excluded by regulation 101(3) of the VAT Regulations 1995.

You must also exclude the value of supplies in the following categories:

(a) any supply made from branches situated outside the UK;
(b) any supply of any goods or services sold on in the same state connected to the making of an advance or the granting of any credit, including for example, goods sold on by a finance house under a hire-purchase agreement;
(c) any supply of goods or services made to connected persons, where the supply is acquired for the purposes of your business and supplied to the connected person without material alteration or further processing;
(d) supplies made where it is intended that the same, or equivalent, goods or services will be subsequently used by the business including for example, goods or services forming part of a sale and leaseback transaction.

[Amend, exclude or add any other supplies that are likely to cause a distortion to the calculation as appropriate to the particular business]

9. Supplies to connected persons

Where the value of a supply made to a connected person is either significantly less than, or significantly greater than, its open market value, then the value of the supply shall be taken to be its open market value for the purposes of this method.

Any question as to whether a person is connected shall be determined in accordance with section 1122 of the Corporation Tax Act 2010.

10. Percentages to be used

All ratios are to be expressed as percentages. They shall be rounded up to two decimal places in each tax period and in the longer period adjustment.

11. Annual adjustments

A longer period adjustment must be carried out and declared in accordance with regulation 107, Value Added Tax Regulations 1995. This adjustment should be included in the first period following the end of your tax year.

12. Requirements

(a) You are required to keep records to show how you have calculated your deductible input tax and enable an Officer of HM Revenue and Customs to verify the amount claimed.

(b) When you have calculated the value of your non-recoverable input tax refer to the "de minimis" limits currently in force.

13. Contact officer

Should you wish to discuss this letter please contact [ ] at the above address.

Yours

a.3.5 Example 5 Sectorised Method

This Example a suggested format for a PESM and is in no way binding

Dear

VAT REGISTRATION NO.

PARTIAL EXEMPTION SPECIAL METHOD FOR THE RECOVERY OF INPUT TAX

1. Approval

Consideration has been given to your request dated [ ] in which you seek approval for the use of a partial exemption special method to determine recoverable input tax and your declaration dated [ ] that to the best of your knowledge and belief your proposals are fair and reasonable. The method is set out in this letter and the attached appendices and the Commissioners approve that method (and hereby record their approval of it) subject to the conditions below.

This method has been approved under Regulation 102 of the Value Added Tax Regulations 1995. It incorporates input tax attributable to foreign and specified supplies as defined in Regulation 103 ·Value Added Tax Regulations 1995.

2. Use of the method

You must use this method to calculate your recoverable input tax for all periods with effect from and must continue to use it until such time as the Commissioners approve or direct the termination of its use.

You should make proposals to this office for a new method if this one no longer results in a fair and reasonable recovery of input tax.

3. Change in business/trading patterns

WORDING FOR NON VAT GROUPS

This approval is given in the context of your current business structure and trading patterns as advised by you to this office. Should there be any changes in the structure of your business

and/or trading patterns, which prevent this method from giving a fair and reasonable recovery of input tax, you must notify this office in writing at once. Planned changes in the above mentioned matters should, wherever practicable, be notified to this office at least 30 days in advance of implementation and in any event, no later than upon implementation.

WORDING FOR VAT GROUPS

This approval is given in the context of your current business structure and trading patterns as and is based on information [name of VAT group] has provided to the Commissioners. Should there be any changes in the structure of your business and/or trading patterns, which prevent this method from giving a fair and reasonable recovery of input tax, you must notify this o ffice in writing promptly. I would ask you to inform this office of the change or changes in writing should:

- there be any material change in the structure of your business;
- any member of XXX VAT group cease, commence, or re-commence trading, or commence a new type of business activity;
- there be any changes in the trading patterns of any member of the VAT group, or any other changes affecting the VAT group, that might reasonably be considered to create a risk that the approved method will no longer produce a fair and reasonable recovery input tax;
- any group undertaking commence or recommence trading with the VAT group. For the purpose of this letter group undertakings shall have the same meaning as in section 1161, Companies Act 2006.

Planned changes in the above mentioned matters should, wherever practicable, be notified to this office at least 30 days in advance of implementation and in any event, within 30 days of implementation.

4. Definitions

For the purpose of this method the words used shall have the meanings defined in Appendix 1, or if not defined in Appendix 1, their meaning as defined in the VAT Act 1994, or if not defined there, their normal everyday meaning.

5. Tax year

Your tax year begins on [ ] and ends on [ ].

6. Attribution

In each prescribed accounting period you shall:

(a) identify all supplies, acquisitions and imports you receive which are used, or to be used, in whole by you exclusively in making taxable supplies; the input tax thereon is recoverable;

(b) identify all supplies, acquisitions and imports you receive which are used, or to be used, in whole by you exclusively in making exempt supplies or in carrying on any activity other than the making of taxable supplies; the input tax thereon is not recoverable;

(c) identify all supplies, acquisitions and imports you receive which are used, or to be used, both in making taxable and exempt supplies and which are used, or to be used, exclusively within a single sector or sub-sector; the input tax thereon shall be allocated in full to that sector or sub-sector;

(d) identify all supplies, acquisitions and imports you receive which are used, or to be used, both in making taxable and exempt supplies and which are not used, or to be used, exclusively within a single sector or sub-sector; the input tax thereon shall be allocated between the sectors on the basis of [ ];

(e) [reallocate input tax allocated to the sectors and sub-sectors listed in Appendix 2 according to the calculations set out in Appendix 3]; and

(f) attribute to taxable supplies such proportion of the input tax on such of those supplies received as are used, or to be used, by you in making both taxable and exempt supplies as is determined to be the deductible proportion of the non-attributable input tax for each sector and sub-sector by the calculations set out in Appendix 3.

[The following wording can be inserted here or as "catch all" sector:]

Non-attributable input tax incurred in respect of activities not covered elsewhere in this method is deductible to the extent that it is incurred on goods or services which are used or to be used to make taxable supplies, expressed as a proportion of the whole use or intended use.

7. Exclusions

You must exclude from the calculations.

[Insert appropriate exclusions, based on the method(s) to be used that are likely to cause a distortion to the calculation, as applicable to the particular business].
[Include the following if there are any values based calculations]:

You must exclude from the calculations the value of any supplies specifically excluded by regulation 101(3) of the VAT Regulations 1995. You must also exclude the value of supplies in the following categories:

(a) any supply made from branches situated outside the UK;

(b) any supply of any goods or services sold on in the same state connected to the making of an advance or the granting of any credit, including for example, goods sold on by a finance house under a hire-purchase agreement;

(c) any supply of goods or services made to connected persons, where the supply is acquired for the purposes of your business and supplied to the connected person without material alteration or further processing;

(d) supplies made where it is intended that the same, or equivalent, goods or services will be subsequently used by the business including for example, goods or services forming part of a sale and leaseback transaction.

[Amend, exclude or add any other supplies that are likely to cause a distortion to the calculation as appropriate to the particular business]

8. Supplies to connected persons

Where the value of a supply made to a connected person is either significantly less than, or significantly greater than, its open market value, then the value of the supply shall be taken to be its open market value for the purposes of this method.

9. Percentages to be used

All ratios are to be expressed as percentages. They shall be rounded up to two decimal places in each tax period and in the longer period adjustment.

10. Annual adjustments

A longer period adjustment must be carried out and declared in accordance with regulation 107, Value Added Tax Regulations 1995. This adjustment should be included in the first period following the end of your tax year.

11. Requirements

You are required to keep records to show how you have calculated your deductible input tax and enable an Officer of HM Revenue and Customs to verify the amount claimed.

When you have calculated the value of your non-recoverable input tax refer to the "de minimis" limits currently in force.

12. Contact officer

Should you wish to discuss this letter please contact [ ] at the above address.

Yours

VAT REGISTRATION No: [ ] (*insert name of business*)

Appendix 1: Definitions Effective date:

Taxable supplies
Where this method refers to taxable supplies it should also be taken to include:
(a) any supply made outside the UK that would be a taxable supply if made within the UK; and
(b) any supply specified in an Order made under section 26(2)(c) of the Value Added Tax Act 1994.

Exempt supplies
Where this method refers to exempt supplies it should also be taken to include:
(a) any supply made outside the UK which would be exempt if made in the UK, other than
(b) any supply specified in an Order made under section 26(2)(c) of the Value Added Tax Act 1994.

Connected persons
Any question as to whether a person is connected with the VAT Group shall be determined in accordance with section 1122 of the Corporation Tax Act 2010.

Attribution
The act of determining whether the whole of the supply, acquisition or import is used, or to be used to make either supplies wholly with a right to recover, or supplies wholly without the right to recover, input tax.

Allocation
The act of assigning a share of the non-attributed input-tax to a sector or sub-sector.

Re-allocation
The act of assigning a share of the previously allocated, or reallocated, input tax to another sector, or sub-sector

Apportionment
The calculation of the amount of the non-attributable input tax allocated to each sector, or sub-sector, that shall be attributed to taxable supplies

[Add any other required definitions - e.g. transactions, headcount, full time equivalent etc.]

APPENDIX C

VAT REGISTRATION No: [ ] (*insert name of business*)

Appendix 2: List of sectors and sub-sectors

Appendix 3, Annex Number	Name of Sector or Sub-Sector	Effective Date	Date Ceased	Comments

Appendix 3: Annex **Effective date:**

SECTOR:

This sector is the business of [ ]

Detail of calculation to be used in this sector
The deductible element of the non-attributable input tax allocated to this sector shall be determined by multiplying that input tax by the formula below, which shall be expressed as a percentage:

Notes

[If any restrictions, qualifications or explanations are needed]

APPENDIX 3: Annex **Effective date:**

SECTOR:

This sector is the business of [ ]

This sector is divided into [ ] sub-sectors: [ ] and [ ]

Sub-sector [ ] is the business of [ ]

Sub-sector [ ] is the business of [ ]

The deductible element of the non-attributable input tax allocated to this sub-sector shall be quantified by multiplying that input tax by the formula below, which shall be expressed as a percentage:

Notes
[If any restrictions, qualifications or explanations are needed]

Detail of calculation to be used in sub-sector
The deductible element of the non-attributable input tax allocated to this sub-sector shall be quantified by multiplying that input tax by the formula below, which shall be expressed as a percentage:

Notes
[If any restrictions, qualifications or explanations are needed]

a.3.6 PESM Template Aide Memoir

AIDE MEMOIRE:

PARTIAL EXEMPTION SPECIAL METHOD TEMPLATES FOR THE FINANCE AND INSURANCE SECTORS

1) Introduction

This guidance note should be read in conjunction with the special method templates and in drafting partial exemption special methods. These method templates are issued with a health warning and should be tailored to reflect the individual circumstances of the business. If you have any queries regarding the drafting of special methods please consult a member of the TAPE team or one of the local Regional Partial Exemption Specialist Officers (RPESOs). Reference should also be made to V1-15 guidance on Partial Exemption.

2) Supplies and Transactions

Supplies and Transactions should be defined in a single pot method or in each sector in a sectorised method. The suggested definition of 'transactions' comes with a health warning, and the terms "transactions" and "supplies" need to be defined clearly within each special method depending on what supplies are being made.

3) Suggested wording for determining the recovery of non-attributable input tax

The following methods of apportionment can be used to determine input tax recovery in sectors, sub- sectors and in single special methods. The methods of apportionment need to be defined clearly within each sector/sub-sector or within single pot methods and should state any weightings (if applicable), inclusions and/or exclusions.

a) Single pot special methods for other methods of apportionment

Refer to Section 6, paragraph (c) (Attribution) in the 'single pot other' template. The following paragraphs refer to suggested wording based on the method of apportionment other than values or transactions.

i) Headcount

$$\frac{\text{Number of staff generating taxable income in the period}}{\text{Total number of income generating staff in the period}}$$

**Where income generating staff is used as a method of apportionment in special methods, this term must be defined clearly. Exclusions and/or inclusions should also be stated.*

ii) Time Spent

$$\frac{\text{Time spent on taxable transactions in the period}}{\text{Total time spent on all transactions in the period}}$$

** The above apportionments can also be used in sectors for multi pot special methods.*

b) Methods for allocation to sectors for multi pot special methods

Refer to Section 7, paragraph (d) of the 'multi pot' template which can be replaced with the following:

i) Values

Identify all supplies, acquisitions and imports you receive which are used, or to be used, both in making taxable and exempt supplies and which are not used, or to be used, exclusively within a single sector; the input tax thereon should be allocated to the fullest extent possible between the sectors on whose behalf the expense was incurred, in the ratio of the value of transactions in each sector as a percentage of the total value of transactions in the nominated sectors.

ii) Headcount

Identify all supplies, acquisitions and imports you receive which are used, or to be used, both in making taxable and exempt supplies and which are not used, or to be used, exclusively within a single sector; the input tax thereon should be allocated to the fullest extent possible between the sectors on whose behalf the expense was incurred, in the ratio of the number of income generating staff employed in each sector as a percentage of the total number of income generating staff employed in the nominated sectors.

iii) Transactions

Identify all supplies, acquisitions and imports you receive which are used, or to be used, both in making taxable and exempt supplies and which are not used, or to be used, exclusively within a single sector; the input tax thereon should be allocated to the fullest extent possible between the sectors on whose behalf the expense was incurred, in the ratio of the number of transactions in each sector as a percentage of the total number of transactions in the nominated sectors.

iv) Time Spent

Identify all supplies, acquisitions and imports you receive which are used, or to be used, both in making taxable and exempt supplies and which are not used, or to be used, exclusively within a single sector; the input tax thereon should be allocated to the fullest extent possible between the sectors on whose behalf the expense was incurred, in the ratio of time spent on transactions in each sector as a percentage of the total time spent on all transactions in the nominated sectors.

v) Cost Accounting System

Identify all supplies, acquisitions and imports you receive which are used, or to be used, both in making taxable and exempt supplies and which are not used, or to be used, exclusively within a single sector; the input tax thereon should be allocated to the fullest extent possible between the sectors on whose behalf the expense was incurred, using the method by which the input is accounted for within your own cost accounting system.

c) Methods for allocation and apportionment for sectorised methods

i) Refer to Section 6, paragraph (d) of the 'multi sector' template for method allocation. You can use some of the suggested wording as listed in (b) above.

ii) Refer to Appendix 3 of the 'multi sector' template for methods of apportionment. You can refer to some of the suggested wording as listed in (a) above.

4) Exclusions

You should insert appropriate exclusions, based on the method(s) to be used, that are likely to cause a distortion to the calculation, as applicable to the particular business.

Refer to the exclusions that relate to values depending on method of apportionment.

5) Contact Officer

This paragraph should only be included where there is an allocated.

Appendix D – Transfers of business as a Going Concern – Legal Extracts

Value Added Tax (Special Provisions) Order 1995 (SI 1995/1268)

5(1) Subject to paragraph (2) below, there shall be treated as neither a supply of goods nor a supply of services the following supplies by a person of assets of his business -

(a) their supply to a person to whom he transfers his business as a going concern where -

(i) the assets are to be used by the transferee in carrying on the same kind of business, whether or not as part of any existing business, as that carried on by the transferor, and

(ii) in a case where the transferor is a taxable person, the transferee is already, or immediately becomes as a result of the transfer, a taxable person or a person defined as such in section 3(1) of the Manx Act;

(b) their supply to a person to whom he transfers part of his business as a going concern where -

(i) that part is capable of separate operation,

(ii) the assets are to be used by the transferee in carrying on the same kind of business, whether or not as part of any existing business, as that carried on by the transferor in relation to that part, and

(iii) in a case where the transferor is a taxable person, the transferee is already or immediately becomes as a result of the transfer, a taxable person or a person defined as such in section 3(1) of the Manx Act.

(2) A supply of assets shall not be treated as neither a supply of goods nor a supply of services by virtue of paragraph (1) above to the extent that it consists of -

(a) a grant which would, but for an election which the transferor has made, fall within item 1 of Group 1 of Schedule 9 to the Act; or

(b) a grant of a fee simple which falls within paragraph (a) of item 1 of Group 1 of Schedule 9 to the Act,

unless the transferee has made an election in relation to the land concerned which has effect on the relevant date and has given any written notification of the election required by paragraph 3(6) of Schedule 10 to the Act, no later than the relevant date.

(3) In paragraph (2) of this article -

'election' means an election having effect under paragraph 2 of Schedule 10 to the Act;

'relevant date' means the date upon which the grant would have been treated as having been made or, if there is more than one such date, the earliest of them;

'transferor' and 'transferee' include a relevant associate of either respectively as defined in paragraph 3(7) of Schedule 10 to the Act.

(a) Schedule 10 was amended by the Value Added Tax (Buildings and Land) Order 1995 (S.I. 1995/279)

Value Added Tax Act 1994

44 (1) Subject to subsections (2) to (4) below, subsection (5) below applies where -

(a) a business, or part of a business, carried on by a taxable person is transferred as a going concern to a body corporate treated as a member of a group under section 43;

(b) on the transfer of the business or part, chargeable assets of the business are transferred to the body corporate; and

(c) the transfer of the assets is treated by virtue of section 5(3)(c) as neither a supply of goods nor a supply of services.

(2) Subsection (5) below shall not apply if the representative member of the group is entitled to credit for the whole of the input tax on supplies to it and importations by it -

(a) during the prescribed accounting period in which the assets are transferred, and

(b) during any longer period to which regulations under section 26(3)(b) relate and in which the assets are transferred.

(3) Subsection (5) below shall not apply if the Commissioners are satisfied that the assets were assets of the taxable person transferring them more than 3 years before the day on which they are transferred.

(4) Subsection (5) below shall not apply to the extent that the chargeable assets consist of capital items in respect of which regulations made under section 26(3) and (4), and in force when the assets are transferred, provide for adjustment to the deduction of input tax.

(5) The chargeable assets shall be treated for the purposes of this Act as being, on the day on which they are transferred, both supplied to the representative member of the group for the purpose of its business and supplied by that member in the course or furtherance of its business.

(6) A supply treated under subsection (5) above as made by a representative member shall not be taken into account as a supply

made by him when determining the allowance of input tax in his case under section 26.

(7) The value of a supply treated under subsection (5) above as made to or by a representative member shall be taken to be the open market value of the chargeable assets.

(8) For the purposes of this section, the open market value of any chargeable assets shall be taken to be the price that would be paid on a sale (on which no VAT is payable) between a buyer and a seller who are not in such a relationship as to affect the price.

(9) The Commissioners may reduce the VAT chargeable by virtue of subsection (5) above in a case where they are satisfied that the person by whom the chargeable assets are transferred has not received credit for the full amount of input tax arising on the supply to or acquisition, or importation by him of the chargeable assets.

(10) For the purposes of this section, assets are chargeable assets if their supply in the United Kingdom by a taxable person in the course or furtherance of his business would be a taxable supply (and not a zero-rated supply).

49 (1) Where a business carried on by a taxable person is transferred to another person as a going concern, then -

(a) for the purpose of determining whether the transferee is liable to be registered under this Act he shall be treated as having carried on the business before as well as after the transfer and supplies by the transferor shall be treated accordingly; and

(b) [omitted by FA 2007, s. 100(2)(c) and repealed by FA 2007, s. 114 and sch. 27, Pt. 6(2).]

(2) Without prejudice to subsection (1) above, the Commissioners may by regulations make provision for securing continuity in the application of this Act in cases where a business carried on by a taxable person is transferred to another person as a going concern and the transferee is registered under this Act in substitution for the transferor.

(2A) Regulations under subsection (2) above may, in particular, provide for the duties under this Act of the transferor to preserve records relating to the business or part of the business for any period after the transfer to become duties of the transferee unless the Commissioners, at the request of the transferor, otherwise direct.

(3) Regulations under subsection (2) above may, in particular, provide -

(a) for liabilities and duties under this Act (excluding sections 59 to 70) of the transferor (other than the duties mentioned in subsection 2A above) to become, to such extent as may be provided by the regulations, liabilities and duties of the transferee; and

(b) for any right of either of them to repayment or credit in respect of tax to be satisfied by making a repayment or allowing a credit to the other;

but no such provision as is mentioned in paragraph (a) or (b) of this subsection shall have effect in relation to any transferor and transferee unless an application in that behalf has been made by them under the regulations.

Appendix E – EU member states as at 1 January 2021

The VAT territory of the EU consists of:

Austria	
Belgium	
Bulgaria	
Croatia	
Cyprus	(including the British Sovereign Base Areas of Akrotiri and Dhekelia but excluding the UN buffer zone and the part of Cyprus to the north of the buffer zone where the Republic of Cyprus does not exercise effective control)
Czech Republic	
Denmark	(excluding the Faroe Islands and Greenland)
Estonia	
Finland	(excluding the Aland Islands)
France	(including Monaco but excluding Martinique, French Guiana, Guadeloupe, Reunion and St Pierre and Miquelon)
Germany	(excluding Büsingen and the Isle of Heligoland)
Greece	(excluding Mount Athos (also known as Agion Oros))
Hungary	
Ireland	
Italy	(excluding Campione d'Italia, the Italian waters of Lake Lugano and Livigno)
Latvia	
Lithuania	
Luxembourg	
Malta	
Netherlands	(excluding the Antilles)
Poland	
Portugal	(including the Azores and Madeira)
Romania	
Slovakia	
Slovenia	
Spain	(including the Balearic Islands but excluding the Canary Islands, Ceuta or Melilla)
Sweden	

Other areas not within the VAT territory include Leichtenstein, the Vatican City, Andorra and San Marino.

Appendix F – Terminal markets listed in VAT (Terminal Markets) Order 1973 (as amended)

London Metal Exchange, London Rubber Market,

London Cocoa Terminal Market, London Coffee Terminal Market, London Sugar Terminal Market, London Vegetable Oil Terminal Market, London Wool Terminal Market, London Meat Futures Market,

London Grain Futures Market,

London Soya Bean Meal Futures Market, Liverpool Barley Futures Market, International Petroleum Exchange of London, London Potato Futures Market,

London Platinum and Palladium Market, and

London Securities and Derivatives Exchange Ltd (OMLX).

Index

www.ingramcontent.com/pod-product-compliance
Lightning Source LLC
LaVergne TN
LVHW090318210926
848480LV00001B/289
* 9 7 8 1 9 1 3 5 0 7 2 7 5 *